THE ETHICS OF
CULTURE

Samuel Fleischacker

CORNELL UNIVERSITY PRESS

ITHACA AND LONDON

First published 1994 by Cornell University Press.

Library of Congress Cataloging-in-Publication Data
Fleischacker, Samuel.
    The ethics of culture / Samuel Fleischacker.
    p.   cm.
    Includes bibliographical references and index.
    ISBN 0-8014-2991-9 (alk. paper)
    1. Culture—Moral and ethical aspects.   2. Multiculturalism—Moral
and ethical aspects.   3. Ethical relativism.   I. Title.
BJ1031.F56   1994
170—dc20   94-6106

Printed in the United States of America

⊗ The paper in this book meets the minimum requirements
of the American National Standard for Information Sciences—
Permanence of Paper for Printed Library Materials, ANSI Z39.48-1984.

For Amy

Contents

Preface

"Culture" and "ethics" are frequent bedfellows, but it is far from clear that they have yet been properly introduced. Writers on culture usually show little understanding of what makes an argument or decision ethical, while writers on ethics have rarely done much serious thinking about culture. This is demonstrated most obviously by the unquestioned assumption, on the part of relativists and antirelativists alike, that cultures *exist*, that the term "culture" is a well-entrenched and a scientific one rather than a fairly recent coinage laden with ethical presuppositions. One aim of this book is to lay out these presuppositions.

The other is to show how the notion of culture, properly interpreted, can fill an important gap in contemporary thinking about ethics. The Enlightenment taught us to seek moral principles by way of philosophy, to abandon the provinciality and arbitrariness of cultural or religious traditions in favor of a universal theory of human nature. But over time we have found that philosophical theories have little to say about real ethical problems, and recently a number of philosophers have argued that philosophy is just not the right place to address questions about how to live. Where else should we turn? Depending on whom one asks: to tradition, to community, to narrative, to culture. Now anthropologists have long argued that culture is in fact the source of all ethical beliefs and practices, so it might seem that the time has come for a marriage between moral philosophy and anthropology. But most philosophers remain suspicious of this move, for want of a satisfactory answer to two questions: How can the fact that an ethical norm is passed down by a culture possibly *justify* that norm? And, more fundamental: What is a culture?

We are back where we started, at the absence of an adequate interpretation for the anthropologists' central term. It seems to me that the philosophical gaps in anthropological thinking and the blindness toward the importance of culture in philosophical thinking complement each other, with consequences for much more than academic debate. The ugly silliness bequeathed to the world by European nationalism, the desperate ethnic pride that today stands in for real ethical conviction in the United States, and the anemic relativism that attempts to respond to both may well follow directly from the failure of Enlightenment moral theories to compensate for the day-to-day guidance of a cultural tradition. As a step toward addressing this failure, and reconciling philosophy with anthropology, *The Ethics of Culture* explores what culture has to offer ethics while proposing an ethical interpretation of culture.

The opening two chapters of the book are introductory, surveying the advantages as well as the limitations of universalism in ethics and defending the intelligibility of a moderate version of moral relativism. I then embark on an analysis and defense of tradition and authority, the two main elements of culture that were intolerable to Enlightenment moral theory. In Chapter 3, I attempt to show what stories and their traditional interpretations can say about the good life that ethical theory cannot; in Chapter 4, when and why appeals to authority might be legitimate. The freedom to question and criticize, it turns out, far from undermining tradition and authority, is essential to their preservation. Chapter 5 brings my philosophical analysis together with the history of the term "culture" to argue that cultures are best understood as authoritative moral traditions, and that they necessarily differ but presuppose with equal necessity that they aim at the same goal. In the remaining chapters, I examine how this interpretation of culture can be useful to dialogue across cultures, dissent and criticism within cultures, and our struggle here in the West to decide what might constitute our own particular culture. Cultures tend to contain both relativist and universalist strains, I argue in Chapter 6, and cross-cultural judgment can take place when two cultures map their universalist strains onto each other—without any appeal to a transcultural standard. Similarly, cultures tend to contain strains telling of their responsibility to a good beyond themselves, and in Chapter 7 I suggest they can use these strains as a basis for self-criticism without developing more than a shadowy idea of what the good beyond themselves might look like. Finally, Chapter 8 addresses our particular self-definition by returning to a historical point touched on in Chapter 5: that a residue of respect for tradition and authority appeared even in the Enlightenment (in the writings of Lessing and Herder) and became the basis for both the study of other cultures and the belief that cultural diversity is valuable. I propose that we regard "multiculturalism," the affirmative attitude toward all cultures, as the heart of the post-Christian Western tradition, worthy of exactly that respect—no more but no less—that every culture owes to its articles of faith.

As I hope is already clear, I write this book not only for professional philosophers and anthropologists, but for anyone interested in current debates over cultural relativism, multiculturalism, and the failure of Enlightenment moral theories. It differs from other literature on these subjects in providing an analysis of tradition and authority rather than merely insisting on their importance, seeing cultures as valuable not intrinsically but insofar as they provide ways of realizing a higher conception of the good, and claiming that cultural relativism is as much a product of the Enlightenment as a reaction to it. By tracing cultural relativism to the Enlightenment rather than to the decline of imperialism or the effects of Nietzsche, I attribute to it a quite different pedigree from the one assigned it by both its major left-wing defenders and its major right-wing critics. I also wind up interpreting the Enlightenment—and, therefore, classical Liberal thought—rather differently from Alasdair MacIntyre, the thinker to whom I feel otherwise closest.

These are not mere academic quibbles, for they lead to an understanding of cultural relativism as a consequence not of the West's loss of faith in itself, but of its most energetic and adventurous attempt at self-exploration. Unlike both MacIntyre and Allan Bloom, I do not think we need to choose between traditions and liberalism. Our liberalism is itself deeply rooted in a tradition. At the same time, since freedom is built into authority and tradition, authoritative traditions elsewhere need not be il-liberal. I believe this moderately relativist position can help reconcile not only various philosophical persuasions, but differing cultures and their representatives in the wider community.

I am grateful to the American Council of Learned Societies for financial assistance, and for the hospitality of Barton and Monique Reichert, whose home in Gommecourt provided the peaceful and inspiring space in which much of this book was written. My thanks to E. J. Brill, publishers, who granted me permission to reuse some of the material in chapter 7 of my earlier book, *Integrity and Moral Relativism,* in Chapter 5 of this one. I also thank Donna Chenail, Shirley Bushika, Charles Buckholtz, and Nicholas Kolodny for help in preparing the manuscript. Roger Haydon, at Cornell University Press, has given me invaluable encouragement from this proj-ect's earliest stages. David Frum, Ernest Davies, and Jonathan Rauch pro-vided vigorous and very helpful responses to the first five chapters. Alan White read the entire manuscript and offered important suggestions par-ticularly for my account of Kant in Chapter 2—plus a much-needed tip on horse racing. My wife, Amy Reichert, has read everything I have writ-ten over the past five years; I would be reluctant to publish anything before it had gone through her careful and sensitive criticism. This book is for her.

SAMUEL FLEISCHACKER

Williamstown, Massachusetts

THE ETHICS
OF CULTURE

What are our natural principles but principles of custom? In children they are those which they have received from the habits of their fathers, as hunting in animals. . . . Custom is a second nature which destroys the former. But what is nature? For is custom not natural? I am much afraid that nature is itself only a first custom, as custom is a second nature.

PASCAL, *Pensées*

"Well, now we will finish talking and go to his funeral dinner. Don't be put out at our eating pancakes—it's a very old custom and there's something nice in that!" laughed Alyosha.

DOSTOEVSKY, *The Brothers Karamazov*

1. Limits of Universalism

Ethical arguments are notoriously hard to settle, but we can usually resolve them to some extent if we can agree that a course of action would improve the neighborhood or betray a friend, that it is courageous or petty, generous or rude, that it is the sort of thing only Mother Teresa would do or even Bart Simpson would not do. That is, we are usually satisfied if we can phrase our ethical judgments in specific terms whose scope we find clear and whose value we consider unquestionable. Trouble starts when someone pushes for a justification of these specific terms. In general, and especially for the last two hundred years, it has been the business of philosophers to start such trouble. They do so of course not solely out of a desire to irritate people. From the time Socrates first pestered Meno to give a general account of his moral vocabulary, the search has been on for universal principles from which to derive moral judgments the way theorems are derived from axioms in mathematics. Universal moral principles, it has been supposed, will explain all specific moral projects, determine how to settle all moral dilemmas, and end the ills that come of separate and enclosed moral communities.

The search has not been a terrific success. For reasons we shall examine shortly, universal principles have actually tended to undermine rather than rationalize our moral practices, to determine either no answer or several contradictory ones to our moral dilemmas,[1] and to be too weak to win the attention of individual agents in competition with more provincial (religious, national, cultural) precepts. In recent years, moral philosophers have begun to turn away from universal theories, toward the local systems and ties that actually guide most ethical conduct. Harking in many cases back to Aristotle, who saw Plato's demand for a comprehensive and universal Good as deeply misguided, such writers as Alasdair MacIntyre, Stanley Hauerwas, and Charles Taylor have argued that universalist theories of morals are empty, and that we ought to attend instead to the role of tradition and community, and the specific terms and judgments that tradition and community make possible, in the pursuit of our daily ethical lives.[2] This turn from the universal to the local has been matched, in our society as a whole, by a renewed interest in culture, as a matter for political discussion and as a source for individual identities.

Rich and promising as it is, the return to tradition or culture has yet to come to grips with several extremely important challenges, and it is those challenges that are the subject of this book. In the first place, universal principles are crucial to the very definition of ethical systems and cannot simply be dismissed. In the second place, no one has yet explained exactly what aspect of a tradition, or community, or culture is morally relevant, and why. Why should the fact that a tradition mandates an act be compelling when all other reasons for that act are not? In addition, we need to consider how we can draw limits to distinguish one tradition or culture from another, and to what degree such distinctions are ethically necessary. And once the distinctions are even provisionally in place, we need to ask how one tradition or culture can legitimately judge another and how any tradition or culture can intelligibly criticize itself. Finally, if we in the modern West, and those who have emulated our secular ways across the world, are in possession of any tradition at all, that tradition surely comprises the very liberal, Enlightenment heritage that has urged us away from all traditions. This paradox must be integrated into any revival of traditions, not simply ignored in favor of the supposedly simpler world that existed in the Middle Ages. Traditions may indeed be crucial to ethical reflection, but their function, after the Enlightenment, is at least problematic. We certainly cannot accept them as self-sufficient, self-justifying sources of wisdom.

These are the issues of the ensuing chapters, but their difficulty and multiplicity may lead many readers to wonder again why anyone would abandon the hope for a universal moral theory. Answers to that question, in recent years, have taken many forms: universalist theories tend to underplay the dependence of the individual human being on society; universalist theories tend to smuggle specifically Western or Christian or male experiences into their supposedly general foundational principles; universalist theories are too rough-hewn, use too coarse a mesh, to capture the fine-grained circumstances that surround everyday moral decisions; universalist theories are too general to be sensitive to historical or environmental differences among human beings; universalist theories are weak or ambiguous, arrogant and imperialistic. These complaints are too multifarious to constitute a diagnosis, but they are surely at least symptoms of a fundamental weakness in the universalist approach.

It is not my intention, however, to examine that weakness in detail. This book is written primarily for those who already share the belief that a return to tradition or community promises a better grounding for ethical practice than has been provided by the theorizing of moral philosophers. It is written as well for those who resist the universalism that comes with philosophical theorizing about ethics (insofar as such theorizing appeals to considerations that are supposed to cut across all human experience). I shall not, on the whole, be arguing against particular theories or the universalism that goes with them. Instead, as already indicated, I shall be addressing problems that arise *within* the proposed new traditionalism, and in the course of addressing those problems I shall try to describe concretely how a culturally based approach to ethics might work. One reason for turning to traditions or cultures instead of theories is to draw our moral thinking away from abstraction and toward the specific tasks and judgments of everyday life. It defeats the purpose of this new orientation simply to write a *theory* of how traditionalism or cultural relativism can be instituted or justified. Yet philosophers, given to abstraction by profession, have been slow to spell out what a return to tradition would mean for practice. I hope to remedy this defect: my central aim is to give a detailed sense of what moral judgment within specific traditions might actually be like.

This intention to describe a traditionalist approach to ethics, rather than argue against universalism, may perhaps serve as some excuse for the all-too-brief, sketchy, presentation of universalist theories with which I shall begin. To attempt to refute all Kantian, consequentialist, natural-law based, sentiment based, and intuitionist ethical theories in the space of ten pages or so is a task that calls for more temerity than I possess and more foolishness than I hope I possess. Other books have been written that criticize such theories in the appropriate detail, and in any case I would not so readily dismiss universalist moral theorizing.[3] In searching for an appropriate justification for moral beliefs, Kantian and utilitarian philosophers have developed a conception of the moral point of view as impartial, rational, concerned with human needs and interests, and concerned equally with all human needs and interests, that has had profound and valuable consequences.[4] From the analysis of impartiality and rationality has come much of our current understanding of procedural justice and the liberal state. From the demand for equal concern has come the notion of human rights. From the emphasis on human needs and interests, together with the analysis of rationality, has come the removal of superstitious obstacles to medical and socioeconomic progress, and the relegation of religious dogma to private rather than public life. And from the very discovery or invention of universal conditions for moral thought has come a hope that human beings have enough in common to be able to overcome their reliance on war. That these successes are all political is, I think, no accident: for reasons I shall note elsewhere in this book, the "moral point of view" of the philosophers is much better at resolving differences between people than at giving any individual guidance on how to live. But the successes are nonetheless real, and among their effects has been an increased conviction, for members of many traditions and cultures, that conforming to this moral point of view is at least a *necessary* condition for any precept to be moral. Beliefs and practices that flagrantly conflict with our ability to maintain an impartial, rational concern for all human beings' needs and interests tend to be regarded as immoral, as customs or rituals that warrant reinterpretation or rejection.

Since I approve of these developments, I am not about to condemn universalist moral theorizing root and branch. But to make clear what lines of the current criticism of universalism I share, and to lay out the precise motivation for my own brand of parochialism, I want to emphasize one problem for universalist theories. This problem, noted in criticism of

Kantianism, utilitarianism, and natural law theory but surprisingly little discussed in its own right, concerns how such theories are supposed to generate an adequate set of concrete precepts. While attempts at universal justification of moral beliefs have offered the profound formal insights enumerated above, they have been a disaster when used to construct a specific guide to how to live. From the totalitarian fantasies of utopia to which the Enlightenment gave rise, to the myriad superficial or bizarre discussions published today as "applied ethics," the theoretical mode of moral thinking has not had a happy history of structuring daily life. Why universal moral theories inevitably fail when called on to generate everyday principles is the topic of the first part of this chapter. The second part sums up what aspects of universalism, of the philosophers' "moral point of view," I will retain throughout my argument for a return to culture.

THIN THEORIES AND THICK MORAL CODES

In a very general way, the problems in the daily application of universal moral theories parallel shortcomings in the justification of those theories. Justifications for a claim about what all human beings ought to do normally appeal to some universal emotion or intuition, a universal capacity for reason, or the rational interpretation of universal facts about the human condition. All these appeals are vulnerable to the fundamental question of why, even if there are any universal features of the human being, those features, and those features alone or above all others, should have a special value or ability to bestow value. Even if, as Rousseau hypothesizes, human beings have a natural tendency to pity one another, why should we rate that tendency higher than our other natural tendencies? Even if, as Kant argues so well, reason can approve of human actions only when they are willed under a certain form, why should we weigh what our reason says more heavily than what our emotions may have to urge against it? And if, as naturalists of many stripes have argued, human beings need to structure their lives in certain ways in order to procreate, or coexist harmoniously, or survive—what shall we say to the individual or society that does not particularly care about procreation, or living harmoniously with others, or even survival, at least for any significant length of time? At all events, human beings cannot be *reduced* to their desire for procreation, harmony, or survival, or to their pity or love or reason, or their capacity, if any, for direct intuition of the good.

The same kind of issue arises when the question of how to apply ethical universals comes around. Appeals to emotion and intuition tend to be unconscionably vague in obvious and dangerous ways: one person's "pity" or "intuition" leads to works of charity while another's assures her that Stalin or Hitler has the light that will save humanity. From reason and the universal facts of human nature, on the other hand, one can perhaps derive some general prohibitions of murder or lying or theft, but little else, unless one builds all the specific mannerisms of Western civilization into the definition of rationality. In practice, the search for universal principles leads us either to undermine our own moral norms or to impose them on everyone else. When we insist on universality as the sole ground of ethical norms, we wind up with such an attenuated set of them that telling the truth and not killing are about all we can expect of a person, and even those virtues turn out to be vague enough to allow for much that we ordinarily want to consider dishonesty and murder. Once we find a real universal consensus on basic ethical principles, on the other hand, we tend to start thinking that we now have a way to show all those other cultures that they ought to be monogamous, Christian, democratic, capitalist, and properly dressed. These two concerns move in opposite directions: the thinner the set of norms we derive as universal, the less will we be inclined toward preposterous claims of the "all people should wear clothes" variety, while the more we allow for such claims, the more can our universalism approach the richness of the ethical lives we actually lead. Both alternatives must surely be unattractive, however, to all except those convinced, on revealed or chauvinistic grounds, that their own way of life is obviously the best for everyone.

To these complaints, many universalists would respond either that a claim to universality is part of the very definition of moral language or that in fact there are some ethical principles that all peoples believe should apply universally. These two quite different responses reflect a crucial ambiguity in the notion of ethical "universality." Saying that an ethical claim "holds universally" may mean that it applies to every human being or it may mean that every human being ought to believe it, and the two are by no means the same. Suppose it were the case that all people with blue eyes ought to eat marshmallows while all people with brown eyes ought to avoid marshmallows. Then it might be possible to persuade all people of what both the blue-eyed and the brown-eyed ought to do, but that very possibility entails that "what one ought to do" will not apply in the same way universally. By contrast, suppose that all people ought to pursue the Grail, but some people have such corrupted minds that they will always construct some casuistic argument to exempt themselves from their duty. Then an ethical claim would hold of all people, but some would be immune to persuasion of it. At the heart of much moral theory, especially of the Kantian variety, lies a belief that these two kinds of universality must and will fall together: all people have the same ethical standards and obligations if and only if they can all be persuaded of the same standards and obligations. Cases appearing to contradict this imply that an individual or people has turned out to be (ethically) stupid or that a claim has turned out not to be ethical. According to the ordinary uses of the terms, however, many such people are of course *not* stupid and many such claims are ethical. The universalist dogma survives by means of a good deal of methodological blindness to the variety of ways in which ethical terms are used and ethical positions staked out in our ordinary lives. In the remainder of this section, I press the claims of ordinary usage against methodology.

Ethical universalists in the twentieth century are especially fond of claiming that moral statements by definition lay claim to universality, that a culturally relative morality is a contradiction in terms.[5] I want to endorse, against this, the kind of definition for "morality" proposed by the political scientist Terry Nardin, who ties it to its etymological root in "mores" and takes the difference between morals and other customs to be primarily the fact that, in a given community, morals "generally override other sorts of considerations."[6] Nardin suggests that any morality "presupposes not only a community of moral agents whose conduct is judged but also a community of judges," and he defines morality, in accordance with this stress on judgment, as the "principles or rules of conduct based on, though not necessarily identical with, the 'manners' and 'morals' of a people, that is, with the generally acknowledged standards of conduct by which the acts and character of a particular community are judged."[7] But is it possible to describe a set of norms that appeals only to the adherents of one culture among others as a "morality"?

The case against this move is generally made as follows: Morality concerns what people should do as people, rather than as Ibos, Italians, whites, blacks, women, men, or other subset of people. Presumably, this claim derives in part from the overriding importance we attach to what we call "morality," on the assumption that what all people should do will naturally trump, in cases of conflict, what this or that subset of people should do. Above all, however, it points out a deep connection between the use of the word "moral" and the use of the word "person." For the universalist, that connection is immediate and clear: the moral "should" always applies to persons and never to types of person. Most human groups with which we are familiar have a conception of how all human beings should behave, which may coincide with, or more probably will run alongside, their conception of what their members, in particular, should do. If the group believes that all people should do precisely as it does, we can call their entire code of behavior "morality." If not, we reserve the term for that part of the code they do universalize, and call the rest "manners," "folkways," "ritual," or the like. "Morality is by definition about personal responsibility . . . , impartiality and the promotion of people's well-being," writes Robin Barrow, and any culture whose evaluative language lacked a demand for impartiality would "clearly be talking about something different from what we refer to as morality."[8]

As it stands, this will not do, although it does bring out interesting features of the word "moral." Certainly, morality is about what people should do, which means that having a morality entails having some conception of "personhood" akin to our own, but this is not a strong enough condition to rule out nonuniversalist moralities.[9] As critics of Kant's categorical imperative have long pointed out, the bare demand that a rule apply to all people can be met much too easily to serve as a significant constraint on moral rules. Consider, for instance, a sexual code that, for purportedly biological or demographic reasons, recommends plural partners for men but single partners for women. Surely we can construe this as a recommendation about what people in general should do: they should (a) recognize that their biological constitution is essential to their decisions about sexual ethics, and (b) act in one way if their biological constitution is of one kind, and in another way if their biological constitution is of a different kind. Similarly, any cultural group can construe its local code of behavior as a guide to all people: "everyone should (a) recognize that their cultural origin is essential to their ethical role and duties, and (b) behave as we do, if they belong to our group, and contrary to the way we do, according to some more minimal standards, or however they please, if they do not belong to our group."

Suppose the Werespecial group divides the world into Werespecialites and Allothers, and holds that Werespecialites should obey the Werespecial standard of behavior, which entails keeping promises and telling the truth, while everyone else need only obey the Allother standard of behavior, which does not entail keeping promises and demands truth telling only in court. Are we to say that the Werespecialites have no morality? That seems absurd. Or that their morality really asks a single standard—"Act like a Werespecialite or like an Allother"—of everyone, merely admonishing each person to decide whether the Werespecial or the Allother aspect of that standard applies to her? But that would be to lump two quite different standards together, for the purpose of preserving a now somewhat vacuous thesis. The universalist often wants to posit a vague and general principle such as "act for the Good" as a foundation for both the local and the intercultural standards of a group, but if the local component of this set is very different from the intercultural one, or if the intercultural one is as uninteresting and uninformative as "act however you please," the assimilation of the two standards will be quite arbitrary and fail to account for or guide any actual behavior.[10]

In response, a universalist might say that, regardless of whether a code prescribes different kinds of action for different kinds of people, to be a morality it must promote all people's well-being. It may at first seem that this is right, that we could not possibly consider something to be a morality unless its principles can be justified as in aid of every person it affects. But this demand runs at least as much risk of either failing to be necessary or failing to have substance as "act for the Good." Consider a teleological version of "act for the Good": the locals see their code as promoting happiness or virtue or wisdom for themselves, while providing some lesser good to others or no good (but no harm) at all. Perhaps they feel that others cannot achieve or appreciate the goods that they can, or that others should choose or attain their goods by their own efforts and code. In such a case, and if the local code is action guiding, ideal based, and overriding,[11] why should we not call it a morality? Without an arbitrary assimilation of goods, however, how can we possibly call its telos universalist?

Turning now to the claim that universal persuasiveness ought to serve as the ground for ethics, we confront a rather different set of philosophical strategies. Few would want to say that ethical statements by definition demand that every human being be actually convinced of them, except as a theoretical presupposition (they must "in principle" be able to be convinced) for their being universally applicable. Rather, the argument here works in a different direction: *if* everyone were convinced of an ethical claim or theory, that claim or theory would then apply universally and provide a standard determining the truth or falsehood of all other ethical claims. If we could find a universally persuasive ground for ethics, or at least some universally persuasive ethical propositions, we would no longer need to worry about the difficulty of resolving ethical arguments. Such purported grounds frequently take the form of a theory of "human nature"; such propositions, the title "natural law."

The first thing to be said about this approach is that if all human beings were to agree on what is ethical, it is not obvious that what they agreed on would in fact be ethical. This, for several reasons. To start with, what people agree on is a fact, and there is no legitimate inference from facts alone to values. In addition, if it makes sense to speak of "truth" in ethics, then it is essential that any agreed-on belief could turn out to be false, so agreement cannot establish truth and must be open to criticism in the light of the truth. And finally, the agreement would have to concern method as much as precept or value, and that means that the agreed-on values (e.g., the legitimacy of slavery, or meat-eating, or "white lies") could be undermined by the agreed-on method (e.g., the presentation of new facts, according to an accepted procedure, about the effects of slavery or the nature of animals or the psychology of lying, or the presentation of an accepted type of story that makes human freedom or animal life or unswerving devotion to the truth appear sacred). I do not want to belabor these points, since it seems to me that a truly universal agreement on values would make argument about values de facto if not de jure superfluous, but it is worth noting that even explicit universal agreement does not immediately establish ethical truth or objectivity.

Much worse, however, are the conclusions often drawn from virtual or implicit universal agreement. The leading current exponents of natural law concede that inferences to values from a scientifically established human "nature" alone are illegitimate but maintain that all human beings implicitly share certain ethical beliefs since *most* human beings explicitly assent to them.[12] Thus, respectable writers on ethics cite findings of anthropologists that all human societies have practices resembling what we call marriage, friendship, courts, education, play and religion, to show that all human beings should participate in those practices and develop ideals and principles in accordance with them.[13] This position thrives on a rather obvious vagueness, on a methodological problem in translation that makes the vagueness irremediable, and on a tendency to use the supposed universals as a fulcrum to make less universal principles seem necessary to those who dissent from them.

The vagueness lies in what to count as marriage, friendship, and so on. Should the word "marriage" cover both polygamy and monogamy, legally sanctioned and informal unions, temporary and permanent ones, unions interwoven with ritual orgies or an indifference toward pre- or extramarital sex and unions interwoven with strict prohibitions on "fornication" and "adultery"? (What does "adultery" mean where marriage is an entirely different practice?) John Finnis gets around this problem by avoiding the word "marriage," with its large number of familiar connotations. "No human society fails to restrict sexual activity," he says. "In all societies there is . . . some opposition to boundless promiscuity and to rape, some favor for stability and permanence in sexual relations."[14] Similarly, he tells us not that all societies prohibit "lying," but that they all "display a concern for truth." The problem with this strategy is that practically anything might count as a "favor for stability and permanence" or a "concern for truth," and the interesting cases we might want to rule out—"free love" or ceremonial rape, deceit to outsiders or to oneself or in the marketplace or by priests—can easily be consonant with virtues so weakly described.

Moreover, Finnis is not always so careful. He says that all societies "know friendship" and "have some conception of *meum* and *tuum*, title or property."[15] But do the Ik, Ugandan tribespeople who betray each other unremittingly and avoid all intimacy, really know "friendship"?[16] And should we really use such entrenched terms of European law as "*meum*" and "*tuum*," "title" and "property," for tribes who see land and homes as "owned" in common or by the gods, for nomads, for societies in which the ruler lays claim in principle and as much as possible in fact to everything in his domain, for kibbutzim and socialist states?

Here the methodological issue enters in. We are interested in finding universally shared practices and precepts precisely so that we can argue their necessity to human life—which argument we will conduct, we must surmise, with people who dissent from these very practices and precepts. Actions that *everyone* performs are hardly candidates for ethical debate, indeed can barely be considered ethical matters, since they presumably require no deliberation or conscious decision. And theoreticians of natural law in our day are usually in fact concerned to argue that whole societies are mistaken about what human beings need.[17] Now it is imaginable that we might have to convince a dissenting *individual* to live in accordance with practices that everyone else in his society accepts as necessary to human life: the individual might be immature or foolish enough to make a mistake about what he or she assents to. But can a society make such a mistake? Does it make sense to regard an entire society as "immature" or "foolish"? Certainly, through lack of information, a society can adapt the wrong means to achieve its own ends, but it is hard to see how it could be "mistaken" in the setting of those ends. (Note that even failure to survive can count as a "mistake" only if the society takes its own survival to be one of its standards. The Shakers do not procreate, but survival as a society is not a prime concern of theirs, and they have now peacefully written their own "death" warrant.)[18] The individual we can judge against the standards of his or her society, but against what standards can we judge the society? To translate what an individual claims to be doing or believing, we need to interpret her words in the light of her society's language: immediately, therefore, we have at least a possibility of judging her actions or words to be a confused realization of her beliefs. But to translate a society's beliefs, we must begin with an assumption that its words and practices are overwhelmingly in accord with each other, else we will never get anywhere, which means that we need *never* reach a point at which we have to say that its beliefs conflict comprehensively with the way its members act. We would question our translations, or what function the society's official declarations of belief are supposed to serve, if we ever seemed to face such a situation.

When we want to tell a society we disapprove of, therefore, that its dishonesty, bestiality, human sacrifice, and the like violate universally accepted conditions for human life, we cannot mean that its members too believe these conditions are necessary, that they are mistaken about their own beliefs. What else might we mean? That human beings die out without these conditions? But, like the Shakers, they may not care whether they die out or not, or they may disprove this claim by surviving. That human beings need certain conditions to "flourish," to avoid becoming "demoralized" or "violent" (like the Ik, again, or the Nazis)? But in question here is precisely what counts as "flourishing," and we are trying to determine it by appealing to a process of universalization on which our dissenting society sheds doubt. Nor can we interpret "flourishing" by holding fixed what we, in our local culture, take to be a healthy and decent life. Our own insecurity about what we, locally, consider true in ethics is precisely what has led us to the search for universals; we cannot now fall back on local beliefs in order to find those universals.[19]

It follows, in addition, that even if we do find a universally accepted principle, we cannot simply assume that others will accept what we take to be the implications of that principle. Because our own moral beliefs are so insecure, because we can so easily see the arguments for variations on our own views and practices, we can never claim that a particular judgment logically *must* follow from an accepted universal. We know that monogamy, or a prohibition of adultery, need not accompany every version of "stability and permanence in sexual relations"; we know that a "concern for the truth" may extend only to the limits of a tribe; we know that a purported "respect for persons" may go together with slavery. Variations like these arise through differences in definitions, or in interests, or in factual but unverifiable assumptions (about divinity, afterlife, etc.), not through mistakes in logic or a lack of understanding as to what the supposed universal truly means. What a universally accepted principle truly means is precisely *what all societies actually agree to*, not what we infer from the version of it we practice in our own society. The fact that the members of a particular society agree to a certain principle is the basis on which we may argue that that society ought to live up to it; that *other* societies agree to it does not, by itself, provide a reason for this one to do so.

The situation is thus not analogous with the discovery that the members of a society want to cure an illness but use an ineffective or dangerous drug. In that case we can show that their desires imply they should do things our way, and if they do not agree, we must question not whether the drug is actually harmful, but whether they are really interested in curing the disease. Questions about what interests one ought to have take us beyond such a consensus about implications. When we find that in most cases interest in monogamy goes with abhorrence of adultery, we cannot infer, as if by induction, that that conjunction will hold for all. For we are establishing not an empirical fact—*that* we do only where there already exists agreement in interest and method—but a consensus, and consensus presupposes free choice, hence the possibility of dissent.

In sum, either universals will merely record the fact that everyone already agrees on something, or they will not be truly universal. The kind of universal we seek here is not an empirical generalization, to be supported by inference where direct evidence is lacking, but a unanimity so complete that should a case arise where we want to appeal to it, that case alone would remove our ground for appeal.

Toward a Universal Definition of "Morality"

A more promising approach to demanding universalism of moral codes begins by looking at the limits placed by the process of interpretation on what we can consider a "morality." It is tempting to regard any conditions we, locally, lay down for interpreting other peoples' words and practices as arbitrary and dispensable, but there is reason to consider this attitude mistaken. The philosopher Donald Davidson has acquired much of his wide reputation by arguing powerfully that the only way we can interpret what other people have to say is to work out from the assumption that they are saying something much like what we ourselves would say in their shoes. This apparently conservative view, which seems to retreat from the last half century's "discovery" of incommensurability among cultural and historical worldviews, actually grows out of a much more comprehensive rejection of foundationalism than those who style themselves "radical epistemologists" have been able to make. If there really are no special, foundational sentences, says Davidson, then we can establish a basis of translation with another language only by assuming a general likeness of *all* beliefs. I do not propose to enter the details of this position, which are complex and extremely subtle, but only to note that, insofar as it succeeds, it casts serious doubt on the very possibility that people might differ significantly over moral questions.[20]

I shall argue in Chapter 2 that we do not need to accept the entirety of Davidson's position for moral purposes, but to a large extent it is undoubtedly correct. We cannot, and certainly need not, recognize any and every system of action as "what we refer to as morality."[21] Some features must be held in common with our own system if the word is to have any meaning. On one level, this is an extremely simple claim. Suppose you encounter someone who insists that the equivalent of "morality" in his language is a word that, in every context in which you find it used, seems quite clearly to mean "elephant." You will have no alternative but to say that he does not understand *our* word "morality" at all. Any equivalent of "morality" must be concerned with human action. The same goes in the slightly more interesting case in which someone insists that the equivalent of "morality" in his language describes a human activity like digestion or the rules for an activity like driving a car. If a set of principles merely describes an activity, or sets rules for an activity that has nothing to do with (what we could recognize as) a people's "values" or "ideals," then those principles are not even a candidate for the name "morality."

We have very quickly drawn out of "morality" the demands that anything claiming that name be at least (1) an action-guiding code and (2) a code that represents some collection of values or ideals. It is tempting to complete the universalist case equally quickly, by adding to these formal considerations the claim that we cannot recognize the values a code pursues unless those values are our own. I do not think this is true, but I do think the values at which any morality aims must bear some family resemblance to our own—specifically and minimally, that they have a telos and that they make enough room for human freedom and dignity for us to be able to imagine each adherent of the code assenting to its tenets.

To appreciate the power of these intuitions, consider the way they are used to persuade us even of moral philosophies that officially spurn any appeal to intuition. Interwoven with argument in Kant's discussion of the universality of moral thinking are gestures directing us toward the intrinsic value of human dignity,[22] and of the emotion Kant calls "respect" or "awe," gestures that at the end of the *Groundwork* issue in a remarkable passage:

> There is no one, not even the most hardened scoundrel—provided only he is accustomed to use reason in other ways—who, when presented with examples of honesty in purpose, of faithfulness to good maxims, of sympathy, and of kindness towards all (even when these are bound up with great sacrifices of advantage and comfort), does not wish that he too might be a man of like spirit. He is unable to realize such an aim in his own person—though only on account of his desires and impulses; but yet at the same time he wishes to be free from these inclinations, which are a burden to himself. By such a wish he shows that having a will free from sensuous impulses he transfers himself in thought into an order of things quite different from that of his desires in the field of sensibility; for from the fulfillment of this wish he can expect no gratification of his sensuous desires . . . ; all he can expect is a greater inner worth of his own person. This better person he believes himself to be when he transfers himself to the standpoint of a member of the intelligible world.[23]

We find this passage moving, if we do, because we like to think that every human being capable of reason is also capable of a certain kind of "inner worth"—the worth evoked by the favorable connotations of the word "person"—and is by that token worthy of respect. We tie "person" to a capacity for free choice, for reflection, and for control over desire, and we see people as in this sense equally deserving of respect. We thus bring together freedom, dignity, and equality as supremely important, if not ethically definitive, characteristics of human beings, and we cannot work up much enthusiasm for any ethical code that fails to share this intuition. It is one of our deepest interests to see human beings universally treated in a way that accords, in some recognizable sense, with their internal dignity.

The West has long had an inclination toward spreading its own way of life, born perhaps out of the cross-fertilization of a philosophy (Stoicism), a religion (Christianity), and a political unit (the Roman Empire) that all aspired to transcend their local roots. But it is not merely out of a desire to spread our own way of life that we demand universal acknowledgment of a certain fundamental dignity in all human beings: we cannot avoid believing that those who do not recognize human dignity are *wrong* about something, that they have failed to understand something about the very nature of morality. Rather than allow for legitimate disagreement over this intuition, we hold it fixed in our interpretation of other cultures and suppose that, implicitly at least, people everywhere do share it, whatever their official ideologies and institutions might look like. Thus anthropologists try to give us ways of understanding other practices and beliefs as at least attempting to respect the dignity of the human being. Human sacrifice, child exposure, killing the aged, and cannibalism can all be given functionalist or symbolic explanations by which they reflect dire necessity, an honor to the victims involved, mistaken beliefs about the world, or at worst the reign of a few crazed or evil individuals, and it is the mark of good anthropological work to give us such explanations, so that we do not find the people who do such things unrecognizably inhumane. Not every individual is humane, of course, but respect for human dignity, and something of our sense of what constitutes human dignity, is in general one of the criteria by which we determine what to count as a human mind at all— certainly a rational and sane human mind. We cannot do otherwise without losing the notion of humanity, and rationality, ourselves.

In addition, we reserve the word "morality" for codes of behavior that societies take very seriously and that they try, at least to some extent, to examine and discuss. To be a morality a code must have some rationale, must aim at some good and make some attempt at explaining how, and why, it attempts to realize that good; otherwise, we call it an etiquette, a custom, a game, or a folkway. A morality must be explainable as having some end, must be open to critique and reflection in terms of that end, and is revealed as merely custom when the end, or the tie between code and end, no longer seems intelligible or worthwhile (as happened with Jewish law for the early Christians, and the Hawaiian notion of taboo for Kamehameha II).[24] Recalling our discussion of the teleological version of "act for the Good," we might now think that a code directed to a good for Werespecialites would become by that very fact custom or (mere) prudence rather than an ethic—at least in our non-Werespecial eyes. But while the notion of a telos does belong deeply to our conception of an ethic, it is not as deep a part of that notion that the telos be shared by all human beings. There are familiar, even noble, codes of life we would normally call an ethic in which the telos is not especially directed toward the good of human beings at all. People may pursue the welfare of all *sentient* beings, like the vegetarian utilitarians; of "the world" as an organic whole embracing both the animate and the inanimate, like some Buddhists, mystics, and Spinozists; or of God, like, among others, Bach (*ad maiorem Dei gloriam*). An ethic with these ends may well produce less of what we familiarly consider "human good" for one group than for another.

If these considerations are enough to make it plausible that a code may count as an ethic even if it does not aim at the *good* of all people, however, they are not enough to allow for a morality that expressly seeks the *harm* of some person or persons. It is at this point, I think, that the need for the values of a code to bear some family resemblance to our own makes itself felt. It sticks in our throat to call the Nazi ideology a "morality" or to say that the Ik currently live by a new morality rather than that they are unable to live up to the demands of their old one.[25] On the other hand, a code that, like Aristotle's, sees slavery as good for the slaves, or, like some religions, sees human sacrifice as ennobling or joyful to the victim, may appear foolish or unpleasant but does not obviously fail to count as a morality at all. Why a group's ethic has this telos rather than that one may well be somewhat obscure, at least to outsiders,[26] but it (grammatically) cannot be so obscure as to bear no relation to what we ordinarily call "good," and that it would be if it required the deliberate degradation or destruction of another set of human beings. "Another set," because we can imagine such degradation or destruction as justified if the victims are members of the group, for the same reason that we cannot imagine it otherwise: that *those persons* might (in principle) accept their own destruction as a possible consequence of their membership in the group and pursuit of its goals.

That to be a morality a code must recognize people's fundamental dignity and cannot be directed against any set of persons of course implies, not surprisingly, that its adherents must share our conception of "person." Otherwise the Nazis could simply say that their ideology is not directed against persons since Jews do not belong to that category. We can imagine some legitimate disagreement here—over the comatose, the severely mentally deficient, the fetus, and perhaps the infant—but the range of such disagreement is not very wide. We can also imagine that a group with no experience of, say, white people might at first conceive them to be gods or beasts, but we expect it to withdraw that conception as mistaken on discovering that the creatures in question talk, have a social life, act kindly, cruelly, lovingly, cleverly, and at all events, intentionally. There may yet be further hard questions. Does the intent to degrade some people necessarily make an entire code nonmoral? Do we say that the hard-line racist of America's antebellum South had *no* morality, was *im*moral, or had a morality in general but failed to have one as regards blacks? In the case of the Nazis, we are probably inclined not to count the ideology as a morality at all, but perhaps that is because there is not much left, nothing particularly distinctive at any rate, once we remove its conception of people as deserving to degrade or be degraded.

We have now a fairly strong, but still minimal, set of conditions for anything to count as a morality or ethical code: it must be action guiding, ideal based, overridingly important, directed toward a conceivable end, accompanied by a conception of "personhood" that does not severely conflict with our own, and not aimed toward the degradation or destruction of any being fitting that conception of "person." We should bear in mind three facts about these conditions. First, that we demand a telos and a respect for persons of ethical norms helps explain why we take them as overriding (merely) ceremonial or aesthetic ones. Second, the conditions derive from central *intuitions* about our words "moral" and "ethical," not from a theory or fixed definition, and from intuitions, moreover, that are themselves part of our ethical code. For *ethical* reasons, not for logical or scientific ones, we refuse to accept as ethical a code that flouts the requirement of not being directed to human harm. Finally, the conditions we have found will not rule much out; many a repulsive or silly code will meet them. We indeed apply these conditions universally, but only to begin the discussion over how to live, not to end it. If universal applicability is made a necessary condition of every ethical precept, we will wind up either with the thin, implausible conceptions of morality that have led some recent thinkers to suggest we abandon the notion altogether, or with the vague universalism that lumps quite disparate actions or ends together under a heading like "always aim at the Good."[27] Instead, universal regard for persons is a *necessary condition* of any ethical code. A substantive ethical system requires something more. Precisely when we come to the limits of ethical universalism do we begin to appreciate the need for ethical traditions.

2. Beyond Universalism

Before we ever hear of universal theories of morality, and after we decide they are not very useful, most of us make our decisions about how to live in accordance with the advice we receive from friends and relatives and the examples of conduct we witness in the society around us. How to treat a spouse, what kind of work is worth doing, what is owed to parents and children, when telling the truth is honesty and when rudeness, when fearlessness is courage and when foolishness—all these questions, about which universal theories of morality, by their nature, have nothing to say, are settled for us by what today we call our "culture." Those who say this is the *right* way to answer ethical questions describe themselves as "cultural relativists." I distance myself with quotation marks from the word "culture" because one of the issues that I think needs exploring, in this approach to ethics, is precisely what a culture is: the word's sanctified connotations today cover over its relative youth and the fact that its short history has been plagued by bitter controversy over what it is supposed to name. The vagueness and revered status of the word make it all too easy to ignore the problem of just what aspect of our society has the right to claim ethical allegiance from us. I will therefore employ the word "tradition" for the practices and standards of conduct that we accept unquestioningly when presented to us by our society, and "authority" for the mode of presentation that seems so readily to deserve our allegiance, until, in Chapter 5, I have an opportunity to show that "cultures," when adequately interpreted, can be identified as authoritative traditions.

A more pressing question is why the fact that our tradition presents a practice or standard of practice to us is any reason for accepting it at all. The argument I shall develop in this and the next two chapters turns on the acknowledgment that strictly speaking it is not a reason. Rather, tradition and authority appeal to us to accept them on faith, and it is that appeal to faith, and not what any given tradition asks us to accept, that can be rationally justified. The justification I shall offer is, however, complicated. Perhaps the greatest, and certainly the central, achievement of the Enlightenment was a critique of all kinds of faith, and we have inherited from that time excellent arguments for the conviction that any limitation on rational thinking, and any division of thought into parts or ways with arbitrary and rationally incommensurable premises, is illegitimate. This conviction, moreover, is largely responsible for the tremendous success of Western science and technology since the eighteenth century. Nevertheless, I shall argue that it is inappropriate for ethics.

THE ENLIGHTENMENT AND ITS CRITICS (I): NEUTRALITY AND INTERESTS

Enlightenment thinkers considered it their mission to redeem people from the burdens of tradition. Traditions, they felt, had entrenched corrupt and oppressive authority structures in church and state, and the need to genuflect to tradition had been the main obstacle, over the centuries, to international peace and the pursuit of economic, medical, and social progress. (In large part, of course, they were right on all these counts.) In place of tradition, the Enlightenment hoped to establish a "science of morals" that would allow individuals to determine goals for and methods of action open to the kind of rational, free, and peaceful discussion characteristic of natural science. If that could be achieved, it would no longer be necessary to accept as a given the aims for life, the interests and projects, passed down through the ages by revealed religions. Instead, one could determine human nature and the human place in the world in the same way one determined everything else. What reason did they have to believe that such a scientific ground for morality was possible?

From the beginnings of the rise of science in the seventeenth century, old Platonic hopes reawakened of providing a single theory that would account for all phenomena.[1] Descartes's and Spinoza's attempts to establish absolute foundations for knowledge and derive all possible scientific conclusions from them, Locke's and Hume's programs for definitively describing both the natural and the moral world in terms of simple impressions, and the Encyclopedists', and later Hegel's, project of collecting everything there was to say about science, art, religion, philosophy, and history in one comprehensive book all point, albeit in different ways, to the attempt to bring together everything knowable under one theoretical rubric. Sometimes that aim was qualified by a warning that knowing everything humanly possible was not the same as knowing everything,[2] but even then the goal and ideal for knowledge was as close an approximation as possible to the sum total of the true beliefs human beings could be expected to discover or derive. Such a standard, clearly and distinctly available to all individuals, together with an *Encyclopédie* in every generation marking how far the approximation had actually gotten, would free people from the tyranny of their particular upbringings. All people begin their lives by being filled with tastes, methodologies, and beliefs about the world by the people who happen to bring them up, although some of the tastes are vain, methodologies foolish, and beliefs wrong. A proper philosophy of science was to cure all that. Developing a touchstone for knowledge free of all prejudices and emotional slants—of all perspective—would enable us all to discover and correct the faults in our individual perspectives. The contemporary philosopher Bernard Williams calls this touchstone "the absolute conception of reality" and says that approximation to that condition is and must be the ideal of science; Thomas Nagel has recently described it vividly as "the view from nowhere."[3]

One result of this attitude was the attempt to produce an account of morality freed as much from the unexamined notions and rituals passed down in families and small communities as modern medicine is from folk remedies and magic. Descartes begins his *Meditations* by remarking that in his youth he "had accepted . . . many false opinions for true, and that consequently what [he] afterwards based on such principles was highly doubtful"; he must look away from all these opinions if he wants "to establish a firm and abiding superstructure in the sciences."[4] Once we realize that the mishmash of superstition and wisdom we imbibe as children steers us wrongly on all sorts of historical, physical, and biological matters, we recognize the need for a more systematic approach to truth. Why should the same not hold for our morals? Among the desires with which our parents and childhood teachers fill us, we later find some to be unfulfillable or dangerous; among the attitudes they instill, we later find some to be ashamed of; among the behaviors they encourage, we later consider some constricting or pointless. Surely such criticism is predicated on the existence of a more fundamental, more absolute standard of how to act, against which the faults of particular perspectives can be measured. If, moreover, ethical propositions are to claim truth—if we can talk of truly right and wrong ways to act—then the justification for such claims must regress to some central and single standard by which they can be finally vindicated or refuted. One ought therefore to examine human nature and the human place in the world just as one examines everything else, and choose one's interests and values only after first acquiring, from a disinterested perspective, knowledge of what interests and values human beings ought to have.

Descartes himself never carried out this program. In his *Discourse on Method,* he tells us he is adopting a traditional moral standard as a convenience while he pursues the fundamental questions of knowledge, but he implies strongly that the results of his cognitive investigations might lead him to revise, or even to abandon, that standard.[5] As it happens, he returns to it, but the possibility of revising morals in the light of philosophy, and especially the notion that knowledge ought to precede and determine practice, was opened up for others to embrace. Thus Hobbes tried first to find the basic principles of human action and then to work out a political and moral system from them; thus Shaftesbury, Hutcheson, Clarke, Wolff, Montesquieu, Rousseau, Hume, and Herder, for all their differences both with Hobbes and with one another, also tried empirically to discover or rationally to derive such a system; and thus, finally, the utilitarians, Hegelian statists, and utopian and Marxist socialists, children of the Enlightenment all, tried in practice to reinvent the moral world around them on scientific grounds.

In the many horrors of Marxist and Fascist governments and the petty failures of democratic welfare programs, we have witnessed in this century some of the moral flaws of Enlightenment ideals, and, in ways I summarized in the last chapter, philosophers have recently begun to analyze the theoretical problems that may lead to these flaws. One of these is said to be the Enlightenment conception of a neutral standard for knowledge. Against the Enlightenment, current wisdom (outside academic philosophy, at least) holds that we are all invested in some set of emotions and moral commitments, that those commitments color everything we believe, that the Enlightenment project of beginning from an objective, neutral, universal ground was incoherent and indeed itself biased. It is supposed to follow that every human group, and possibly every individual, thinks differently, according to the different interests to which their thought is directed.

This vague relativism is, however, unsatisfactory. Taking the anti-Enlightenment position, a little coarsely, as saying that all claims to knowledge are relative to some set of interests, consider three points that those who hold such a position generally overlook. First, to say that interests are antecedent to knowledge does not take seriously enough the way in which we tend to change our interests on the discovery of new facts. Certainly, people may interpret the world around them to accord with desires they desperately want to maintain, but they also adjust their desires to accord with the world when they think that they otherwise face a life of dissatisfaction. I will have more to say about this later on, but for the moment we might simply bear in mind that even sexual desire generally fades upon the discovery that it is not going to be returned.

Second, what is supposed to be the evidence for the anti-Enlightenment claim? Its supporters cite psychological studies to show that people have difficulty understanding, much less accepting, facts that contradict long-held or emotionally charged presuppositions; that people will seek out evidence or pursue whole research projects to defend their prejudices; that people will accommodate data any which way rather than let it disturb beliefs they deeply want to be true. The studies showing these things are striking, certainly, but they are still *studies*—empirical data that for their interpretation presuppose the truth of the scientific method. And this will be so for any fact purporting to show that our emotions blind us to the facts: to accept it as evidence at all, we must take ourselves to be standing enough beyond those emotions to know that our acceptance of *this* fact, at least, is a response to the truth and not just more blindness. Bernard Williams has made this case well: "Anything that can be empirically explained, as that . . . we (as opposed to Hopi Indians, or again as opposed to cats) see things in a certain way, or deal with things in one way rather than another . . . [must] fall *within* the world of our language"; there could be no "sociological . . . or zoological, or materialistic" explanation of our world-picture itself because the very notion of such explanation presupposes that world-picture.[6]

Finally, in order to recognize merely *that* there are many interest-bound perspectives on knowledge, that I occupy one of them, and that it differs from those of others, I must presuppose that there is some common position against the background of which the differences among perspectives, the contrast between mine and others, can appear. Donald Davidson, combining this proposition with a deep commitment to holism, makes movement beyond perspectives a condition for the possibility of all interpretation. We interpret a person's words adequately only when we can fit them into what else we know. We understand a sentence only when we understand a language, and we understand a language only when we can make sense of the speaker's beliefs, desires, and words as a whole. We can make such sense, in turn, only by applying the principle of charity, assuming that on the whole the speaker either believes truths or errs in readily explicable ways. This entails not that there is one correct or overarching perspective, but that the very idea of closed and thought-determining perspectives is incoherent: "It would be wrong to summarize by saying we have shown how communication is possible between people who have different schemes. . . . For we have found no intelligible basis on which it can be said that schemes are different. It would be equally wrong to announce the glorious news that all mankind—all speakers of language, at least—share a common scheme and ontology. For if we cannot intelligibly say that schemes are different, neither can we intelligibly say that they are one."[7]

It follows that if we are going to find an alternative to the Enlightenment's neutral and universal standard for knowledge, we will have to do better than the bald insistence that knowledge depends on human interests. We need a more sophisticated view of interests and some answer to Williams's and Davidson's objections, which amount to a fairly strong defense of the Enlightenment attitude. I suggest we will have more success if we look to some peculiar features of the knowledge one needs in order to make moral decisions, an issue raised against the Enlightenment approach implicitly by Kant and explicitly by Søren Kierkegaard. To see what it amounts to, we need to return to our characterization of the Enlightenment.

The Enlightenment and Its Critics (II): Comprehensiveness and Limitations

We considered above the neutrality of the Enlightenment's scientific ideal. Ultimately, that neutrality is what we want to shake up, but let us get at it more indirectly this time, by considering a different characteristic of that ideal: comprehensiveness. Whether or not it would be neutral with respect to our interests, a comprehensive picture of the world would enable us to settle the factual questions that underlie our fundamental moral decisions.

Regardless of the view one takes of the fundamental terms of ethics, it is hard to deny that our ethical conclusions are always in part a function of our beliefs on certain factual questions. Alfred Ayer pointed this out with glee, believing it helped make his case that all intelligible questions are fundamentally factual ones:

> When someone disagrees with us about the moral value of a certain action or type of action, we do admittedly resort to argument in order to win him over to our way of thinking, but we do not attempt to show by our arguments that he has the "wrong" ethical feeling towards a situation whose nature he had correctly apprehended. What we attempt to show is that he is mistaken about the facts of the case. We argue that he has misconceived the agent's motive, or that he has misjudged the effects of the action, or its

probable effects in view of the agent's knowledge; or that he has failed to take into account the special circumstances in which the agent was placed. . . . We do this in the hope that we have only to get our opponent to agree with us about the nature of the empirical facts for him to adopt the same moral attitude towards them as we do.[8]

On a deeper level, there may be factual questions about the very terms of ethics. For Platonists, the existence of absolute values is a factual one of sorts, just as, for naturalists such as Ayer, it is a matter of fact that Platonic arguments are erroneous or incoherent. For most Europeans until the nineteenth century, the truth of the Bible, with its promises of a future and better life, was probably *the* crucial factor in the decision about how to live—both for those who believed in it and for those who denied it. Today the factual issues underlying ethical attitudes might include whether people can be adequately understood as animals or machines, whether there are important emotional or intellectual differences between men and women, whether and how "happiness" can be scientifically defined, and whether, in general, science, or scientifically based philosophy, can comprehensively answer our questions.

So when the thinkers of the Enlightenment maintained that comprehensive knowledge of the world would help settle ethical questions, they were certainly on to something. Gather enough physical, biological, historical, psychological, and anthropological data and we might have the means to determine with finality the accuracy of the world's purportedly sacred texts, the nature of the human being, and the likelihood of there being any trustworthy source of truth outside science. In their different ways, Hobbes and Spinoza, Hume and Bentham, Herder and Marx—all the Enlightenment thinkers we listed earlier and more—shared this belief and offered their work as a contribution to its fulfillment.

The culminating figure, philosophically if not chronologically, of this approach to how one should live, the one who held out the most audacious hopes for a comprehensive picture of the world, is surely Hegel. Hegel attempted, more thoroughly than anyone before or after him, to produce a system that would bring rationality and unity not only to the theory of science, politics, art, morality, and religion, but to all the details of how people have pursued these activities throughout the history of the human race. When the system was complete, he believed, it would be quite literally self-evident, and among the things it would show would be the fact that our ethical duties are contained in our political (civic) ones. It is to this system—indeed, to the very brilliance with which it was carried out—that Kierkegaard took bitter exception, and his response remains the most powerful rebuke to all attempts at using scientific means to settle ethical questions.

Kierkegaard does not regard what Hegel says as false. Far from it. Rather, he thinks the very closeness to truth of this comprehensively rational system is what makes it so terribly dangerous when it overlooks something.[9] And what Hegel's system overlooks—as will any system that attempts to synthesize all knowledge—is the relationship of individual knowers to what there is to be known. Kierkegaard makes two points over and over again: that the Hegelian system is dehumanizing and that it is incomplete. Who is supposed to use all the information a Hegel has to offer? Whose life will it help, and how? Kierkegaard says he wants an answer from a human being, not from "speculative philosophy,"[10] implying that those who spend too much of their time immersed in such philosophy forget that they too have lives to lead and that the mere possession of so much knowledge will not necessarily help them decide how to lead those lives.[11] He also asks, repeatedly and with the scornful misery of one who once shared the systematists' hopes, when the system is going to be finished. An unfinished system, after all, lacks the self-evidence Hegel claimed for it, since that was to be a product not of any of the system's parts but precisely of the fact that it explained everything. (Exactly analogous claims are made for modern science.) One surd, one acknowledged truth that the system just cannot accommodate, would utterly invalidate its claim on our intellects. And in the brilliant stroke for which he is best known, Kierkegaard makes clear that the one truth a comprehensive explanation of the world will never be able to include is the very one hidden in his accusation that such systems are dehumanizing: the truth about what use someone who understands the explanation ought to make of it for his life. Hegel's system could be completed only by a being for whom knowing and doing exactly coincide—only by God:

Whenever a particular existence has been relegated to the past, it is complete, has acquired finality, and is in so far subject to a systematic apprehension. Quite right—but for whom is it so subject? Anyone who is himself an existing individual cannot gain this finality outside existence which corresponds to the eternity into which the past has entered. . . . [Who then] is [the] systematic thinker? Aye, it is he who is outside of existence and yet in existence, who is in his eternity forever complete, and yet includes all existence within himself—it is God.[12]

What is it about us, as opposed to God, that unsuits us for the attempt to survey the whole world? I have hinted that it has something to do with the distinction between knowing and doing (what Kant, as we shall see, called the difference between the speculative and practical points of view). For Kierkegaard, thought about action is marked by the fact that it must always be done by individual human beings—as opposed to God and as opposed to "humanity at large." In the short span in which we are alive, the problems for which we need knowledge will inevitably grow out of characteristics and situations specific to us as individuals, not from the general characteristics and situation, or the history, of the entire human race.[13] Humanity as a whole may accomplish many things, but that neither takes away nor adds to the fact that I am responsible for what *I* do and that the suffering and joy *I* witness and participate in have more importance for me than anything happening beyond my ken. Science, whether of the Hegelian variety or of the modern, empirical sort, cannot pay much attention to such particular matters, cannot pay much attention to me, or what I ought to do. Its business is with the development of an adequate set of general terms with which to explain and predict what all members of a class do (or must do or should do). Hence the workings of science are a great temptation for those who want to forget about their individuality, with its responsibilities and limitations.

Especially its limitations: Kierkegaard stresses more than any thinker before him that what we do as individuals is done in time, not eternity. Furthermore, by the time we realize we are responsible for our use of time, we have already wasted time, and before we have a chance to overcome our many faults and failures, we will die. Kierkegaard felt that we need knowledge forcing us to focus on our individuality, while the Hegelian system only encourages the all-too-ready inclination to flee from that individuality, with its reminders of what we cannot do and the death that awaits us. Kierkegaard's favorite word for these grim concerns is "Sin," and for the answer to them, "Christianity," but that takes us into territory I have neither the ability nor the inclination to enter. Instead, I shall try to put the issue between him and the champions of science in other terms.

The scientific ideal of the Enlightenment cannot serve as an adequate standard for what the individual ethical subject needs to know. I, in my lifetime, am not going to acquire anything like the totality of available scientific knowledge, and it is I, not the whole of humankind, who must make, live out, and take responsibility for the decisions about how I am going to live. There are two reasons why Enlightenment scholars might have overlooked this fairly obvious consideration. One is simply that they themselves knew so much. The other is that they never adequately understood the importance of the individual.

Newton was not only a supremely gifted mathematician and physicist; he also studied the Bible thoroughly and deeply, engaged in learned philosophical debate, and possessed fine literary skills. Newton was of course the icon of his time, the mind to which all others aspired, but his *breadth* of learning was not exceptional. Descartes, Spinoza, Leibniz, Locke, Hume, Goethe, and Kant, along with many of their lesser contemporaries, were all able to acquaint themselves with the highest levels of philosophical, religious, scientific, and historical scholarship available in their generation, and the notion that each individual could and should attempt to acquire all available human knowledge had been a commonplace since the Renaissance. That belief contrasts sharply with the view that prevailed earlier, according to which all human beings were barred by God from certain kinds of knowledge and each human being required traditional guides to attain the knowledge he or she needed, as well as with the modern assumption that individuals can master only a small part of the total knowledge available and must allow experts to give them access to the rest. What individuals could determine about the world seemed much greater to the people of the Renaissance and Enlightenment than to their forebears, much smaller—more easily contained—than to their successors, and this moderate view of the sum of possible knowledge allowed people to see that sum as something they could attain themselves.

At the same time, for all their own individual achievements and for all their belief in the dignity of every human being, the scholars of the Enlightenment consistently underestimated the significance of the individual subject.[14] With uncharacteristic fuzziness, they posited such entities as a *Volksgeist*, a "general will," or "humanity" as some kind of vague whole, to serve, instead of the individual, as the subject that would have a cognitive and volitional relationship with the absolute object. The historian Carl Becker has demonstrated how "posterity"—"humanity" transplanted to the future—was addressed as practically a divinity: "O posterity, sweet and tender hope of humanity, . . . it is for thee that we brave all the blows of tyranny; . . . often discouraged by the obstacles that surround us, we feel the need of thy consolations; . . . Make haste, O posterity, to bring to pass the hour of equality, of justice, of happiness!"[15]

If this bringing of human beings into a sort of quasi-divine unity was virtually a religious dogma for the Enlightenment, as Becker suggests, then perhaps it is understandable that it went unexamined, but such carelessness bequeathed serious problems to the oft-invoked posterity. Two descendants of Enlightenment vagueness about the individual subject—the utilitarian belief in adding up human satisfaction, as if two people's misery could be canceled out by one person's bliss, and the nationalist and Marxist view of society as one large organism—have justified, respectively, gross economic inequities and some of the world's most horrifying tyrannies.[16] On the cognitive level, we rediscover every day that the accessibility of knowledge only decreases as the total amount increases, and that "social" or "generally human" knowledge, for all the interesting parallels that can be drawn between society and the individual mind, is not truly knowledge at all. Beliefs stored away in some social analog of memory (libraries, lab reports, professional journals) do not really become knowledge, in the sense of true beliefs with a connection to other true beliefs and some possibility of use in action, unless some individual mind takes them up, synthesizes them, corrects other beliefs by means of them, and shows how they can have an impact on how we guide ourselves around the world. And if all currently available human knowledge cannot be simultaneously known by one person, then the gaps any given individual has in his or her knowledge cannot be compensated for either by any other person or by any group, however large. For whatever each person learns, whether from a group or from another person, she herself needs to synthesize, interpret, and apply. So beliefs that are merely distributed across various people, in one mind or another but not in all, are like scraps of informative paper lying around uncollected and unread.[17] They cannot make any difference to the settlement of a question unless either the person asking the question has access to the beliefs or the people who have the beliefs are acquainted with the question. Of course, people can cooperate in the pursuit of knowledge, but only if they share enough interests, procedures, and background information to seek answers to complementary questions. Information is useless, hence impossible even to interpret, unless it can answer some question. But the questions human beings have ultimately regress to the single question of how to live. And the answers to that question, gathered collectively or no, must ultimately be judged by each of us individually. An absolutely accurate picture of reality, even if humanity as a whole could attain or approximate it, would be inaccessible to all individuals and thus could not help anyone plan how to live. The absolute picture of reality would be a picture *for* no one.

It is as though the Enlightenment wanted to replace our reliance on traditions for guidance with a comprehensive map of the world in which we could first locate everything we might need to know and then decide what aspects of the mapped world, what regions or types of terrain, we would like to spend our time exploring. But we have to ask whether such a map, even if it could be constructed, would be of use to any one of us. Kierkegaard writes: "To exist under the guidance of pure thought is like traveling in Denmark with the help of a small map of Europe, on which Denmark shows no larger than a steel pen-point."[18] The real situation is that we must make a choice between different kinds of maps before we find out anything we need to know. One map depicts, say, demographic and political features; another, rivers and valleys, mountains and plains; a third, mineral resources. Or one shows a city or two in great detail; others, the rest of the country more generally. We cannot opt even for a map of the whole country over a map of one city unless we know that we do not want to spend all our time in that city—as we cannot decide, in general, what kind of information we need unless we know what we need it for.

The idea that knowledge must be *for* someone, that some connection must be established between the knower and what there is to be known, brings us to what Kierkegaard calls "subjective truth": the subjective appropriation, in feeling and action, of objective claims to truth. Kierkegaard's positive proposal is that since religious belief requires faith, and since its quality, as faith, is determined by how much risk it entails, science can neither prove nor disprove its rationality; indeed, the more improbable it makes the object of faith appear, the more it gives the religious person an opportunity to strengthen his or her faithful commitment to that object. Translating this out of his theological language and toning the anti-rationalism down a bit, we might say that our commitment to the factual claims most important to our ethical lives is a sort of bet, and the fact that we must bet on these matters frees us from being strictly bound by what science has to say for and against them. It is in the need for betting that interests come to play a role in our rationality, for what we may rationally bet on is no less a matter of what our stakes are than of the chances we will succeed. The gambler's perspective thus opens up an alternative road to relativism.

BETS

In a sense, all our beliefs are bets, even those for which we have the most evidence. Return, for a moment, to Ayer's claim that ethical discussions are really all about facts: they may well be about facts, but the reason for the disagreements is often that different people make different bets about where to find trustworthy sources for factual information. And when they

decide which witnesses to trust, which facts to focus on, and what inferences to draw about factual matters on which no evidence is available, their
choices are normally colored by their interests in a case or ethical judgment
of it. Thus left-wingers see the world through the self-righteous suspi-
ciousness of *The Nation* or the *Village Voice*, while right-wingers look
around them with the amused condescension of the *Wall Street Journal;*
pacifists talk a lot about the First World War while their opponents focus
on the Second; and those convinced that sexual harassment is a pervasive
evil construe the circumstances of an accusation of harassment, and project the consequences of conviction and acquittal, very differently from
those who think women "ask for" such treatment. Wherever there is uncertainty, we have to bet, and wherever we have to bet, our stakes in the
outcome, one way or another, come into our decisions.

The sense in which all our beliefs are bets, therefore, is the sense in
which uncertainty is everywhere. When I go out of the house in the morning, there is a small chance I will be struck by lightning; to the extent that
I am aware of this chance, I bet against it by going out. When I cross the
street, I am betting against the probability of being run over by a car. I live
above ground to the extent that I bet against tornadoes; I go below ground
to the extent that I bet against my house collapsing. I bet on the *New Eng-
land Journal of Medicine* or the kinds of newssheets one finds in natural food
stores, the *New York Times* or Noam Chomsky's latest conspiracy theory,
Steven Jay Gould or the creationist movement. I bet on how the universe
began and how it is likely to end, what human beings are like and what
will make them happy, whether there is anything worthwhile other than
happiness, whether the arguments for and against the existence of God are
flawed, how likely it is that what we now think we know will be overturned
in the future, how likely it is that all these bets will come out successfully
and what my alternatives are if they fail.

Most fundamentally, perhaps, since the Enlightenment we in the West
have bet on the scientific method. I draw here on the work of the philosopher of science Hans Reichenbach, although I believe the uncertainty
involved is greater than he would allow.[19] Responding to Hume's dem-
onstration that there can be no proof the future will resemble the past,
Reichenbach claims that we can bet on the uniformity of nature even if we

cannot prove it, and goes on to try to show that the scientific interpretation of that claim is in fact the best bet we can make. We have better reason to place our bets on normal scientific induction than on any alternative mode of prediction, he says, because if there are any uniformities in nature at all, our familiar inductions will be able to pick them up at least as well as any alternative. Suppose a "clairvoyant" turns out to make consistently correct predictions. Then those predictions themselves will constitute a regularity in the world over which we can make scientific inductions. Indeed, Reichenbach argues, we would only come to rely on the clairvoyant at all if we could "test" her by checking her predictions against other inductions.

But all this assumes that we want to use the alternative mode of prediction recurrently, as a regular *method* comparable to our familiar scientific methods of induction, rather than that we might one time, or under a few special circumstances, break away from our familiar inductions for a sudden appeal to oracles or prophets. Certainly, a regular use of an oracle presupposes a regularity in the world which scientific induction will ultimately be best suited to pick up. The use of an oracle on any one specific occasion, however, may presuppose precisely the opposite: that here, for some reason, the practices we normally endorse will break down, that a super-natural structure or being is displaying its super-natural status precisely by overruling what is otherwise the natural order. And the reason for appealing to the oracle in such a case may have nothing to do with prior success. We might choose the person because of her ethical qualities or charisma, because she occupies a social role hallowed by tradition, or because we simply have a strong affection or love for her.[20] The assumption that we choose the oracle because of her prior success already builds in a subtle prejudice in favor of scientific induction. Reichenbach says that scientific induction "corresponds to a procedure the applicability of which is the necessary condition of the possibility of predictions,"[21] but if it is actually the necessary condition only of *most* predictions, and of any *exceptionless method* of prediction, there is nothing illogical about trusting a seer in exceptional cases. Reichenbach assumes that the world is either absolutely orderly or utterly chaotic; one may reasonably assume, instead, that the world is governed by regular patterns together with a sharp break, here or there, in those patterns. But if that is true, if the breaks are important enough, and if one has some inkling as to when and how they occur, then it will make sense to guide one's life by *combining* scientific induction or common sense with some extraordinary mode of prediction bending one here and there away from what science would prescribe. Which is what non-Western societies and religious traditionalists in the West tend in fact to do.

The reference to the importance of the breaks that might exist in nature brings out the other flaw in Reichenbach's position. Strangely, Reichenbach pays almost no attention to the role of the stakes in determining the rationality of a bet. It is certainly unreasonable to run through a battle zone in order to pick up a pound of butter, but it is not unreasonable to run through a battle zone in order to save one's family. Those who bet against science believe that their life in another world, or the whole quality of their life here, is at stake. When the stakes are as high as all that, even a bet at very poor odds may be reasonable.

Now why, given that science has almost nothing to offer as regards future lives or intrinsic "qualities" to life, does anyone bet on science at all? Well, in the first place, science has a good deal to offer that alternative methods of prediction do not: not only much more successful technology than other systems have produced, but a mode of organizing society that is more open and egalitarian than any society hitherto. The Enlightenment conception of the human being on which science is based holds that "anything of which the intelligibility, verifiability, or actual affirmation is limited to men of a special age, race, temperament, tradition or condition is [in and of itself] without truth or value, or at all events without importance to a reasonable man."[22] If we accept this, then the power of those who claim special access to ghosts, spirits, deities, and the like is immediately removed. Insofar as such power has been used to maintain corrupt and oppressive human hierarchies, we therefore have a stake in the very method of betting that science endorses.

In the second place, since science wins so overwhelmingly when pitted against alternative modes of prediction of events in our experience, people tend to assume that it is correct on all subjects, including its bet against other worlds and modes of experience. And this assumption is buttressed by the fact that scientific explanations of religious systems (in sociological, psychological, anthropological terms) tend themselves to be borne out in experience, to issue in successful bets. Of course, on the argument I have given against Reichenbach, neither of these points is conclusive, but it does allow many people, including most people in the West, to regard the odds as very much in favor of the bet on science, and in that light to opt for what it has to offer against the rather more dicey, and in some ways less desirable, promises of alternative methods. But they are still making a bet, not drawing the only rational conclusion. Unless they are philosophers, moreover, they are usually conscious of this fact: most people who have a firm belief in the ability of science to explain everything value future lives and the like very little, or consider the likelihood of their attainability so small as to be not worth thinking about, or find their interest in a free society and the material benefits of science outweighing these other matters.

On the view I am recommending, when scientists maintain that the evidence for a particular claim is as conclusive as scientifically possible, they mean that it is as good a bet as any other scientific claim. Each time scientists carry out a study, they are betting on the reliability of their equipment and the honesty and accuracy of their researchers. To the extent that questions might be raised about these factors, scientists should, and generally do, qualify their results with notes about margins of error and the like. But to the extent that their results are also subject to the uncertainty of the scientific paradigms that determine what they regard as good evidence at all, and to the extent that this is a concern that can be stretched wider and wider, from, say, questions about the reliability of specific experimental techniques, to questions about underlying principles of biochemistry or astrophysics, to questions about the entire scientific method, it makes no sense for any particular study to record this uncertainty, and we must simply presume that all scientific conclusions at a given time share pretty much the same level of risk, in the service of pretty much the same interests. Thus medical reports do not, and need not, tag on to their findings a reminder that those findings are valid if and only if normal scientific induction over sense-data is indeed the best way to obtain facts about the world that human beings are interested in.

But each scientific conclusion does for all that express our interest in a certain way of proceeding and the practical results promised by that way of proceeding, as well as our belief that that way can in fact produce those results. And when, as individuals, we modify the general bet of our society on the methods of science to accommodate here a traditional religious dogma or practice, there a piece of astrology or a New Age reworking of Eastern rituals, we are also weighing what we desire out of reality against what our experience tells us is likely to constitute reality. So in a very strong sense, stronger than Reichenbach's, our view of the world is fundamentally a bet, a function of hunches about reality measured against interests in it. Knowledge depends on our interests not in the sense that people consciously or unconsciously skew their observations according to what they want to believe, but in the sense that we put our faith in an approach to knowledge on the basis of how we value what it promises in addition to how well we think it can deliver.

INTERESTS: DESIRES AFTER THE FACTS

With this talk about bets we have already finessed the second of the objections we encountered earlier to relativistic approaches to knowledge (pp. 25–26, above). The criticism I attributed to Williams focused on the circularity of using scientific evidence to show that interests blind us in the very pursuit of science. In holding that scientific claims are bets, we make no appeal to the self-defeating suggestion that human interests are blinding. Nor do we deny that the search for knowledge presupposes an openness to all manner of facts and an awareness of as many of them as possible. We simply maintain that out of the total facts of which we are aware we must always bet on the superior significance of some of them for explaining or moving among the ones that remain unknown. Kierkegaard said that as long as Hegel's system remained incomplete, even in the smallest detail, the fact that one's entire salvation depends on its falsehood means that one is rationally entitled to bet against it. Similarly, as long as modern empirical science cannot explain everything, its claim to be able to do so remains a hypothesis, and that means that where it threatens claims we consider essential to the significance of our lives, we are entitled, if we dare, to bet against it.

But only *if we dare*. We come now to another (the first) of the objections to relativism we encountered earlier: that it had too thin a notion of the interests that are supposed to lie behind knowledge. It is ridiculous to allow any and every desire to set the stakes in our attempts to grasp reality. Where the chance of a claim's being true is very slim, according to the system by which we have hitherto, and successfully, looked for facts, to bet on it anyway is reckless, and reckless bets are hardly rational. We may bet at terrible odds when the stakes are very high, but normally we bet according to some weighing of our stakes in a result against the odds of its coming to pass. This notion that a bet may be reckless, and the process of adjustment that corrects for such a possibility, opens the way for us greatly to enrich our understanding of the "interests" to which knowledge is supposed to be relative.

First of all, as I indicated earlier, to a considerable extent we correct our desires against our views of reality. The types of motivation and desire that guide our long-term planning and with which we most closely identify our "true selves" are not mere immediate feelings. Desires track facts, as Robert Nozick has said about beliefs: if I desire something I increasingly come to think is impossible or self-destructive to attain, I try to direct my desire toward a more plausible object, or to eliminate it altogether. Generally, I try to match my desires to the options open to me, taking an interest in my father's business, perhaps, if that seems my best shot at a career. Of course, at times I just "feel" a strong desire, but I usually try to exercise control over my desires, molding them so as to cohere with my notions of what, in the natural and social world I inhabit, is attainable. When I take a serious interest in obtaining a car, I have a certain conception of what a car is, what purposes it serves, and what I might have to spend or otherwise give up for it. A set of factual beliefs goes automatically with the desire.

Second, we correct desires against other desires and against the models of what to desire that our society offers us. My desire for a car is normally limited by my desire not to have to steal in order to obtain it—and even if that doesn't particularly bother me, there are probably some constraints on from whom or with what amount of violence I am willing to steal. More generally, my desires must on the whole cohere with one another if I am to have a chance of fulfilling any of them, and I will usually try as well to bring them into as much coherence as possible with those of my neighbors, or at least with what my neighbors hold up as paradigms of an appropriate desire.[23] I try to do this partly because other human beings may be able to teach me how to bring my desires into harmony with one another and the world, but also because, for a great many reasons—from the vulnerability of the individual human creature to the bald fact that many of the things that satisfy human beings are social by nature (art, love, games, philosophical dialogue)—I want as much as possible to have desires that my society will respect and help me fulfill.

I reserve the term "interest" for the long-term, deeply considered, and socially informed desires that are not so much feelings as complexes of feelings, beliefs, ways of proceeding, and histories of social and individual judgment. There can be slack between any of the parts of these complexes, but it is hardly rational to allow any part to persist in defiance of the others. It is irrational to desire the impossible or the impossibly cruel or offensive ("irrational" in a strict sense, since one will not in fact be as satisfied as one imagines if one's immediate desire is fulfilled at the cost of society's permanent hatred or contempt). It is also irrational to bet on methods of seeking truth that have nothing to say either about the fulfillment or about the changing of one's desires. And it is irrational, both for individuals and for societies, to act in ways that persistently ignore either how the world works or what one seeks to achieve in it.

This claim has two important consequences. First, it corrects the well-entrenched mistake of regarding the rationality of the passions in such a limited way that, to use Hume's notorious example, it would not be contrary to reason "to prefer the destruction of the whole world to the scratching of my finger."[24] On the basis of this claim, Hume, like the twentieth-century emotivists who admired him, assumed that once he had shown ethical values to depend on the passions, he had also shown them to be outside the realm of rational discussion. Perhaps those desires that are really nothing more than a momentary feeling are indeed beyond the purview of rationality, but interests are not, and it is interests, not immediate desires, that are crucial to ethical judgment.

The second consequence is more troubling. I have argued so far that interests not only inform ethical judgments—judgments of "value"—but set the stakes for our judgments of fact. If interests are themselves informed by our bets on the facts, however, do we not face an inescapable and vicious circle?

Inescapable, yes; vicious, no. Belief, desire, and action may well be inextricably linked to one another,[25] but that does not mean that every configuration they form is as good as every other configuration. There is such a thing as equilibrium within the complex, as well as equilibrium between it and the experience of the individual or society maintaining it. To see what this means, we need to return to our gambling comparison.

Bets can be interlocking in many ways. If Hurricane romps home in the Derby, then I have reason to think she will also win the Belmont; if I have bet successfully on horses many times in the past, I have reason to make secondary and tertiary bets on my skill at the track; and in some cases the terms (the odds or the stakes) of one of my long-term bets may be renegotiated as a result of wins or losses elsewhere. In quite a different sense, my bets may be tied together by the fact that I use the winnings of one as the stakes for the next, and occasionally—if, say, I am rich enough to buy or sell a huge number of shares in a particular stock—how I bet in one place may affect the odds available to me in another.

Now imagine a set of interlocking bets such that not only does one always bet with one's winnings from previous bets, not only are the terms of each bet correlated with the terms of similar bets, not only can one renegotiate the terms of one bet on winning or losing another, but among the things on which one is betting is just how—with what stakes and at what odds—one will be willing to bet in the future. One may bet initially that one will only stake one's money, but after losing a lot of money, or winning a lot and getting surprisingly tired of the stuff, one starts betting on love instead, at the cost of conceding, or renegotiating, one's original bet on how one would bet. In real life, we bet with our love, our honor, even our lives, and we bet *on* our love, our honor, and our lives as well.

On this model, it is not hard to see how I can bet on facts and desires at the same time. I may set my health at stake on a particular medical adviser. In the background, I have a bet on the truth of science. If my health worsens, my investment in the background bet may diminish; if my health improves, my investment may increase. But the background bet does not depend solely on my health. I am also invested in the scientific method because I desire, perhaps, to live without the dogmas of religion, or because I desire to live in the open, largely egalitarian society that goes with science. At the same time, I am betting that the conclusions of science, and the scientific interpretation of my own experience, will bear out my belief that I do indeed desire to live in such a society, and that nothing else, nothing outside science and the scientific interpretation of my experience, will lead me to change that desire.[26]

Something similar happens when I buy stock in a particular company. In the background of such a bet are other bets on, say, a particular journal's advice in business matters, on the approach to business represented by that journal, on the rationality of playing the market in general, and on the value of a free market, private property, and the whole enterprise of trying to make large amounts of money. If my investment in the stock fails, I may abandon one writer for another in the same journal, I may abandon the journal altogether, or I may abandon a wider and wider circle of the underlying investments that led me to this particular bet. But I may also do any or all of this even if my particular investment succeeds: my bet that I want to make large amounts of money may fail instead. Here my interest in a mode of gathering evidence is upheld or shaken by the success of a particular bet that mode supports; it is a condition for my belief in the mode of evidence that I approve, and will continue to approve, of the ends at which the mode aims and the social and psychological configurations that make it possible; and my approval can quite clearly be shaken up by the very mode of evidence it supports: my journal, or the results of the life I have interpreted in its light, may lead me to believe that the business point of view is itself a "bad investment"—for society, for my health, even for my material happiness. But here it is also obvious how factors quite outside the workings of business, and the business interpretation of my experience, can interact with that viewpoint to lead me to change my commitment to it. Whether any experience lies "outside" the scientific point of view in the way it can lie outside the business point of view is debatable but for that reason is itself one of the things on which we bet. In general, it is surely true that the desires on which we bet are supported and can be undermined both by the factual methodologies for which they set the stakes and by other factual methodologies taken together with other desires.

It follows that whenever I make particular bets on what to consider real and what to seek out of the real, I do so not against any unshakable groundwork, but against a general framework of interests and factual methodologies that I take, at least for the moment, to be reasonably stable. If desires can always be corrected against facts and factual methodologies, and facts and factual methodologies against desires, then there can be no end to the process of seeking a firm foundation for my approach to the world. If I want to make any limited and particular decisions, however, in the service of my quite limited and particular life, I must be able to call a halt to the process of examining my interests and methodologies and regard them, at given moments, as "good enough" *for* the moment. Although an encounter with a startling fact or frustration of a deep-seated desire may lead me radically to revise the very framework against which I normally interpret facts and develop desires, I could hardly carry out such activities at all, normally or in the extraordinary cases, without relying on a framework in which factual, emotive, and normative judgments seem to me for the most part to cohere, succeed, and remain stable over time.

It is here, I propose, that traditions have their part to play. In practice we resolve the problem that the adjustment of interests and methodologies can go on indefinitely by relying generally on the interests widely propounded, established in institutions, and represented in custom by a particular society. A society can spend a longer period adjusting desires to facts, and vice versa, than can any individual, and it will express its conclusions in practices with which we in any case want our interests to cohere. The political slogans of the society, the presuppositions of its discussions, what it tells us as children and recommends we tell our children, and especially its customary practices teach us what factual propositions are best supported by our shared experience and what we ought, and are permitted, to desire. "Especially its customary practices" because practice, for societies as for individuals, represents the decision or bet that brings together fact and desire, because convictions represented in practice are more likely to be sincerely held than those merely propounded in doctrines and slogans, and because to participate in activities that can be socially shared is, as we saw earlier, one of the prime aims of the correction of our desires. Moreover, the specific ways into which custom breaks up a day, a year, and a lifetime—when, what, and how to eat; how long to work and at what; what to do with one's leisure time and when to take it; when and how to celebrate and to mourn; what distinguishes summers from winters, youth from age—resolve the greatest problem we face, as individuals, in filling up our lives: how to reconcile our limited knowledge about how to live, at each moment of decision, with our limited ability, once we know more, to correct for our mistakes. At every stage of maturity, we find ourselves unsure how to act at that stage, but once we decide how to act, and learn how we like our decisions from their consequences, that stage will already be over and we will be hurried along, a little closer to our deaths, without getting the chance to go back and try again. I argued in the last chapter that general beliefs about the world, human nature, or the purpose of life do not have enough content to bear on these specific decisions. Socially established practices can correct for our most particular desires and beliefs and in any case give us something to do, some way to carry on with our lives while, around these activities, we try to come up with an interpretation of what the whole activity of living is about. Even if an individual's interpretation then issues in a call for rebellion against the society's customs, only a set of such customs could have provided a view of the world and how to live in it in terms of which *to* rebel.

A set of customs passed down over the generations, and a set of beliefs and values endorsing those customs, is commonly called a "tradition." I suggest it is this aspect of society—the aspect that is more a matter of inheritance than of argument, and manifested more in action than in profession of belief—that is most directly responsible for the shaping of our interests. "Tradition" and "society" are not interchangeable terms. Traditions are passed down by societies, but not all societies are characterized by a specific tradition. Indeed, short-lived societies (inhabitants of a refugee camp, survivors of a shipwreck) may maintain no tradition. Traditions differ from society to society, moreover, in part as a result of the different interests people have and different bets they are willing to make, in part simply because, being constellations of very specific actions and judgments, there is much more room for difference among them than there would be if they consisted of general principles. If it is true that traditions provide the terms from which all our everyday questions and decisions begin, then it will be obvious why universalism—by its very nature, abstracting from the doubtful and the particular, the basis of all our bets, that which gives content to them and explains why they have to be bets in the first place—cannot satisfy our ethical demands.

Is it true? One natural question we might consider is why the standards against which interests are corrected need to be something social. Can we not each individually come up with our own considered compromises of desire and belief, interest and methodology? I do not want to dismiss this possibility entirely. The main point of this chapter is that factual beliefs, including beliefs about the exceptionless application of the scientific method, are fundamentally bets rather than conclusions any rational person must accept. That the stakes for our bets should be set by traditions rather than individually (or by some empirical investigation of human interests, such as psychology) is a subsidiary point for which I shall argue more fully in the next chapter. But our consideration so far does indicate that interests are informed by and directed toward a social group, and my more extended argument will suggest that the choice between tradition and individual reflection is in part falsely framed: societies come about as much because people share interests as shared interests come about because societies shape them that way. When they can, people drift toward traditions that make the same bets they do.

Thus traditions come to be maintained by people who make similar bets on where to find reality and how to live in it. Since there are different bets to make, there are different traditions, and we may expect that *as long as* there are different bets to make, there *will* be different traditions. Relativism at this level follows readily from the obscurity of life and is not antipathetic to reason: equally rational people can easily gamble differently.

LIMITED PERSPECTIVES AND THE MORAL POINT OF VIEW

There remains a serious challenge to any kind of relativism. Of the three objections we encountered earlier to attempts, against the Enlightenment's hopes, to cut knowledge up into distinct, interest-relative parts, we now have a more sophisticated understanding of interests and a response to Williams's claim that such attempts are self-defeating, but we have said nothing yet about Davidson's arguments. On Davidson's view, it would seem that all traditions must regress to the same, tradition-free process of interpretation. And there is something to this. Whether we are talking about the evaluation of facts or desires, it is hard to make good sense of the idea that the standards of evaluation might form separate and closed systems. Suppose I want to show that system or scheme A differs from system or scheme B. Then I must surely be able to see enough of both of them to know that they are in fact both schemes and do in fact differ. But, from the perspective of A alone, B will appear as just a set of wrong or incoherent utterances, and the same goes for A from the perspective of B. We need some view of what they have in common, not itself invested in either of them, to make the point that they *are* different and incommensurable frameworks. Let us call this view, and the information on A and B it contains, scheme C. Now to recognize C as itself a scheme, a particular view of the facts rather than the absolute truth itself, we need to contrast it with some other, actual or possible, scheme D, and this contrast in turn will require a regress to the wider scheme E . . . Hence, merely to make the point that there *are* varying schemes—or "frameworks," or "traditions"—we need to presuppose a scheme-free background, containing and delineating the differences among all the schemes. This is an old antirelativist argument, of which Davidson's theory of interpretation is a version.

My response to it, in brief, is that while the antirelativist argument is irrefutable, there is an equally good argument for the relativist position, that we may therefore choose one position with quite as good grounds as the other, and that, from the moral point of view, the relativist one is preferable. These claims rely on what Kant called an "antinomy" and on the distinction he drew between moral ("practical") and scientific ("speculative") points of view. To clarify them, therefore, we need to turn first to Kant.

After laying out the conditions that make scientific knowledge of the empirical world possible, Kant maintained that precisely because we know these conditions structure our science, we cannot suppose the world "in itself" to resemble our scientific conception of it. To understand our knowledge as limited by certain conditions is to understand that we cannot have knowledge outside those conditions, but it is also to posit a mode of access to reality beyond our limitations by which they make sense *as* limitations at all. In other words, Kant accepted the argument that the very notion of perspectival views of the world presupposes the possibility of a point beyond perspectives, but he insisted at the same time—consistently, I think, with a deep understanding of what it is for knowledge to be perspectivally bound—that that absolute conception could never enter our knowledge; it could function only as a limit ("ideal," in Kantian language) outside of, and defining the outside of, what we know. Absolute reality, reality as it might be for God, can be thought but not known, although to think about something is always to try to know it. We therefore continually attempt to know the unknowable. As a result, human reason is "burdened by questions which, as prescribed by the very nature of reason itself, it is not able to ignore, but which, as transcending all its power, it is also not able to answer."[27] This is how Kant accounted for the endless arguments people have over the existence of God or free will. They are antinomies, attempts to settle questions by nature unsettleable, in which equally good proofs can be given for propositions on opposing sides. Kant offered proofs for the thesis and antithesis of four antinomies—there is/is not a beginning to the world, there is/is not a simplest possible part, there is/is not freedom of the will, and there is/is not a God. These four, he claimed, and they alone, meet the proper conditions for an antinomy: they each address a question that human reason necessarily encounters; raise an unavoidable, not an artificial, contradiction; and arise from attempts to seek the absolutely unconditioned that makes possible, but eludes, all conditioned knowledge.[28]

I suggest there is a fifth antinomy, in the debate between absolutism and relativism: the thesis holds that knowledge must be grounded in an absolute description superseding and accounting for all background conditions,[29] while the antithesis, equally plausibly, shows that claims to knowledge must always be judged against some limited set of background conditions (interests, methodologies, perspectives). Proofs for this antinomy, in Kant's own reductio ad absurdum fashion, might run roughly along the lines (1) that insistence on background conditions leads to an infinite regress making explanation impossible, while (2) an absolute description of the world would lie beyond all finite determination and consequently be empirically useless.[30] Alternatively, we might construe the antinomy as a debate between the Hegelian (and Davidsonian) demand for comprehensiveness in our attempts to grasp and communicate truth (no limited chain of justifications and explanations can be recognized as even provisionally legitimate except in the light of a method of evaluation beyond that limit) and Kierkegaard's insistence on an ineradicable knot of obscurity in each of those attempts (in actuality, we always have to bring our justifications and explanations to an end at some point short of the infinite series that would illuminate and legitimate them).

However exactly we phrase and defend it, putting the contradiction between absolute and interested conceptions of knowledge as an antinomy has several important implications. In the first place, Kantian antinomies are neither questions for further study at the end of a textbook on metaphysics nor Hegelian contradictions to be somehow overcome. Rather, they are permanently irreconcilable, in principle immune to what Kant calls "dogmatic solution";[31] at the same time, they express essential and ineradicable features of what it is to seek knowledge. It follows that to premise an argument, as I am doing, on one side of an antinomy neither invalidates nor is invalidated by arguments, like those of Williams and Davidson, premised on the other side. Where I assume for moral purposes that our thought begins with and regresses to distinct and incommensurable frameworks of interest, others may equally well assume, for scientific purposes, that those frameworks must be commensurable in light of a more fundamental, perspective-free gathering of the facts in the world.

In the second place, Kant bases his strict distinction between practical and speculative reason on his antinomies, and accepting the significance of antinomies will enable us to make rich use of that distinction. The terms "practical reason" and "speculative reason" derive from Aristotle, but Aristotle used them to characterize two among several different kinds of thought, which he distinguished in a fairly rough and ready way. For Kant, by contrast, practical reason and speculative reason can come to radically different conclusions: in particular, practical reason holds that there is free will and there is a God, while speculative reason insists on the antitheses of these propositions. On my account, the distinction between practical and speculative thought yields a similarly radical difference in one's attitude toward incommensurable frameworks of interest.

On the simplest level, this distinction amounts to the difference we notice in everyday life between the viewpoint of the spectator and the viewpoint of the agent.[32] The spectator may know exactly how a situation will come out, or believe, without knowing, that everything in a given situation, including what the agent chooses, is fully determined, but the agent cannot make a choice without assuming that—without acting *as if*—her choices can change things and are dependent on her deliberations rather than on external circumstances determining those deliberations. In addition, the spectator claims his disinterest as an advantage for his viewpoint: he can see what the agent is too frightened, too angry, too much in love to see. The agent, however, may claim interestedness as an advantage as well: the spectator, in his Olympian position, may miss the details of what it is *like* to be an agent in the situation and consequently misjudge what agents are likely to do. Finally, the spectator is theoretically able to survey many situations and then decide which he would most like to act in, but while the agent may not be able to afford this luxury, at least she has a chance of attaining some goal, some object she has evaluated as worthwhile; the spectator, like some of Dostoevsky's and Kafka's characters, could sit forever, trying to decide what to do.

Kant stresses the differential place of free will in these two standpoints, suggesting ingeniously that it is visible only from the practical one but is nonetheless truly visible for all that. I want to stress instead the relative function of the unknown and of interests in the two standpoints. From the ethical point of view, concerned as we are with what to do, we cannot forget that we are all limited individuals, most interested in those facts relevant to the course of our lives, having to make decisions before we have all the information a pure seeker after knowledge would require, and having, in those decisions, to determine simultaneously what we are willing to believe given the objects of desire we have at stake and what we ought to desire given what we are willing to believe. Even though it is a potentially infinite process, and one demanding that we transcend all interests, we must always bring our thinking on an ethical question to a definite, interest-bound close. It is therefore incumbent on us, as ethical beings, to presuppose the antithesis of the fifth antinomy.

None of this is true for science, or any other methodology seeking knowledge in a purely "speculative" way. To rest satisfied with limited information is poor science, and to bet on data according to how one assesses the stakes involved is dishonest science. Scientists come to provisional conclusions, to be sure, and indeed philosophers of science view all scientific claims as in some sense provisional, but these provisional claims are left open as much as possible to future correction. The scientist tends to hedge and qualify answers until they are thoroughly researched, and not to answer questions at all if they are not amenable to research, while in ethics this would make action, and responsibility for action, impossible. Insofar as it is simply a search for knowledge, science projects its completion infinitely far into the future and as something no individual need be able to grasp: it can afford to rely, and ought to rely, on the thesis of the fifth antinomy.

One consequence of this is that the contemporary divisions between those who accuse science of being itself a product of human interests and those who dismiss ethics as merely a fact of human life deserving scientific investigation are simultaneously irresolvable and pointless. Ethics and science view each other with suspicion because the one always relies on incomplete and interested information while the other strives to be comprehensive and disinterested, but the debate between them represents nothing more than their dependence on different sides of an antinomy. Scientists purport to be able to give a disinterested account of our evaluation of our interests, and hence of ethics, by showing it to be, say, a biological development that evolved to preserve human life in community.[33] But one can judge the scientific method ethically, as serving certain interests, tying the rise of the experimental method, perhaps, to the individualism of sixteenth- and seventeenth-century Protestants or to the desire of later generations to direct human attention from other-worldly to this-worldly pleasure. Alternatively, science can claim to be the "broader" perspective, because it answers questions about more phenomena than ethics does. But ethics can also claim to be broader than science, since it answers more of the questions human beings actually ask, including ones about the nature and function of science. From the scientific perspective, interests are a distraction and the standards by which we evaluate them are utterly incapable of being judged true or false. From the ethical perspective, science is but a servant of our interests and is unable to attribute objectivity to ethical judgment only because it must suspend the interests of which ethical standards are the object. These are not settleable arguments. There is no more possibility of showing, ultimately, whether science is interested or ethics an illusion than there is of proving or disproving the existence of God and free will.

So when making ethical claims we can assume them to be objective, and if I am right to add a fifth antinomy to Kant's four, we can also assume the legitimacy of relying on interests, or limited frameworks of interest, in the service of our limited ethical decisions. This does not of course mean that in ethical discussions we may ignore what science has to say, only that such discussions must always refer back to our conception of ourselves and our role in the world and never merely rest on scientific results as if they were a neutral given. Agent and spectator, relativist and absolutist, practical and speculative reasoner have much to teach each other, although the conclusions to which they finally come may differ sharply. Kant in part realized this, in part ignored it at the cost of serious confusion as to how his various viewpoints were supposed to come together in one person. Factual considerations about the natural and social world will be very important, in the next two chapters, to the case I shall make for tradition and authority in ethics. That I approach those considerations from an ethical rather than a scientific point of view means only that the interpretation of the facts I present gives the requirements of action priority over the requirements of knowledge.

Finally, reliance on limited frameworks of interest goes with a recognition that the world is very obscure to us. We know we are merely positing these frameworks as a legitimate stopping point: we know that much lies beyond them and that we could go further. We know, as we know if we posit God or free will, that the proof on which we are relying is not the only one around on the issue. Antinomies, and the bifurcated notion of thought to which they are related, suggest that reason can leave matters radically unsettled. I shall argue in the next chapter that we need more than a scientific conception of human nature in order to act, but from Bernard Williams's or Donald Davidson's position, premised on the perspective of speculative reason, one could argue quite the opposite. And even within the perspective of practical reason one can come to very different conclusions depending on what tradition, what limited framework, one is willing to accept. How then can any position carry conviction? How can anyone decide where to place his or her bets? Kant himself spoke of a place in practical reason for a certain kind of faith, a "rational faith," and to a considerable extent I shall follow him here.[34] We place our bets on the basis of a trust, a rational faith, in our frameworks of interest. It is something of an offense to reason, however, certainly to the Enlightenment ideal of reason, to allow faith to settle conviction where argument still has room to go—and nothing I have said denies that we *can* pursue our investigations of fact, and evaluations of desire, well past the point at which traditions are content to stop. Why insist on what we do *not* know, why rein in reason with limits, rather than allowing it to go as far as possible on its infinite journey? In anticipation of those who might find "rational faith" an oxymoron, and an unpleasant oxymoron at that, I want to end this chapter by quoting Kierkegaard, in this respect Kant's closest intellectual descendant:

> What then is the Unknown? It is the limit to which the Reason repeatedly comes, and in so far . . . it is the different, the absolutely different. . . . When qualified as absolutely different it seems on the verge of disclosure, but this is not the case; for the Reason cannot even conceive an absolute unlikeness. The Reason . . . conceives only such an unlikeness within itself as it can conceive by means of itself, and hence conceives only such a superiority over itself as it can conceive by means of itself.[35] . . . The Reason will

doubtless find it impossible to conceive [that the Unknown could in any way be revealed,] . . . and when it hears [such a revelation] announced will . . . sens[e] merely that its downfall is threatened. In so far the Reason will have much to urge against it; and yet we have on the other hand seen that the Reason, in its paradoxical passion, precisely desires its own downfall. . . . Consider the analogy presented by love, though it is not a perfect one. Self-love underlies love; but the paradoxical passion of self-love when at its highest pitch wills precisely its own downfall. This is also what love desires, so that these two are linked in mutual understanding at the passion of the moment, and this passion is love. Why should not the lover find this conceivable? But he who in self-love shrinks from the touch of love can neither understand it nor summon the courage to venture it, since it means his own downfall.[36]

That reason might need something beyond itself, that reasoning might depend on something unreasoned, is a paradox, but to shrink from this paradox, while not an intrinsically irrational attitude, might be as crippling to reason as egocentrism is to our egos. For Kierkegaard, the something unreasoned that restores us as if with the power of love is religious faith, specifically Christian faith. I suggest that it is ethical faith, the faith in traditions that makes ethics possible.

3. Traditions and Their Stories

I argued at the end of the last chapter that, for moral purposes, we may allow our thought to regress to frameworks of interest. We need now to explore in greater depth why we should want traditions, rather than individual reflection or psychological theory, to provide and shape those frameworks.

DRAWBACKS OF PRAGMATISM

People who defend the importance of traditions usually do so on grounds that followers of those traditions cannot themselves maintain. Defenders of tradition tend to be political conservatives or anthropologists with a moral commitment to cultural relativism, and in either case the grounds they give are pragmatic ones. Political conservatives, taking their cue from Edmund Burke, argue that one ought to rely on traditional ways of doing things, in making laws and formulating policies, because traditions contribute to social harmony and prevent individuals from introducing changes that the society is unable to accept. In *Federalist* No. 14 James Madison asks, "Is it not the glory of the people of America, that . . . they have not suffered a blind veneration for antiquity [or] for custom . . . to overrule the suggestions of their own good sense, the knowledge of their own situation, and the lessons of their own experience?" This kind of Enlightenment boast makes political conservatives shudder. A veneration for custom, they feel, allows the people of a society always to know what they

can expect of one another and their government and is a much better political guide than "the suggestions of [one's] own good sense." An individual's own sense, in significant political matters at least, is generally anything
but good. Unlike custom or the wisdom of "antiquity," it has not been
tested against a very long stretch of experience and tends to be driven by
an excess of optimism and a lack of patience. Far better to humble oneself
to the regimented and slow ways of tradition.

In anthropology, tradition goes by the name of "culture."[1] Defenders of
tradition here are principled cultural relativists, whose arguments constitute a more sophisticated version of the conservative claims. Cultures, they
maintain, have over time worked out ways for their adherents to adjust to
their physical and social environments. Endogamy is a way of preserving
tribal identity, exogamy of increasing a tribe's membership or preventing
inherited birth defects, food taboos of avoiding health problems or con-
serving scarce resources.[2] The beliefs and practices promoting this adjustment are tightly interwoven, moreover, so an attempt by reform-minded
individuals to interfere with one piece will often bring down the whole
system. Some anthropologists stress the function of traditions; others, the
way in which the pieces of a tradition are woven together; but the bottom
line is always the same: cultures ought to develop out of their own internal
resources because anything else will bring degradation, and perhaps physical destruction, to the people brought up in them. And, indeed, this is
often true. The rampant alcoholism and despair among contemporary
Native Americans and Australian aborigines give striking testimony to the
wisdom of the relativist prophecy.[3]

But for all the accuracy of this prophecy, pragmatic cases for preserving
traditions have a crippling flaw: they use universalist reasons to support a
nonuniversalist ethic. When conservatives and anthropologists are
pressed, they generally have a pretty straightforward notion of the goals
of human life: to be healthy, to be free, to be happy, where "freedom" and
"happiness" take their most obvious, uncomplicated sense. The value of
traditions, much as they emphasize it, is then subordinated to these goals.
If that is the case, however, it is hard to see why traditions *must* be preserved. Meddling in custom and hallowed belief has often wreaked havoc,
to be sure, but could that not be because the meddling was poorly

performed? The sciences of human life with which, over the past two centuries, we in the West have tried to replace tradition—psychology, sociology, economics, and the like—are but young; as they gain maturity, they may be able to lead people out of their old-fashioned ways more easily. Indeed, one approach might be to get people to abandon their traditional cultures altogether, instead of trying to construct some precarious middle ground between tradition and modernity. A reasonable explanation of the aborigines' suffering, after all, is that they have not gone *far enough* from their old ways; if they gave them up completely, their children might be able to assimilate happily into the West. In any case, if the human telos is as universally recognizable as health, pleasure, and political freedom, it can hardly be *necessary* to work through traditions to attain it. And since many traditions actually perpetuate illness, misery, and oppression, there is good reason to find an alternative way.

In addition, pragmatic considerations cannot easily maintain the loyalty of a culture's members. A Jew who believes that her ancestors avoided pork out of fear of trichinosis should find this a silly practice to maintain in the light of modern sanitation. If she dislikes pork or enjoys having restrictions on her food, then she may follow it anyway, but these are not motivations that will hold up well against any strong reasons to abandon the practice; they will certainly not long persuade her children. The same goes even for those who are taught by more subtle anthropologists to view their culture as an elaborate set of symbols. If that is *all* it is, why not simply study it?— and guide one's practice by more direct routes to the common human ends.

I come to the traditionalism I am advocating from a suspicion of the very notion of "common human ends." It is certainly true that human beings generally desire health, pleasure, and freedom from political oppression. It is also true, I believe, that an ethic, to be a framework by which people ought to structure their lives rather than a mere arbitrary result of evolution, must aim at some end beyond itself by which it can be judged. What is not so clear is that the things all people desire, and the ultimate telos by which ways of life are judged, ought to be identified. Perhaps social scientists have accepted the Enlightenment's emphasis on health, pleasure, and political freedom simply because these naturalistic goals lend themselves to scientific study. Perhaps health, pleasure, and political freedom are subsidiary goals on the way to some other end—either prerequisites for that end or things we value for themselves but less than we value something else. And if we have some other, ultimate end, it could turn out that traditions are essential, rather than accidental, to the attainment of that end. But then, what could our ultimate end—our highest good—be? How do we define the word "good" when we conceive it apart from all our actual desires?

The best alternative I know to defining "good" in straightforward, naturalistic terms is the claim that "goodness" is and must be in part obscure. "In part" because one cannot give an account of a word that bears no relation to the meaning we pretheoretically assign to it. Any definition of the good would have to allow that health, pleasure, and political freedom are goods and would presumably relate whatever else is good to them in some fashion. But the whatever else, and the structure by which the various parts of the human telos might hang together, need not be so clear. So, at least, claim theories that regard the good as obscured from us.

Of course, to skeptical eyes this looks like a smoke screen. Philosophers unwilling to acknowledge that an ultimate good, if it exists at all, can consist only of the objects that all human beings actually desire, will naturally want to describe their own candidate for the good as mysterious. That way they can avoid explaining or defending it. The oldest trick in the book for getting people to do something they would not otherwise want to do is to say there is a mysterious prize at the end. And since ethics is a lifelong task, one who uses this trick to win support for his conception of the ethical life need not fear he will ever have to explain what happened to the prize.

There are, however, strong reasons for considering obscurity of purpose essential to ethics. To begin with, our ethical practice and evaluation depend significantly on the presence of risk. Our respect for a great many actions diminishes if the agent has complete knowledge of and control over the results. It takes away even from one's choices on behalf of others if those choices all wait on a strict calculation of how much happiness or other benefit they will bring. Such choices reveal no virtues, nor do they express any evaluation of one good over another. Evaluation comes in when there is a possibility of loss, when there is risk. Choice notoriously gets its meaning from risk, and commitment means nothing except against a background of risk. Perhaps if we lived in a world without any risks this would not be so, but in a world without risk there would also be little point to ethics. We might be able to regard a God or an inanimate object as good although it took no risks, but that is precisely because such a being would by nature have no choices to make. A good *life*, as we know it, is inevitably a series of choices, evaluated according to the virtues revealed in those choices, and that entails the presupposition of a world of risk. The presence of risk is thus a condition for ethics—the practice of deliberation over goodness—even if it is not one for goodness per se. And as limitations on knowledge are a condition for risk, so they too are a condition for the ethical life.

But this presupposition of risk is just a phenomenological fact about the way we evaluate action. Nothing I have so far said goes to show that risk and the limitations on our knowledge that go with it are themselves "a good thing," that we are better off with them than we would be attaining, or trying to attain, the choice-less existence of a God. And nothing I have so far said goes to show that the limitations on our knowledge need include limitations on our knowledge *of the good*. We might know the goal at which we should aim while still taking risks as we try to overcome partially obscured obstacles on the way to that goal. Why should obscurity, in particular, of *purpose* be essential to ethics?

THE HIGHEST GOOD—AND TRADITIONS

I want to suggest that a complete description of the good would defeat the very function of ethics as a guide to action. This is a hard point, and I shall try first to make it comprehensible before attempting a philosophical defense of it. Consider therefore what would happen should you discover that the definition of "goodness" is, in fact, "whatever gives you pleasure." You would surely feel free not to pursue that goal, if you didn't feel like striving after pleasure. You would probably be disappointed and consider, not that you had finally found the true significance of the ethical, but that there was no "ethical" at all, or at least that it made not nearly the difference you had imagined it might. Now suppose someone offers you a different definition of the ethical goal—perhaps a more sophisticated version of pleasure (Mill's rather than Bentham's), or pleasure for a certain number of others as well as yourself, or something like Christian salvation, or Marxist utopia, or freedom from neurosis, or contemplation. You might request of your informant to describe what life at that endpoint would look like. Whatever the description, you can then ask, "But why should I desire such a life? Why should *I* take that as my goal?" If the answer is, as it often is, "Because otherwise you will be burnt in hell fire" (or some equivalent: "massacred by the proletariat," perhaps), then the game is up. The good has been translated back into terms of pain and pleasure and you are free, once again, to measure it against your preferences; it does not serve as an objective counterpoint to, and correction of, your interests. If, on the other hand, the answer is, "Because otherwise you will just be immoral," you can dismiss this as obscurantism. The person proposing a conception of the good is thus placed in a double bind: either she confesses to not being able to describe it and raises the suspicion that it does not make sense, or she leaves you with the option of saying that what she describes does not interest you. A conception of the good can seem important as long as the reasons why it is important are concealed, but once the reasons are given, you feel free to ask what is important about these reasons, and in pressing that question inevitably find that both the reasons and what they are reasons for cease to have any hold over you.

One response to this dilemma is to claim that it makes nonsense of the notion of an objective good, but what Kant calls our "practical faith," the faith required for and manifested in practice, resists this approach. In our choices we show that we consider things objectively valuable, some more valuable than others, and that we consider our desires and interests, far from being the source of this hierarchy of value, to be themselves subject to evaluation and correction. We use a hierarchy of evaluative standards, which we derive from and refer to some vaguely imagined ultimate point.

Since this ultimate point seems essentially obscure, philosophers who accept its existence have tended to say that it is something mystical, and the object of a mystical insight that requires great training (the Neoplatonists), or that, while not mystical, it is a nonnatural quality perceivable only through nonnatural intuition (G. E. Moore), or again that, while it is natural and akin to what we naturally consider happiness, infirmities in our present condition prevent us from being able to see and accept it properly (a wide range of philosophers, including Spinoza, Hegel, and Freud). I do not want to opt for mysticism here, and all attempts of which I am aware to define nonnatural ethical intuition, or to say who might have it and who not, have ended in failure. I have more sympathy with the suggestion that the reason we cannot properly perceive the power of the good is a matter of our psychological limitations, but this approach does not take seriously enough our feeling that we do not merely in *fact* lack a definition of the good—we cannot even conceive of something that might fit such a definition. We see something as objectively valuable when it leads us to something else we are seeking; the phrase "self-sufficiently valuable" sounds disquietingly like an oxymoron.

It is not literally an oxymoron, however, simply an expression for which it is hard to imagine an appropriate referent. I shall not attempt to offer a specific candidate for that role here. For the purposes of this book, I need to establish that traditions *may* provide access to a highest or ultimate good—something "self-sufficiently valuable"—not that they actually do so. I am in fact convinced neither of a realist nor of a nonrealist position about this good. The question seems to me unsettleable: another antinomy. But if realism is a *possible* position, then acting as if it were true may be reasonable. The possibility, if not the truth, of realism is thus a necessary condition of practical faith. Only something self-sufficiently valuable could convey value to the more limited goods we seek in everyday life, so we must establish at least the intelligibility of that notion if we are to take seriously ethical deliberation as I understand it. What a description of this ultimate good *might look like* is therefore essential to my project, even if an actual description of it is just as essentially unavailable. But what kind of story can plausibly explain both what the highest good might look like and why in fact it seems irremediably obscure?

Try imagining how you might come to recognize a state or thing as the "good" or purpose of the universe. In principle, it seems to me, you would need either (i) to feel, on encountering it, that all your desires, and all the desires you can imagine having in the future, were satisfied by it, or (ii) to see how all lesser human purposes could be explained and justified by it—perhaps, indeed, how its existence gave a "point" to the existence of every other object and event in the universe. You might, in viewing it, lose all your desires (achieve "nirvana"), feel all your desires satisfied, or find your desires changing such that you now desire something you can fully attain. Or you might suddenly understand how something could make human life, and in particular your life, absolutely worthwhile despite the fact that you continue to have restlessly unsatisfied desires. So the recognition of a highest good could come by way of either a change in feeling or a change in knowledge.[4] For Plato, the source of most discussion of this issue, these two routes ought to come together. There is good reason to question whether such convergence is possible—what intellectual recognition could still the restlessness of our desires forever? and why should something that did bring such "peace" necessarily answer our questions about human or natural purposes?—but aside from that, there are problems in meeting the demands of even one of the two routes. In the first place, it is hard to be clear on just what those demands are. My formulations are vague (what does "point" mean, for instance, when applied to nonhuman beings?), but others have not tended to be much better. In the second place, nothing has ever in fact met either condition (i) or condition (ii).

Why not? I offer seven different possibilities, all with forceful and well-known defenders. (1) There is no ultimate good. (2) The ultimate good exists, but only those with access to the special mystical intuition or training mentioned earlier can perceive it, or can perceive why it is self-sufficiently valuable. (3) The ultimate good is a perfectly natural phenomenon—a certain kind of sensation or activity, say: we just haven't found it yet. (Most of us haven't, at least: scientologists, transcendental meditators, and other cult followers are notorious for proclaiming their access to a kind of experience that removes all dissatisfaction with life.) (4) We are unable to perceive the ultimate good because of various evils that we tolerate or perpetuate in the world. One might take this to mean that a God withholds vision of the good from us as punishment for the violence and cruelty we inflict on one another, or one might take it simply as an unsurprising, natural fact: beings immersed in violence and suffering are likely to mistake their immediate ethical goals for the ultimate good on the rare occasions in which they find the leisure to engage in reflection on such matters at all. If the evils of war, poverty, and hatred could be overcome—by a divinity or by "historical necessity"—either we might find what we are looking for in our lives or the dissatisfaction that leads us to keep looking for something might disappear. (5) Our desires are so structured that we never fully desire anything once it is within our grasp. Thinkers from Plato to Lacan have talked about the inevitable development of new objects of desire every time a particular set of desires is satisfied. Perhaps (a) we have not yet found the proper means by which either to restructure our desires or to rid ourselves of them. Or perhaps (b) this structure is so much a part of our biology or psychology that we will never find the means to change it. (6) The good, being after all the good *of* all the world, or at least of all human life, cannot be perceived as such until all the world or all human life is completed. Perhaps this good consists in Leibniz's ideal: a world of as much variety as is compatible with a rational order.[5] Then it would clearly be reasonable to suppose one could see what such a good amounts to only by surveying the entire universe. The picture of the complete world might itself be something we could wholeheartedly desire: taken as a whole, our world might obviously be the best of all possible worlds and that fact, or our part in it, might give us joy. If this is the case, or if in any other way the good is something that emanates from the history of the universe or human race, then we may expect never to grasp it, regardless of whether we change our desires or overcome our immediate evils. The nature of the good would then be necessarily beyond our grasp in exactly the way that the whole of the universe, according to Kant's antinomies, is necessarily beyond our grasp. (7) Perhaps the very pursuit of the ethical life bars us from perceiving the good; perhaps action is incompatible with full perception of the goal of action. I do not understand why this would be so, unless it is merely a consequence of hypothesis 4 or 5 above (*given* our current desires or the evils of our current condition, action may be structured thus), but many people have supposed it to be so and have reserved contemplation of the good for a state beyond this life—for God, for the soul after death, or for a kind of meditation completely divorced from action.

Now suppose the truth about the highest good involves some combination of hypotheses 4 through 7. The last three positions can be combined: as Goethe suggests, our desires may be insatiable (5) precisely so that they can keep moving us to action, and in action we may never perceive the complete good (7) because that good requires an infinity of world and time (6). Suppose, in any case, that the true good of the universe, or of human life in the universe, cannot be properly perceived or desired without the completion of the universe of which it is the good. Then, if the universe is infinite, we can never properly perceive and desire the good, and if it is finite, we can at least not do so until there is no further action to be performed. Yet we might well expect to perceive *more and more* of the good as our history in the universe continues—and to desire both what we do perceive of it and the very process of coming to perceive it. This would be a goal that, by perpetually evading completion, would satisfy the constraints on action and desire of hypotheses 5 and 7. It would also allow us to give value to the more limited goods we use every day without giving them ultimate value: we could see the kinds of pleasure we include under "happiness," the kinds of knowledge we include under "wisdom," and the kinds of behaviors we approve of as "courageous," "just," "generous," or "loving" either as parts of the true good that is being progressively revealed or as aids to the perception and desire of that good. The ultimate good would then be like a giant jigsaw puzzle into which our various limited goods fit (or to the construction of which they aid)—and the variety of interpretations of those limited goods represented by the variety of our ethical traditions would then correspond to the fact that people may collaborate on a jigsaw puzzle by working on different pieces of it. We may posit that all traditions will come together explicitly at some point, or we may suppose the point of their convergence to be, like the good itself, something to which we aspire but can never reach, something "at the end of time." Traditions would be the appropriate bearers of the limited goods because they continue over time and, as we shall see shortly, display on their face the very limitations that allow us to posit a good beyond all limited goods. Finally, to bring a version of hypothesis 4 into the picture, the possibility *that* this scenario about the good is correct, or at least a "reasonable bet," may be something we can perceive clearly only once the various traditions stop fighting one another, once they find a role in public life in which they can simultaneously be effective and avoid tyranny and corruption.

There are two obvious problems with this picture: Does the account of "the good" it offers make any sense? And is there any reason at all to think it true?

Talk of an "ultimate good," of the Platonic sort I have in mind, can easily seem nonsensical. How can we name something that by hypothesis we have never really known? Put another way, how can the use of our ordinary word "good" depend on something outside all our experience? These sorts of considerations have led most twentieth-century philosophers to insist that we either reinterpret the notion of an "ultimate good" or abandon it altogether. There are, however, quite familiar cases in which we name things we do not adequately know. In everyday life we often grasp that something is a name of a person before we have a clear idea of what kind of name it is (nickname, patronymic, kinship term, title, etc.), or that something names a kind of object before we have a clear idea of what kind of object. On a more sophisticated level, the causal theory of reference, in contemporary philosophy of language, has maintained that we discover the essential properties of natural kinds only long after we name them; we learn what constitutes our reference, in these cases, long after we set up the relevant referential chains. So it is hardly absurd to suppose we might use "the good" to gesture vaguely in the direction of some purpose that all people seek, while discovering the analytic a posteriori truths about its essential properties only much later. A similar response can be made to the analogous question about use: it is not implausible that the use of some of our terms is precisely to drag us beyond our normal patterns of use. If, as hypothesis 5 supposes, our desires continually drag us beyond every stable point we reach, then that is itself an ordinary fact about ourselves which we might expect linguistic communities to reflect in some fashion. Perhaps the phrase "the good" functions to challenge accepted conceptions of human virtue when a community's discussion of such matters threatens to become complacent and stifling. In any case, neither reference nor use has to be perfectly clear for a word to have meaning.

And the second objection? What can plausibly be said in defense of my story about the good? Nothing directly, I think, but the failure of alternative accounts speaks well for it. Hypothesis 1, as has already been mentioned, renders ethical discussion unintelligible. Hypothesis 2 is unlikely, on the available empirical evidence, as are 3, 4, and 5a, when they are taken to imply, as they were in the Enlightenment, that an empirical, scientific search will eventually reveal our "common human ends." Socialism, Rousseauvian educational reforms, psychoanalysis, sexual liberation, "mindexpanding" drugs—none has lived up to its promise of leading people to the "purpose of life," either in the sense of producing contented individuals or in the sense of eliminating social conflict and corruption. Treating the good as an object of science is an approach that demands empirical evaluation rather than a priori judgment, so it would have been premature to reject this approach in the eighteenth century, but good empirical practice virtually demands such rejection in the late twentieth century. But if rejection of the notion of the good wreaks havoc with ethical language, while naturalistic accounts of that notion's obscurity seem empirically false, then an account building obscurity into the essence of the notion begins to look attractive. Furthermore, such an account fits well with the phenomenological facts about desire and action on which hypotheses 5 and 7 are based. So my story has going for it the implausibility of other stories as well as coherence with a number of facts that are otherwise difficult to explain—both generally taken as strong marks of truth. I do not pretend to have anything stronger in the way of proof for it: I assert not that my story is incontrovertibly true but that it is a *reasonable bet,* and in particular a better bet than its purely naturalistic, antitraditionalist rivals.

On the bet I am offering, therefore, the good is mysterious not because it is nonempirical, but because it is essentially a project for action, hence something that remains incomplete as long as there remain actions to take. When we pin it down as anything static, even a mystical vision, it fails of its primary role as a guide for practical faith. That virtues glow more strongly when they reflect commitment rather than calculation, that naturalistic accounts of human goals are too weak to explain most of what we do, that we seem always to need new objects of desire, all reflect, within the phenomenology of action, the fact that any ultimate goal for action must remain partly obscure.

How obscure? If we hold it entirely obscure, that will be the same as having no goal at all and a ground for scoffers to call our faith empty, our commitment deluded. Herein lies the temptation to introduce a complicated Platonic training into ethics or a special nonnatural intuition: better some access to the good than a goal so mysterious it could just as well not exist. I suggest instead that it remains always just beyond our reach, elusive but ever more distinctly visible. Translated out of metaphor, an adequate conception of the good to suit a practical faith might be one in which limited concrete goals—a ritual, a marriage, a job—keep appearing as worthwhile (measured by one's pretheoretical intuitions and standards as well as what one has reflectively worked out about the nature of and means to happiness, decency, and beauty). Those limited states then prove themselves to be as good or better than anticipated (by the pleasure they give, the anticipated notions of goodness they fulfill, and the contribution they make to the perception and fulfillment of future goals)—but they are always succeeded by new limited goals, which appear necessary for a fuller achievement of the good but could not, or at least did not, so appear until the first effort was completed. Then the good for an individual life would be a series of particular good states, one behind another, such that they could not be known as a whole. Each state would hold our interest because we would know that something else, and better, lay behind it. It would of course be vain to seek full knowledge of our ultimate end, but trust in a specific tradition could take the place of such knowledge as a day-to-day ethical guide. Traditions are structured to suit a good of precisely this kind: they provide guidelines, at each moment of our lives, that help us respond to the question of how to live at that moment, while always concealing, or at least refusing, any overall, final answer to that question.

Alasdair MacIntyre proposes a similar vision of the good, in the course of a similar move toward traditions as a basis for ethics:

> To ask 'What is the good for me?' is to ask how best I might live out [the] unity [of my life] and bring it to completion. . . . The unity of a human life is the unity of a narrative quest. . . . Two key features of the medieval conception of a quest need to be recalled. The first is that without some at

least partly determinate conception of the final *telos* there could not be any
beginning to a quest. Some conception of the good for man is required. . . .
But secondly it is clear the medieval conception of a quest is not at all that
of a search for something already adequately characterized, as miners search
for gold or geologists for oil. It is in the course of the quest and only through
encountering and coping with the various particular harms, dangers, temp-
tations and distractions which provide any quest with its episodes and incidents that the goal of the quest is finally to be understood. . . . The virtues
are to be understood as those dispositions which will . . . sustain us in the
relevant kind of quest . . . and which will furnish us with increasing self-
knowledge and knowledge of the good. . . . We have then arrived at a provisional conclusion about the good life for man: the good life for man is the
life spent in seeking for the good life for man, and the virtues necessary for
the seeking are those which will enable us to understand what more and
what else the good life for man is.[6]

That is, according to MacIntyre, the telos of an ethic, while it must be
vaguely recognizable to be an ethical telos at all, need not be fully known
and may in fact guide our lives most successfully if we come to know it
better only in the search for it. Taken together with his definition of a
tradition (a "living tradition" at any rate) as "an historically extended, socially embodied argument, and an argument precisely about the goods
which constitute that tradition,"[7] this account of the good allows for the
following conclusion: that traditions acquire their ethical value precisely
by providing us with a working conception of the telos of our lives. We
might call them "midlevel generalizations" about the good: neither as obscure as the ultimate purpose to which they refer nor as ill-formed as our
immediate desires and beliefs, they provide reasonably general standards
of how to live that are at the same time detailed enough for our particular
daily questions to regress to them. If this is so, it will be vain to seek the
point of every tradition in the light of some universalist conception of
people's goals. Each tradition, if it functions at all, *will establish for its followers the way all goals are to be conceived.*

That is the position I shall defend here, but it is not exactly MacIntyre's
own argument for traditions. MacIntyre argues powerfully for the role of

a narrative in making action intelligible and providing a framework for the Aristotelian virtues. He adds, reasonably enough, that the narrative we tell about ourselves ought to include our place in the various communities to which we belong; and then, rather lamely and certainly too quickly, he suggests that the community with which we identify needs a tradition to give it a specific character that endures over time.[8] The connection between narrative and community is weak: MacIntyre claims only that the narrative I pick for myself will be less rich and less accurate if it does not reflect the life of my community. Nor is the connection between community and tradition any stronger: why should the community care about failing to retain a particular identity over time? It can provide the background for individual lives and carry on an argument over the nature of the good, even if it intermingles freely with other communities, borrows from the wisdom of those other communities, and merges, either eventually or as fast as possible, into a society comprising all the human beings in the world. Why should a community, or an individual, identify with a *specific* past, a *specific* narrative or history? MacIntyre brings in traditions and communities in the first place to provide a context for the life of the Aristotelian virtues. Ultimately, however, this is again an external, universalist telos for the maintenance of traditions, albeit an ethical rather than a pragmatic one—they are justified in that they make possible the attainment of qualities to which all human beings aspire. Like other universalist views, this position can do little to mitigate the arbitrariness to which actual traditions, in their specificity, are prone.

We will do better if we can show the arbitrariness of traditions to be essential to the discovery of one's telos. To do this, we need to explore the function of arbitrariness and its place in lives that are also subject to rational discussion and evaluation. If a tradition is an ongoing argument, as MacIntyre says, why should its origins in an arbitrary history and its arbitrary differences from other traditions be so important to it? How can its participation in the space of reasons not overcome these nonrational limits?

To put it another way: how can the truths of ethical reasoning take their beginning from the accidental facts of history? I choose this phrasing to echo a theological claim of great importance in the eighteenth and early nineteenth centuries: "Accidental truths of history can never become the proof of necessary truths of reason." That was how Lessing expressed the difficulty of bringing Leibnizian religion together with Christian revelation, and it was in response to that claim that Kierkegaard produced the best, if also the most eccentric, defense of the "accidental truths of history" that Christianity has ever known. While I want to keep ethics separate from religion,[9] their problems in reconciling reason with history are much alike. How Kant's ethics goes together with the history of any given way of life is indeed a question with almost exactly the same features as the theological issue that troubled Lessing. So a theological morass shall serve as our starting point, and we shall use that as an excuse, later on, for returning to Kierkegaard to help us out of our ethical one.

STORIES

To call traditions historically extended "arguments," as MacIntyre does, is a paradox, since traditions are first and foremost the sum total of what is *not* argued in the transmission of knowledge and practice from parents to their children. I think MacIntyre is right—at the end of a long day, we shall come back to the way this authoritative transmission depends crucially on the possibility of argument—but we can hardly begin with his insight and certainly not use it as a definition. "Tradition" is a word for "passing down," and we employ it in its most familiar sense when we talk of practices—rituals, customs, superstitions—that are passed down, more or less closely bound together, from generation to generation. What goes along with those practices are stories, and it is that aspect of tradition I want first to consider.

Traditions tell stories about the origin and workings of the natural world and about the history of the community with which they are associated. The stories vary widely from tradition to tradition, more widely than the practices themselves do, and they serve a variety of functions. They may offer quasi-scientific explanations of the way things work; they may present a theory of the community's role in history; they may provide models of human vice and virtue; or they may constitute a metaphysical view of the world and of what one ought to seek in it. They may, and usually do, perform all these functions at once, but different communities, and different spatial and temporal segments of a community, tend to focus on some aspects of their stories to the virtual exclusion of others.[10] But in all cases they provide a context for a way of behaving. The wanderings of Australian aborigines along the "songlines," singing up the earth as they go, are utterly unintelligible without the creation stories that make such activities a condition for the fruitfulness of the earth.[11] Clifford Geertz has shown beautifully how stories about the meditative savant Kalidjaga, in Indonesia, and the sardonic marabout Lyusi, in Morocco, have helped to structure forms of both political and religious practice in their respective countries over the subsequent centuries.[12] Jewish practice, of course, is incomprehensible without the supernatural history in which it is embedded, while Christianity (perhaps Buddhism as well) is virtually all story—indeed, it could be said to be a story about the overcoming of practice by story.

Now these stories are usually packed with literal falsehoods, at least by the standards of modern science, and are always strongly biased in favor of certain themes and of the good or ill of certain communities. It is a mistake to underestimate this fact,[13] since there is no sharp distinction between literal and moral truth in daily life, and communities are often severely shaken by the discovery of scientific challenges to the views of nature and history they have always taken for granted, but on the other hand literal falsehood rarely robs a tradition's central narrative of all its power. For one thing, the fact that the narratives serve varying functions allows them to be reinterpreted so that their falsehood in one respect only lends color to what they have to say in some other respect. Thus Genesis 1:1–2:3 has been understood as a way of putting metaphysical rather than scientific truths, Greek mythology was reshaped by Athenian dramatists into discussions of fate and justice, and those same myths were transformed by Virgil into an interpretation of history. Communities may change the aspect of their central narrative that they care about—think of the way religion turns into nationalism and vice versa—and they often prefer to do this than to give up on the story altogether.

Why these efforts to preserve a story? The simple answer is that the stories are interesting and that they provide interesting reasons for doing whatever one does in one's daily life. A more adequate answer must explain why they are so interesting, why they grab our attention. I propose two main reasons. First, they offer a concrete conception, a usable interpretation, of the good. Second, they enable us to develop a concrete conception of ourselves; they help us decide, and in part help to determine, what kinds of people we are.

The most striking thing about accounts of revelation, in everything from tribal cults to Judaism, Christianity, and Islam, is that the all-embracing, universal Good, hard to attain and even harder fully to understand, is given a humanly intelligible face. Not necessarily a human face—pace Kierkegaard, incarnation is but one way by which traditions signify divine intelligibility—but at least something on the order of a human voice, a means of communication, by which individuals can be relieved of the twin fears that nothing they do will be adequate to the demands of the good life and that whatever they do will satisfy those demands. We looked at some universal conditions for ethics in the first chapter, and there is every reason to believe that people universally recognize those conditions. But the conditions leave much open, too much for one to have any idea of what kind of life, specifically, is worth pursuing. One knows, perhaps, that one ought somehow to work, to love, to learn, and to worship. *What* work, however, is worth doing? What should one learn? How—in what format or with what mode of expression—should one love? How, and to what end, worship? Or one knows that courage is a virtue, but is it more courageous to risk death in war or to risk humiliation by holding stoutly to absolute pacifism? Is it more courageous for *me*, in *this* situation, for *these* reasons, to fight in or resist this particular war? These kinds of questions no universal notion of the good will answer, although if, as we tend to believe, there are so much as better and worse answers to them, there must be some general account to which arguments over specific cases can regress. This middle level of generalization about the good is occupied by traditions.

Traditional stories tell us in considerable detail what human life is like, give us a multitude of specific paradigms for how to structure our daily activities and how to act in or resolve typical human crises, tend consistently to highlight some virtues over others, and almost always, as a whole, suggest one or more general models for how, among all these details and crises and virtues, the good life is conducted. The Jewish tradition, in contrast with the Greek, praises a kind of fortitude in the face of persecution rather than military courage and, in contrast with the Christian, emphasizes dignity rather than humility. It also establishes a series of practices designed to add historical and theological resonances to the way its community eats, makes love, dresses, works, and marks the seasons. It suggests in general, using its own history as a model, that the course of human life is a series of exiles: of going down from the home of one's birth into luxurious foreign enslavement, of being redeemed from that to be educated by renewed wandering, in a condition of barrenness and self-denial, of returning home with what one has learned to fruitfulness and triumph, only to be thrown out again at the height of one's maturity and power, to wander again, this time indefinitely, and transform one's source of security altogether from a place to a communal and behavioral structure.[14] This can in turn be understood, as my language in describing it implies, as a parable about childhood, adolescence, the promise of young adulthood, and the need to come to grips, at a later age, with the inevitable failure of that promise, or it can be understood as a political metaphor, a description of the course of love, among human beings or between human beings and the divine, or in any of a number of other ways. In all realms of human endeavor, there thus tends to be a distinctively Jewish way of looking at and living through the facts—of picking what is important out of what does happen, of anticipating what will happen, and of prescribing how to behave throughout it all. In addition, however one interprets it, the Jewish story provides a clear alternative to the happier homelessness—more an absence of home than a loss of it—depicted in Australian myths, to the Christian tale of suffering and rebirth into freedom, to the Muslim account of progressive revelation culminating in one lifetime's flash of mystical insight, or to the quite different account of both freedom and progress that Enlightenment Europeans shared with one another.

One does not do justice to the fineness of these stories or to what they do for practice in their communities by summing them up in this cursory way, but one can thereby bring out how clearly they are alternatives to one another, and that is the point I want to stress. Our traditional stories often come to have appeal for us precisely when we look at other traditions and feel, "*That* can't be right! *That* can't be the whole story!" Indeed, this is a standard way by which new cultures and traditions get their beginning. Judaism is founded on the condemnation of its idolatrous neighbors, Christianity on the condemnation of Judaism, Islam on the condemnation of Judaism, Christianity, *and* certain idolaters. And it is not only the mono-theistic faiths that share this characteristic. Greeks defined themselves against "barbarians," Persians against Assyrians and Babylonians, and communities all over the world against their neighbors up the road. Even the syncretic Hindus (so at least their social structure, obsessive purifica-tion rituals, and agonistic writings would suggest) have layer on layer of denial and rejection buried within their embrace of incoming faiths. That one people's culture usually unites around the rejection of some other way of life is an embarrassment to most apologists for culture, who would rather find the "positive" in every world-view, but nonetheless it is a fact, and I suggest it is a revealing and valuable fact, not an embarrassment at all. For the specificity of every tradition's vision of the good not only allows for contrary visions to exist alongside it, but positively demands such con-tradictions.

Why? Well, in practically all traditions there is an explicit recognition of the fact that the good by which they want their stories of the world and how to live in it to be measured must be broader, more comprehensive, than whatever they describe of it in their stories, else it could not serve as a measure. And where explicit recognition of this line of argument does not appear, we may still insist that it ought to be introduced, as a part of the logic by which something can claim to be an ethic at all. (Plato, who formulated the argument for his own social context and from whom we in the West have all inherited it, insisted that he did not invent it or even discover it for the first time, that the Socratic method merely brought it out of people who could and should have been able to develop it for them-selves.) So the fact that Greeks gave priority to military courage, and Jews to structures of ritual, practically demanded that Christians come along to say, "No! That's not what's important at all!" And the fact that they then produced an account of the world subsuming all human events under the rubric of sin and redemption made it equally necessary for non- and post-Christians to insist that this cannot be the whole story either. One might think that eventually we would come to some overarching narrative in which all the partial ones would be comprehended, but this point—like Hegel's Absolute, which is a version of it—is a position that cannot be occupied, and indeed contradicts the nature of the process by which narratives arise.

Perhaps, in the order of time, there was a first, purely positive tradition, a choice by some person or persons, possessed of a sense of an ineffable overall Good but with no particular idea of how to live, to say, "Here's how the world might work, and here's what one might do in it." This is difficult to accept even as a hypothesis, since people tell stories when they need to explain the bad things that happen to them and then develop practices designed to avoid, if not someone else's bad habits, at least the bad habits of their own that got them into trouble. But suppose, once upon a time, it did happen. After it had been done, after one of the many possibilities of envisioning the good life had been chosen, the world was open for other people to prefer another possibility. And when the bad sides of the first view became evident, when the children of this society with the first tradition saw some of their parents, as inevitably happens, using the tradition as an excuse for cowardice or selfishness or violence or corruption, then surely they rebelled, splintered off, with a view of their own meant to correct the evil in the old one. Rousseau, discussing the growth of divisions among individuals and nations, says that one person, fencing off a piece of land for his own private use, forced others, for their own protection, to do so as well, and that one group of people, banding together into a nation for their mutual protection, forced others to do likewise. "It is easily seen how the establishment of a single society made that of all the others indispensable, and how, to stand up to the united forces, it was necessary to unite in turn."[15] In my story the stakes are more ideas and modes of behavior than land, but the sequence of events is the same.

My story is only a myth, however, and unlike Rousseau's, it is not meant historically, even as a possibility. For the original "positive" view, if it were to survive its splintering at all (as Hinduism has survived Buddhism; or Judaism, Christianity), would have to show why it remains of value, and that means setting itself against its own offshoot, serving as a corrective to the ways in which that offshoot, perhaps in the very effort of correcting its parent, developed overemphases and blindnesses, yielded to corruption or violence. Retrospectively, then, we must interpret the original view as intending to deny whatever came after it, even if the latter existed, at first, only *in potentia*.

The myth I am telling about myths is valuable in two respects. First, by hewing closely to the way Rousseau imagines the birth of nations, it points up a weakness of his account. Rousseau makes the origin of cultural difference look accidental, a mere matter of convenience for obtaining security once private property had destroyed the original world of indifferent individualism. This does not begin to explain either the intense attachment people have to their cultural differences or the widely varying ways in which such institutions as religion and art have developed. Nor does the typically eighteenth-century appeal Rousseau makes to climate get the explanation of culture any further.[16] Rousseau has been taken by many to be the father of ethnology;[17] as I shall show in detail later on, I think one of his contemporaries, Herder, whose account of cultural origins is similar to the one I have offered, has a considerably stronger claim to that position.

Second, the myth I have told stresses the neglected truth that cultures are in part formed by the choices of individuals to adhere to them. There are good reasons why this truth is neglected. Contrary to the notions that informed Enlightenment social contract theories, most people, at most times in history, neither think about what society to join nor have much option of changing their social allegiance should they decide they want to. But individuals did band together to follow Jesus, the Buddha, and Mohammed; individuals have often left their homes to intermarry with or emigrate to other communities; individuals remaining in their homes have chosen either to assimilate to conquerors or to entrench themselves all the more in their local ways; and individuals in every society, both today and in the past, have chosen orthodox or heretical, fervent or lackadaisical, modern or old-fashioned, cosmopolitan or provincial approaches to the tradition in which they were raised, according to their personal desires, reflection, and experience. Especially at the formation of new communities, but also in the form of immigration, conversion, assimilation, revivalism, and the day-to-day interpretation of practice, individual choices about how to live determine cultures as much as cultures determine them.

But cultures do also determine individuals, and it is that fact that gives the lie to social contract theories and the bite to the Herderian myth I have told instead. For individuals do not arise with their moral notions and ability to make moral choices fully formed and then decide what society to join. Traditional stories embody the vague notion of a general good in specific terms, but they also help create the specific individuals who can have a relationship with that good. This was the second factor, I suggested earlier, making such stories interesting. Many things determine my specific views of how and how not to live—the tastes I acquire and examples I see, the crises I witness and participate in, the long-term results of the way those crises are resolved—but among the most important pieces of this history, and the one most capable of making sense of the rest of it, is the traditional story with which I grow up. I may identify with particular characters—Miriam or Samuel or John of Patmos or Teresa of Avila or Hanuman or Arjuna or Ben Franklin or Lawrence of Arabia—and try to model the role I want to play in my society on them. I may bear in mind key phrases or incidents whenever I have to resolve a certain kind of crisis or meet a daily situation I find difficult. I may interpret my setbacks and triumphs in terms of what I take to be a theme or overall thrust of the story. But by far the deepest of its effects on me will be *that it shapes me, and thus sets limits on me, at all.* The particularity of stories, the way in which they cannot include everything worth saying about how to live, mirrors my own particularity, reminds me of it, and provides a framework within which I can struggle against its limitations. One who identifies, say, with King David's youthful joy and generosity may have to wrestle with the vengefulness with which that hero died; one who takes up the Jewish emphasis on justice may have to come to terms with its concomitant deemphasis on compassion for wrongdoers. But the very embrace of a particular story both relieves individuals of the burden to perform all good in one lifetime and forces them to face how much they will miss, in how many ways fall short or fail, before passing away from the world of action altogether.

I return to Kierkegaardian concerns here because it is one of Kierkegaard's most striking points that only trust in an obviously inadequate ("absurd") portrayal of the good can force me into an adequate recognition of my own inadequacies—and can enable me to recognize that even with all my inadequacies I can commit my life to that good. I acquire an adequate sense of my possibilities for action only when I accept the fact that my place in the world is given by my emotional and historical circumstances, while I adequately recognize the limitations of this position only when I measure it against the universal good that I shall never achieve. These various and conflicting requirements can be met by trusting a particular narrative that gives me my place in the world rather than allowing me to imagine I have created that place, while reminding me how absurd it is for the achievement of the good life to have to work within the limits of a particular place. The very submission to a story, the very turn to faith over reason, humbles me whenever I am tempted to suppose I am some "universal" (Hegelian) subject rather than the specific person, with specific limitations, that in fact I am, while the particularity of the story forces me to recognize, constantly and disquietingly, that I ought not rest satisfied in my limitations but push within and against them toward the attainment of a broader, more universally relevant good. So the particularity of a story points toward the universal, while its pointing at the universal only demonstrates that that universal can and must be sought in particular ways. These are some of the paradoxes by which Kierkegaard interpreted the Christian Incarnation; I think they can be equally applied to any "incarnation" of the ultimate good in a specific way of life. And I suggest that practically all entrenched communal ways of life, all "traditions" or "cultures," can be understood as such an incarnation.

How? Well, in the first place, it is not merely a fact but a necessary assumption that actions central to people's lives tend to come with some rationale. We cannot understand something as an action at all, let alone a human action, if we cannot find reasons that might motivate it. An action is not the same as an "event" or an "accident" or a "mistake," and it is the existence and nature of motivating reasons that accounts for the difference. It follows that the distinction in kinds of actions performed by different groups of people must be accompanied by a parallel distinction in motivating reasons, and that implies both that there will always be motivating stories to go along with specific sets of practices and that those stories, while they need not be appealing rationales for action to everyone, must at least be universally recognizable *as* rationales for action. And a rationale for action must meet some standards that we, the interpreters of it, take to be conditions of a reasonable practical aim. That means it must bear some relationship to what we understand, naturalistically, as what human beings need to do in order to survive, and also cohere, as we saw in the second part of Chapter 1, with at least the minimal conditions for what we take to be a good life. In this way, specific stories about practice demand to be considered an interpretation of some more universal conception of the good.

On the other hand, I have had to use the adjective "appealing" rather than "convincing" to describe the rationales that stories offer because they are not in any real sense *arguments*. At most, a story may say, "The world is thus and so, you want or ought to want thus and so out of it, and you can attain that only by behaving in thus and so a way." Usually stories are not this direct, and usually their account of the world is at best unprovable, but even if these objections could be overcome, their claim of what one wants and ought to want would always be open to the response, "But I don't happen to want that," and a consequent lack of interest in the prescription that follows. Stories are thus best not construed as arguments. Rather, as my Kierkegaardian remarks have tried to show, if one puts trust in a story *instead of* demanding an argument, one can bring one's array of "accidental" features, and not merely one's capacity to argue, into the pursuit of an ethical life. For this reason, stories cannot simply provide universally acceptable rationales for action—their historical and arbitrary, "revealed" or "incarnated" aspect is as important to them as their rationality.

In actual practice, narratives about human action crop up for all sorts of reasons, in all sorts of places and times, and often find followers regardless of their nature, but they found communities only if they aim, or can be made to aim, at some universally recognizable notion of the good. Charles

Manson in our own day, Joseph Frank in the seventeenth century, could attract believers, but only at the most desperate fringes of a troubled society and only for a short time, as has been the way with hundreds of cruel or excessively ascetic cults in the past. These unsuccessful cases demonstrate that, while functionalists are right to say that stories about practice must meet the needs of a community, the story often comes before the adaptation to function. Far from being called up by function, stories must often be adjusted to meet its demands. To establish an ongoing community, a narrative must turn into a tradition, something passed down from one generation to another, and to do that it must come to be understood so that it allows for the satisfaction of the fundamental needs of human life in society. These are considerable: they include not only permission for individuals to eat, drink, and procreate, but provisions for an economy that can furnish food and shelter to the whole society, for some form of educational system, and, if only to allow the economy and educational system to operate, for a general absence of internal and external violence. (And this need for peace alone entails that the society come to terms, at least to some extent, with common human notions of justice and decency.) Hence Islam has reinterpreted its original demand that war continue until the whole world becomes Muslim,[18] and Christianity has abandoned or reworked its original tendencies toward extreme antinomianism and absolute celibacy. There is a difference, then, between a story *tout court* and a traditional story, and it is only traditional stories that merit prima facie consideration as legitimate foundations for a moral view.[19]

TRADITION AND AUTHORITY

Traditions and their stories do not constitute the starting point for ethics all by themselves. They sustain and are sustained by communities, histories, and structures of authority, all of which are in turn interwoven with one another. I want to focus especially on the notion of authority. The ethical importance of community has been much discussed; the importance of history to a community, and body of ethical judgment, is fairly obvious. Relatively little has been written about authority, on the other hand, although reliance on it seems the very paradigm of an offense to reason. Yet without such reliance, traditions cannot gain a grip over us. If traditions help us decide who, specifically, we are, and in that way give us a basis on which to make all our daily choices, then we can hardly hope to choose the tradition to which we adhere. Ordinarily, at least: we saw earlier that traditional communities are, to a degree, formed by individual choices. But for the most part we do not reason to our communal affiliation; it comes to us authoritatively. Normally, we accept a tradition, community, and history on the authority of our parents; normally, also, the interpretation of a tradition proceeds by one generation's establishment of a set of judgments as precedents that the next generation takes as fixed. On the whole, this is reasonable enough. If traditions are to be something for us to work from, to humble ourselves to rather than to control, then they ought to be somehow given, both from society to individual and from generation to generation. And if they are to provide us with and remind us of our historical and emotional place in the world, then the appropriate story for each of us must surely engage with the desires, beliefs, and ways of proceeding we acquired from our parents.

Traditional stories are also meant to constitute a vision of the good, however, and the fact that they inform the world of our parents is not enough to show that they meet that criterion. We used this consideration above to demonstrate the need for stories to be adapted by a tradition to meet more general naturalistic and moral concerns. Now we need to say something about how communities adapt their traditions to meet the specific concerns of their individual members, and how those individuals interpret and apply what their communities teach them in their everyday lives. How does an individual determine which aspect of a tradition— which characters, which practices, which themes—actually shape her, and how does that shape affect her practice?

Tradition and authority, as Hannah Arendt has pointed out, are intimately interwoven.[20] Traditions make possible institutions of authority, while authorities convey, to each new generation, the power and daily application of a tradition. We interpret the tradition to which we belong as much by accepting the authoritative word of its spokespeople as by reflecting on it ourselves. Recognition of authority lies at the heart of the trust or "faith" that I have described as our characteristic relationship to traditions.

But authority is a position in which we regard a speaker as representing the truth regardless of whether he can offer reasons for what he says. How can a reasonable person acknowledge the legitimacy of such a position? That reason should be substituted for the bare say-so of our parents is one piece of Enlightenment dogma even its most virulent critics tend to accept. It is one thing to suggest that traditional stories set the stage for ethical reasoning, that ethical reasoning cannot get under way unless such stories are accepted without reasons. It is quite another thing to maintain that, even to a limited extent, we must submerge reasoning in the ordinary practice of thinking about and negotiating with our tradition. We turn in the next chapter, therefore, to an exploration of authority, and of how authority, in moral reflection, can be incorporated into reason.

4. Authority

"He speaks with great authority." We say this as a compliment, similar to "He has great presence." In both cases, we mean to bring out something theatrical, as if having authority resembled the way in which a character can become present, can appear to command its own life. To speak with authority would then seem to be a matter of one's acting ability. If one convinces someone with one's authority, one will have pulled off a triumph of fiction, drawn on a truth that has been *made* (*fictio*), shaped, enacted, rather than on the truth about, say, illnesses or dangerous objects or violence, which lies beyond the making of all human beings and imposes itself on us regardless of our will.

In stark contrast, when we say, "He is a great authority on pharmaceuticals or astrophysics," we mean that he has access to precisely that kind of truth, truth we all need and have to respect. Once we spoke also of authorities on how to live and considered the citation of such authorities a trump card in ethical and religious argument; today we call the citation of authorities a logical fallacy and abjure it in serious philosophy.

These are not the only uses of the word "authority." We speak of a police officer or judge as being in a position of authority; we speak of texts as authoritative; we consider the rules of a game or the decisions of a referee authoritative in some situations. In the political sense, the sense in which the judge is authoritative, there are certainly people with authority today. But insofar as it is supposed to reflect wisdom rather than arbitrary power, the authority of judges is derivative from a notion of authority that we have on the whole abandoned. Neither the police officer nor the expert on pharmaceuticals represents authority in the sense relevant to ethics. To revive that notion, to delineate its workings and show its beauty, I shall draw on the fragments we still retain of belief in the possibility that one might have to learn how to live from others. It is important to bear in mind, however, that neither the qualities nor the institutions I am about to describe exist in full form in post-Enlightenment societies—to their moral cost.

In "What Is Authority?" Hannah Arendt suggests that "authority has vanished from the modern world," undermining our ability to pass traditions on to our children, indeed threatening the institutions of child-rearing and education altogether.[1] But she is interested in authority only as a political idea, while I believe we must establish its moral, even episte-mological, validity if it is to regain any purchase on our sensibilities. In fact, the authority I want to examine is in important ways *non*political. Arendt rightly says that true authority entails the absence of both force and persuasion. If all authority is ultimately a matter of power—if the priest has authority over the worshiper, as the Marxists would have it, only by dint of socioeconomic position or the construction of mass delusions—then there is no such thing as legitimate authority and all pretensions to it ought to be unmasked and shattered. And in the practice of persuasion (conversation at least in principle free and equal) we treat others as author-ities only provisionally. In any case, coercion and conversation are both quintessentially styles of politics, whereas the relationship of authority is quintessentially the relationship of teacher to student, parent to child, priest, and perhaps God, to worshiper: if genuine, it marks a place where status and interests do not matter and where a concerned and observant public (the "spectators" of Arendt's polis) is not at all welcome. Authority is often conceived of as a political matter, but I hope to make it evident that politics and authority ought fundamentally to be quite wary of each other. Authority proper is a powerless way of bringing about submission, and the individual who accepts it submits only to the truth—although since it is, after all, not persuasion, to an unclearly known, disguised, or otherwise partially hidden truth.

The difficult question, which Arendt did not answer, is precisely what kind of truth there is that does not allow for persuasion. Only a truth of which we could in principle not be persuaded is one for which authority, in principle, would be the right vehicle. I stress "principle" here because in many cases in which in *fact,* right here and now, we cannot be persuaded of a particular claim, we regard any trust we place in an authority as merely provisional, a makeshift or shortcut in the conveyance of a truth for which ultimately we demand a possibility of persuasion. When a doctor tells me what I should do for an illness, I accept what she says as true with a minimum of persuasion, but only because I expect her to be arriving at a result of which I, were I to go through the same medical training, would be persuaded myself. When a physicist tells me something about quarks or the solar system, I may doubt that I could in fact successfully complete the training she has undergone, but I continue to hold out, albeit with vanishing hope of realizing it, a theoretical possibility of being in the position to understand and argue for such truths myself. The physicist and doctor save me time, as I, perhaps, do in some ways for them: we participate in a division of cognitive labor enabling each to draw truth from the richer and more efficiently distributed supply of it that a market can provide. I want to call what passes for authority in these cases "expertise" and by that term distinguish it from authority in the essential sense, the sense in which I respect the teacher as the author of my belief without feeling we could trade places.[2] There are good arguments, however, not only that the latter position, from an "enlightened" and egalitarian point of view, is morally and politically offensive, but that a truth incapable of commanding persuasion would not be truth at all. "Truth" is a term that applies to our beliefs, and it is not clear we can have a belief in something we cannot be persuaded of. How can we so much as *understand* what we are supposed to believe, unless we can fit it in with the other beliefs we have, the grounds on which we determine when something is meaningful and when it is true or false?

The place for authoritative speaking, I shall argue, lies in reflection and discussion directed toward the radical changing of one's interests. On the one hand, as we saw in Chapter 2, we want our interests to be corrigible and often try to shape or redirect them. On the other hand, we are interested in whatever we happen to be interested in; we identify ourselves by our interests, and they comprise the motivations on which we act even when we try to change them. It follows that to overhaul them comprehensively, we may need the help of an outsider, and need more to trust that outsider than to be persuaded by him or her.

Before proceeding to the details of this position, let me make one note about procedure: We usually consider "authority" to have two quite different senses, one in which people serve as authorities, the other in which traditions or ideas have authority over people. I shall eventually want more or less to identify these two senses, certainly to tie them closely to each other. Both people and traditions can speak to us, and it is their speech that can be authoritative. For reasons of presentation, however, I begin with the authoritative people. This allows me to postpone the issue of why tradition and authority are so closely linked until I have clarified the notion of authority itself.

ACTION AND THE NEED FOR AUTHORITY

People do not in general think carefully about the ethical values on which they act. This is not a matter simply of laziness or lack of time (although the latter is not a triviality, given that our acts and choices take on importance precisely because of the limitations on our time). Rather, once we think about our values, we find we are no longer able to take them as seriously as before. Bernard Williams has said—controversially, but I think correctly—that ethical reflection destroys what it reflects on.[3] When you work hard for the liberty of a nation, that liberty seems important *because* you are working so hard for it. The same is true even if the goal is something as limited as the performance of a play: it gains importance in your eyes precisely as you put more and more effort into it. Should someone stop you to ask why the performance of that play, or the liberty of that nation, is so terribly significant, you may be hard pressed to answer. Certainly there are pat responses that you give in the very course of pursuing the project, to win supporters and fend off critics—"because it turns feminism into high drama"; "because the people have been exploited by imperialist powers"—but these answers only place one specific object behind another, only exchange one unquestioned premise for another. If the questioner keeps pressing ("Why is feminism so important?" "What do you mean by 'exploitation'?" "What's wrong with imperialism?"), your answers may soon give out, and if you do not finally insist, "This is simply what I do," you may feel, at least for the moment, that your efforts are all a bit lame, your goals faintly ridiculous.[4] Or you may try to derive your purposes from more general principles: "happiness," perhaps, or "freedom," or "the survival of the species." But these general aims seem, when pressed, considerably *less* important than the specific goals they are supposed to explain.

There is no help to be found, either, in grounding values frankly on the efforts of those who seek them, as Nietzsche and his followers tried to do. The paradox of values is that, while they appear important only when one is striving for them, they then appear *objectively* important, important independent of the striving. The notion that the play or the nation is important only because one considers it important is depressing and tends to erode one's very ability to consider it important. A more satisfying account of values might say that their importance exists independently but appears only when one is acting on them. Of course, that independent importance can then not be demonstrated, except to the agent, who is already invested in it, and even he can see it only insofar as he acts.

All this is mostly a way of putting Kant's conclusion that thought outside the context of action and thought in the course of action are radically distinct: good and bad, and all the specific things we consider good and bad, appear real only when one makes choices about action, although it is no less rational to consider them real for all that, and real independent of one's choices. Especially once we give up on the Enlightenment notion of attaining a comprehensive and disinterested view of the world, it is not unreasonable to hold that we learn much of importance for our lives simply *by* living, by acting and discovering the consequences of what we do. I suggested in the last chapter that people will more often accept the traditional story in which they are raised than choose a new one: one reason is that what a story has to say can be found only by living it out. Even its blindnesses and failings appear only once it has established a way that people actually live. So both individual agents and new generations in a community generally begin with a "practical faith" ("practical" because necessary for practice, and "practical" because demonstrated in practice) in a given structure of objective or quasi-objective values by which actions and their ends are to be judged.

Now interests, the complexes of feelings, factual beliefs, and ways of proceeding that motivate us to act, are simply the flip side, the subjective or quasi-subjective side, of values,[5] and we are just as unable to comprehend our interests as our values. An interest is a way of living out a desire or choice about what is important. As a way of living, it cannot be constantly and fully open to reflection on its nature or on whether one ought to abandon or amend it. This is so not only because of lack of time and the enervating effect of reflection, but because to have a way of living, as Aristotle showed, is to have certain habits and to feel the emotions appropriate to those habits quite spontaneously. It may take some training to become generous, but *being* generous is not a matter of painstakingly working out what one ought to give people and then reluctantly handing it over. One is even less able to love in this manner, or create art, or provide strong and efficient leadership. And one cannot become any distinct kind of person, or pursue any distinct kind of action, without developing some such habits and emotions. So when Adam Smith noted, astutely and well ahead of his time, that we cannot fully acknowledge our true characters because when acting we are too caught up in the passions moving us to act, and when reflecting on past action we reignite those passions in order to justify what we did, his only mistake was to regard this as a weakness of human psychology.[6] Rather, the one is a structural feature of action; the other, of having a character. Of course, at times I can reflect hard enough to change my character, but if I do not regard myself as on the whole "all right," at least for long stretches of time, then I cannot act at all, even in the direction of repentance and reform.

In addition, my interests are heavily shaped by my society, and societies are hardly more able to combine action and speculation than are individual agents. When societies act, they also develop habits and ways of spontaneous reaction (expressed in applause and Bronx cheers, celebrations and mourning rituals, posters, referenda, riots and demonstrations), and they can also not be too open to critical reflection on those habits. This time, of course, the competition between having interests and reflecting on them takes place on a different level. Some individuals may spend all their time criticizing their societies' projects, while others pursue the projects whole-heartedly, and the mere existence of the former does not mean that the society as a whole is critically examining itself. In a society that as a whole wants to pursue a project vigorously, the major forums of opinion (main-stream literature, the mainstream press, the places of political debate) may ignore or soften the views of critics, or the critics may make themselves innocuous. Consider how convinced Communists in America have gener-ally become cranks, playing a stock comic role in the social drama of uni-versities and public debates.

A project or institution that a society is pursuing too busily to reflect on might be called an "idol," with all the Baconian, as well as Old Testament, connotations of that word. It is an idol because it stands in, unshakably and unquestionably, for the full as well as the true good, but it is also an idol because it has something good about it and draws its strength from the piece of moral purpose it embodies. Idols serve the individual as mark-ers for interests he or she can legitimately pursue. I can go into advertising; I can have sexual affairs before marriage; I can spend my spare time watch-ing television; I can count volunteering once a month at a homeless shelter as an adequate contribution to social welfare; and I can structure my life this way without thinking too deeply about it because the value, or at least ethical acceptability, of these projects is not seriously in question in my society. They cannot be deeply questioned by those for whom the very choices in their lives are made possible, the very questions in their lives made intelligible, by the unquestionable legitimacy of these and similar alternatives. In order to act at all, we must normally act in preset grooves, rather than each carving out a new path for ourselves. We find certain values important, and make others think they are important, by acting on them, but we try not to think too carefully about their foundations lest we lose all sense of why, or indeed how, to act on them sincerely. We rather accept them as given, and if our society offers them to us in established grooves, why that is better than not being given them at all. Yet the importance of values need not be reduced to the interests and efforts of our society any more than to our individual interests and efforts: if values can appear important in our action without acquiring their importance from that action, then they can also appear important in socially set grooves without acquiring their importance from those grooves. (The society, like practice itself, becomes a mode of ethical vision or knowledge, rather than the locus of ethical ontology.) Thus we can keep deliberation from making practice impossible, abjuring comprehensive speculation to work out instead this or that narrow tactic, narrow negotiation around one particular fact or another detail of custom, while our standards for action are held firmly in place by our society, unquestioned so unmoved. And if the good is at all as I described it in the last chapter—necessarily obscured from us in part, necessarily appearing to us only in discrete stages or elements, such that the practices and stories of a tradition express it better than any theory—then these unquestioned social standards may as reasonably belong to it as the consequences of any moral theory.

It is in the passing down of these standards that I want to claim there is a need for authority. In one sense, this is obvious: the resistance to speculation that belongs to their essence entails that the standards must ordinarily be transmitted authoritatively—from parents or other teachers to children, without much question. The nature of this authoritative teaching comes out most sharply, however, not in such ordinary transmission, but in the extra-ordinary cases in which an agent's relationship to the standards is in crisis. Suppose, in the first place, a society undergoes an ethical upheaval, as periodically happens when the world to which its standards are meant to fit changes radically, when influential skeptics arise to question them, when many or certain leading actors betray their supposed values with hypocrisy or corruption or violence, or when the society as a whole, ridden with internal dissension and discovering alternative ways of life in other societies, finds its set grooves appearing not so set. Then the agents of the society need someone to think about values, to guide them back to their values, to show them which ones they might successfully consider important. And, in the second place, consider the versions of these societal crises that occur in the ordinary life of practically every individual: there come moments when the values we have do not seem to work the way they should or seem to have legitimate alternatives we have never before considered. One person has been taught as a child that Christians are decent and Muslims are dishonest, but as an adult she meets dishonest Christians and upright Muslims. Another has been taught never to use violence or always to tell the truth, but he encounters circumstances, unlike any described to him in his youth, in which violence seems necessary or the truth misleading or cruel. It is in these cases, as well as in the broader social crises in which all values seem in danger of losing their grip, that the role of authority becomes clear.

An authority is a person who can think about values without losing faith in them. Authorities tend to be people who, while immersed in the practical world, have more opportunity than others to think about action; who, in that thought, see the possibility of abandoning ethics to which such speculation often leads; but who, either despite this possibility or after passing through it for a while, come to enslave themselves to a particular set of values nevertheless. It is only in and by this extra-ordinary commitment that they are able to see the world from an evaluative standpoint at all—in their speculative thought alone, that standpoint seems unintelligible. But because their commitment is so consciously chosen, because it is not an enslavement out of habit, they are also able, as it were, to see "around" the values they have chosen, to understand the alternatives to them and hence the specific differences they make to how one finds one's way about the world, better than those who merely live the values without examining them. Authorities on a set of values are usually people a little farther removed from the life of those values than the people who consult them. At least in thought, they are more aware of—and that means, given the nature of practical awareness, more tempted by—alternatives to the way of living for which they speak than those who come to them to avoid such alternatives.

I had better confess immediately that the model I have in mind for this relationship is that of an orthodox rabbi to a congregant who seeks a definitive opinion about a matter of Jewish law (a *p'sak*), although the notion of consulting the wise was hardly invented in this context.[7] A rabbi who offers such opinions lives between speculation and practice: he participates in the daily lives of many people but at the same time has more inclination and time for reflection than those he observes and helps.[8] From this relationship to practice, he can acquire qualities of immense value to the interpretation of his tradition. A good rabbi has not merely expertise about a tradition but a sense for how the tradition ought to apply in daily life, what values in it ought to take precedence over what other values, and when and how to balance its specifically mandated concerns against such general, more vaguely defined objects as health, the success of a marriage, or the preservation of property. A good rabbi feels the pull of all interests, including those his system officially resists; he is then able to interpret and hone the system with a sense of the kind of path it is trying to carve out in the world, while interpreting and honing people's lives to conform as much as possible to the system. A good rabbi sees the point of his values and can therefore make them interesting; he can make them tell an intelligible and gripping story about the world precisely because he does not have them so deeply ingrained in him as to be habitual. The good rabbi is not a therapist, or an Emily Post, or a prophet, but has something about him of all three. And since ethics is a matter that must simultaneously address human interests, delineate a specific way of life, and represent a good ultimately beyond every particular interest and way of life, this combination ought to characterize authorities of all kinds, in all traditions and faiths.

Authorities, then, stand between the ethical life proper and the skeptical speculation in which all alternatives are open, and their strength consists in their efforts to bridge this gap. As a result of these efforts they receive three gifts, which provide them with all they have to teach, but they are also open to three dangers. The three gifts are: a sense of the beauty of the ethic to which they are committed; a grasp of how, in detail, it works; and a passion for it that can be communicated to those who feel its grip on them fading. The sense of beauty arises from the mere position of standing between—as we shall see shortly, via a discussion of Kant's *Critique of Judgment*, the joy that attests to beauty is constituted by a kind of freedom in moving between opposing perspectives that yet belong together. The grasp of detail comes with the fact that authorities, having to force themselves to live by values that others merely accept, take a greater interest in exactly what they are thus committed to. Knowing the alternatives, moreover, they have a clearer picture of what difference their values make. Finally, moral passion comes to them out of the very effort with which they must sustain their commitment. A thing appears important when you work for it, and authorities must work for their ethical commitment. The need to commit oneself, and to keep that commitment constantly renewed, thus appears more important to them than it does to one for whom commitment comes naturally.

And the three dangers: Should authorities fall firmly into one or the other of their two opposing sides and not know it or not admit it, should they become, de facto, ethical skeptics or blindly dogmatic agents, their very gifts may turn harmful. Authorities have a sense for how and why things are beautiful and powerful, they can make an idea or way of life tremendously appealing to someone, but that someone may include themselves, and they may fall in love with the beauty of a struggle or goal regardless of its true value, or simply with their own skill for making things beautiful. Then they may direct their capacity for evoking beauty to their private ends or to ends that, if they thought them through, they would find silly or abominable. All the while, those who have followed them heretofore, or who now hear the power but not the substance of their words, are swayed in the very opposite of a moral direction. Because they are submitting to authority, they suspend or abandon their individual interpretations of values, but because the authority is self-interested (Jimmy Swaggart) or ethically lost (Jim Jones), what they substitute for their individual interpretations is something they would never, in a sober moment, accept on their own.

Similarly, if authorities lose the broad thoughtfulness that enables them to see more clearly than most agents, while retaining their strong moral passion, that passion may become blindly directed to a goal that, while perhaps a legitimate part of the moral life, does not quite deserve such single-minded devotion. Such a person becomes a crank (Ralph Nader) or a fanatic (Savonarola). While she conveys the impression that her conviction is wedded to a deep understanding of the traditions, human interests, and vision of the good into which any ethical goal is supposed to fit, she is in reality as blind as the average agent. If a veneer of authority persuades others to discount this blindness, they will find it harder, not easier, to see than if they followed no authority at all.

Finally, authorities may become obsessed with the details of a text or tradition to the detriment of their eye for its beauty and power. They may become thoroughly acquainted with what one ought to do according to a certain system while losing all sense of why that system is appealing, what the alternatives to it are, and what the essence of a commitment to it might look like. Then they become pure Emily Post, or the caricature of a rabbi, making their tradition look ridiculous because entirely without shape or reason, while using the appearance of authority to make their thoughtless interpretations become a way of life for their followers.

When authorities succeed, when they do not succumb to their characteristic dangers, they are people we consult for their remarkable wisdom about human nature, for their erudite and subtle understanding of the tradition within which we want to act, and for the passion and clarity with which they can see the ethical point of that tradition. In modern liberal society, the closest thing to someone we treat as an authority is perhaps the psychotherapist (or the psychologically trained "expert" on marriage, education, career success, etc.), but authorities cannot simply be therapists. If authorities are in a position to raise serious questions about interests and projects, they must stand somewhat outside their society's idols. *Somewhat* outside, because they must be able to appreciate the goodness an idol provides enough to speak persuasively to one whose life it shapes, at the same time perceiving enough of a broader ethical picture to shatter it when necessary. For idols are false images only insofar as they are limited. An authority is one who shares enough of our idols to speak to us about them, but who is aware enough of their status as idols to take us out of them when they blind us to other interests we have or values we should have.

Insofar as authorities advise us about our interests, therefore, it is with the intent not of merely clarifying them or of helping us in the process of "socialization," but of leading us toward what they and we both would most deeply consider a good life. Unlike a therapist, an authority is willing to criticize both our individual interests and the accepted social paths they may reflect. A therapist takes turning her client into a normal member of society to be an end beyond which she is not permitted, and would not know how, to venture. An authority's therapeutic qualities, by contrast, are inseparable from her prophetic ones. This might mean the authority is willing entirely to revise a society's understanding of its own commitment to nonviolence, as Gandhi did, reworking an idol in both its own terms and terms borrowed from other societies, or it might mean, and more commonly will mean, that he or she will advise an individual to avoid or defy some societal idol, in spite of the fact that this will not conduce to "well-adjusted," well-"socialized" behavior. Authorities stand between the general good to which our ethical beliefs ultimately refer and the particular feelings and ways of living by which we try to realize that good. This is a standing-between like the standing between living values and reflecting on them, with the difference that one of the two poles here is not only incommensurable with the other but intrinsically beyond a full grasp. Authorities should thus not suppose they fully grasp the ultimate good any more than ordinary agents should, nor should they communicate what they do grasp of it in such a way as to eliminate the agents' feelings of ignorance. Like prophets, they must communicate with images, preserving the sense that there is more to learn than whatever they say and that we ought to stand before both what we have grasped and what we have not grasped with some awe. In this position, authorities tell us truths that we recognize as true only when we have, in trust, acted on them. Authorities thus widen the horizons of what we can consider good, although to do this they must work out from what we already consider good.

But we cannot properly see how this might be done until we determine how, in general, authorities ought to speak. What kind of person speaks authoritatively? Or what kind of speech, what kind of thinking, marks a person as an authority?

JUDGMENT AND THE IDENTIFICATION OF AUTHORITY

Within the traditions in which authority flourished, there were easy answers to the question, Who is an authority? Set procedures produced authorities, set ceremonies marked the fulfillment of those procedures, and set hierarchies enabled such informal guides as elders, parents, and teachers to submit to the occupants of the formal positions in return for a certain derivative authority over their families and students. There is no room within our liberal, post-Enlightenment world for the constricted social systems to which this way of determining authority led. There is also no philosophical need to accept it. Even in pre-Enlightenment traditional societies, it was generally understood that people might occupy authoritative positions without really deserving them, that (whether or not they ought to be obeyed in any case) their authority properly belonged to them only by dint of the possession of certain moral and intellectual qualities. One found true authority in a person who had good judgment and who conveyed that judgment with a ring of truth. We still look for the ring of truth, and if we can say more about what might constitute that ring, we will have the beginning of a way to recognize authority.

You hear the ring of truth when, first of all, you find someone who can speak in your own ethical terms—who "speaks your language"; when, second, that someone is a knowledgeable, sensitive, and decent interpreter of an ethical tradition you can accept; and when, finally and most important, you find in that someone's thought and speech outstanding "judgment," with all the Aristotelian and Kantian connotations of that word.

When you consult an authority, you want someone who can speak to your interests. And when you cast about for someone who shares your interests enough to speak to them, someone who knows and shares your tastes, your ways of doing things, your purposes and your values, you will, not surprisingly, often come up with someone much like your parents. Indeed, your first authorities will be your parents. They may be ignorant or erudite, foolish or wise, but in any case they shape your tastes, present and represent goals and ways of acting to you, and fill you with proverbs and phrases that for a long time you repeat, and try to live up to, without much understanding. I am not suggesting that your childhood environment determines you in such a way as to leave no room for freedom and responsibility; rather, it provides the terms with which your mature self, whatever its source, has to begin. As we are weaned from self-centeredness to communication, so, with luck, are we weaned from a child's selfishness to an adult's sense of answering to a larger good.[9]

Although your parents may not be your highest authorities, it is whatever trust and respect you have for them that enables you to put trust in other people, and insofar as other authorities correct you as to your own nature, they will have to start from an understanding of the interests you acquired in the presence of your parents. Hence one prime candidate for later authority is someone representing the education of your parents—a spokesperson for the books your parents read, the institutions they admired, the customs and activities they loved. If they spoke from a Bible, then a priest of that Bible may be an authority for you even if you think you have rejected religion; if they spoke from German literature, then a sensitive reader of Goethe or Rilke may be an authority for you; if they instilled in you a love for the outdoors, then you may find yourself drawn to environmentalists or nature mystics. Here Freud had the story of religious authority exactly reversed. *Of course* the teachers, priests, and even gods of religious institutions tend to resemble our fathers, but the resemblance must be seen from the opposite direction: our fathers (and mothers, although Freud's schema did not include them) strive to participate in, ought to participate in, and to some extent almost always do participate in the authority of the wider social institutions and values that are the ultimate progenitors of our ethical selves. Our childhoods constitute a small part of our wider authority relations, rather than our authority relations being a mere mirror or extension of our childhoods. That, as Freud says, we attempt conquest in our relations with our fathers does not change this picture of reverence, for "conquest," in Freud's own terms, is a matter of becoming like the father. We do indeed struggle with, attempt to conquer, our authorities, but success in that attempt is a matter of so imbibing their ways and views that we see through their own eyes. (Then, but only then, are we free of blind trust in them. But then we also know that blind trust can be traded only for a seeing trust, that modes of thought or action without any beginning in trust do not exist.)

It follows from this need for authorities to engage with our interests that people cannot all have the same authorities. As upbringings differ, so will the authorities who can speak to those upbringings, and although good authorities will have something to say to many people, the more people they can speak to, the less will they be able to gauge what each one needs to hear. Partly for this reason, authorities always speak for specific traditions.

Engaging with our individual interests entails also engaging with the social paths that shape and direct those interests, and social paths, like upbringings, tend to differ widely. I argued in the last chapter that these differences are necessary—not only do ethical traditions have to respond to the needs and habits that different histories and environmental conditions breed in different societies, but the very process of developing an ethic is a matter of responding critically to whatever one's neighbors are doing. In any case there certainly is in fact no single human way of life, and the attempt to find what we do all have in common tends to conflict with the ability to immerse oneself fully in any one tradition. Authorities must always prefer the latter course. The ethical guidance they have to offer requires knowledge of a way of life specific enough to address the many complex and fine details that constitute everyday moral problems.

At the same time, they cannot merely be experts on a text or set of customs. A gift for memorization will not help people reawaken their ethical passion, unscramble confused interests, or apply apparently conflicting values. Traditions usually have general ethical themes, of one kind or another, alongside their specific practices—a view of life as aiming at self-negation, say, or holiness, or happiness, or freedom, together with some rough outline of how the practices are supposed to get one to that goal—and an authoritative interpretation of a tradition always reflects some understanding of at least these general views. The interpretation will still lack the ring of truth, however, unless the authority shows herself to be acquainted as well with the general nature of human interests, to be passionate about seeking the good in both those interests and the tradition, and to be deeply enough interested in bringing about good that she respects the pragmatic considerations with which ethical ideals must negotiate if they want to be realized. The Emily Post in an authority must unite with the therapist and the prophet, and all three must go together with a deal of common sense about the natural world. No authority who proposes ridiculous fantasies as ethical solutions, or who pooh-poohs such concerns as how much an action will cost can retain an accent of truth.

Common sense is the ordinary, and one of the philosophical, meanings of the word "judgment,"[10] and with it we come to the more general criteria by which authority may be recognized. We have seen so far that, although authorities represent the individual's ethical given, to some extent individuals have to find their particular authorities according to their own personal criteria. We now turn to standards that any authority must meet, and we begin with a faculty that belongs both to the use and to the recognition of authority. Individuals rely on "their own judgment" when they seek people who speak to their own interests and tradition. They thereby draw on the quality by which they come closest to themselves partaking of authority.

What is this quality? Judgment may be characterized as the process by which general terms and principles are applied to particular cases, and cases are interpreted so that they can fall under general categories.[11] We may recognize that it is necessary without being able to explain very well how it works. This, for a simple but essential reason: if we explain how to judge in general terms, those terms again require application, so one who lacked judgment would miss the point of the explanation, whereas if we explain it by giving specific examples, only judgment itself will enable one to see how the various examples add up to a general explanation. Charles Larmore, a philosopher who has recently stressed moral judgment for much the same reasons that I do, writes, "Although we can understand what kinds of situations call for moral judgment, the kinds of tasks that moral judgment is to accomplish, and the preconditions for its acquisition, there is very little positive we can sáy in general about the nature of moral judgment itself."[12] Aristotle suggested that we learn how to judge only by *practicing* judgment (*phronesis*), by actual experience with many particulars, and that this is quite appropriate since judgment is a faculty peculiarly needed for practice rather than theory. I agree[13] but would like to add another point, drawn from legal rather than philosophical accounts of judgment: we learn how to judge *from past judgments,* from authoritative "precedents." This in itself ties judgment to authority.[14]

Not only do our judgments thus depend on authority, however—people acquire authority through their judgment. I can sum up my discussion so far by agreeing with Larmore's suggestion that descriptions of judgment are really negative in character, that we can say "only what judgment is *not,* and not what it *is.*"[15] But from those negative descriptions we know at least that people who lack experience, who love abstract principles for their own sake, or, on the contrary, who observe and remember many particulars without being able to put them together into any general picture will tend on the whole to lack judgment. And we may say positively that good judgment is a rare quality, hard to learn, hard to teach, requiring great skill and great humility, a knowledge of details as well as a feeling for the whole: all the virtues we have so far sought in authorities. It is good judgment, above all, that appears in authoritative deliberation and speech at its best.

Authorities must share our interests and idols yet speak beyond them. They must speak to our interests but, in speaking to them, be capable of lifting us out of them. They must be firmly committed to certain values but know what alternatives to those values look like. They must have a good enough feel for the natural world to know how things happen in it while seeing nature from the removed standpoint that ethics demands. And they must speak the ordinary language of ethics, use reasoning that makes sense to our everyday interests, traditions, and ethical theories, while looking beyond all these things at the elusive telos to which they point. How can one pull off these various tricks, these various ways of standing between? I suggest one needs something much like what Kant, describing aesthetic judgment, calls "disinterested satisfaction."

Unlike Aristotle, who takes judgment to be the prime faculty of ethical wisdom, Kant restricts it to the aesthetic realm, but his account of it there excellently suits our ethical purposes. Kant distinguishes between determinant judgment, which applies rules to particular cases, and reflective judgment, which seeks the rules we might want to apply.[16] Determinant judgment strikes him as easy and rather uninteresting, while reflective judgment, an indefinite process without any clear end, lies at the heart, he believes, of our appreciation of beauty. And that process, although by nature resistant to definite description, can be generally characterized as aiming at "disinterested satisfaction." To be "disinterested," for Kant, means that one is not prejudiced "in favor of the existence of things."[17] Normally, we take pleasure only in objects we use; their existence, therefore, is essential to our pleasure. To separate this kind of pleasure from the sensation leading us to call an object, in itself, "beautiful," Kant argues that we must make such judgments out of a "disinterested satisfaction" in the object. He thus brings aesthetic judgment in line with legal judgment (although he does not mention this comparison), in which a decision is considered fair only if the judge acts without regard to any stake he may have in the matter.

Now someone who is to speak to my interests with an intelligence and fairness of which I am not capable myself must obviously not be as caught up in my interests as I am or consider, in his judgment, any stake he may have in what I do. But there is a paradox in the "disinterested engagement" I want to recommend that is not immediately evident in Kant's "disinterested satisfaction": the authority has to share my interests as well as separate himself from them. As it happens, however, it is on this paradox that the comparison with Kant sheds most light. For "disinterested satisfaction" presents Kant with a similar problem, given that he believes satisfaction normally comes in response to a natural desire or need for an object. This naturalistic meaning of "satisfaction," moreover, underlies Kant's use of it even for the judgment of beauty: taste (the judgment of beauty) "plays with the objects of satisfaction" although "without attaching itself to one of them."[18] And just as one must have a lively awareness of ("play with"), but separate oneself from, the natural connection to objects in order to see them as beautiful, so must one have a lively awareness of, but separate oneself from, the natural tendency to be swept up in an interest in order to judge it worthwhile.

How this can be accomplished may be seen if we consider the process Kant calls "reflection." Reflection is a matter of seeing a potential for harmony between two categorically different kinds of things: the sensations one receives from an object, in the "imagination," and the concept one has of it, in the "understanding." Although necessary, it is paradoxical that these two aspects of knowing should have any connection with each other. Sensations are particular, concepts are general—they require each other but have nothing in common. What brings them together, according to Kant, is reflection, a process that consists in moving from the sensations of an object to an understanding one constructs out of them, then back to the sensations to correct the understanding, back to the understanding to reinterpret the sensations, and on in this way indefinitely.[19] This is how he resolves the problem of beauty, how he suggests that disinterested pleasure in an object's sensations can be distinguished from the (interested) pleasure of those sensations themselves. The pleasure of reflection requires only the sensations of an object, not the object itself, and is indeed disrupted by any desire we have for the object, since desire presupposes a concept. Hence reflection is essentially disinterested, while, as the resolution of an important intellectual problem, it is also deeply satisfying. Consider how we take joy in a work of art. We look at an abstract painting, say, or read and reread a difficult poem, until the lines or colors or phrases that please us fall into a kind of order, and then we interpret the work as about certain themes, as making a statement with a clear meaning. But if the work is truly beautiful, we find our interpretation inadequate and return to revise it or discover something new, and take pleasure both in formulating the ideas and in changing or abandoning them, both in capturing a rich sensory elusiveness in concepts and in letting the sensations turn us back to silent wonder. The pleasure is an intellectual pleasure and an endless one, never to be used up as purely sensory pleasures are, and stimulating to the mind rather than enervating.[20] It is removed from sensations themselves, while remaining responsive to them, and it trains us to free ourselves from the immediate power of sensations, as well as to interpret them intelligently, in our daily course of life.

This notion of reflection, as a mental process that moves from one axis to another as if between two literally reflecting surfaces, and in the course of that motion comes ever closer to a point representing some sort of equilibrium, greatly facilitates the negotiations between interests and the world they have to suit, idols and the values they serve, specific traditions and the elusive good at which they aim. If interests determine what information we attend to but are at the same time aimed at ends for which we need a disinterested grasp of the facts (Christianity may be a way of interpreting the facts, but facts are essential to determining what is a Christian act, who a Christian priest, where salvation and its opposite lie), then a potentially endless but constantly enriched reflection between one and the other is our only hope of bringing the two somehow together. If the patterns of a society can become idols but the higher good in terms of which they must be questioned makes no sense except in terms of such patterns, then a thoughtful judge must move from the "sensory data" of her society's customs, laws, and specific beliefs to an interpretation of what the overall concept of that life might be, then back to the patterns, or the historical facts into which they must fit, then back again to enrich the old or attempt some new interpretation . . . In this reflection, moreover, she must be somewhat removed from the grip of the interests and patterns, all the while coming to understand that grip more deeply than those who live in it. As a critic (judge) of a way of life, she can help the agent see more in it, clarify its workings, and gain a greater appreciation of its point than he could on his own, just as the critic of beauty often finds more in an artwork than the artist can himself.

This applies just as much to the way authorities speak for the ultimate, obscure good as to the other aspects of their role. The elusive telos of ethics cannot, on any account, be separable from the things of which it is the telos, and on the account I have given, it would not be good at all unless it addressed our interests and prescribed specific ways of life. So a person who widens our horizons of what to consider good must also be a person capable of disinterested engagement with our interests, a person knowledgeable about and committed to our tradition, a person sensitive to both ethical and natural details, and a person who can at the same time bring the details of interests, tradition, and nature into an intelligible whole. When such a person then recommends something radically new, it will always be a new particular, which somehow or other relates closely to the ethical whole for which she or he has spoken before. Authorities may, to a community, recommend a new kind of project, or even whole way of living (a republic, a kibbutz, a satyagrahi ashram), that makes sense in terms of the community's traditions but has never been tried before. Or they may suggest, to an individual, something that that individual has never considered ("Take up drawing!" "Get married!"). We have a need for such new particular suggestions frequently, since societies change in haphazard or only unconsciously rational ways, and our particular values take on different shapes, different emphases vis-à-vis one another, and different overall interpretations in accordance with these changes. To apply our values, and our theories about values, to radically new circumstances requires judgment in the highest degree, and we can anticipate that gift only in one who has already shown it before, albeit on other levels.

Finally, authorities must be able both to communicate well and to communicate sincerely. These two qualities often do not go with each other. People skilled in eloquent speech easily sacrifice whatever sincerity they have in favor of how things sound. People trying seriously to speak for moral truth face the problem of finding an appropriate means of communication for what they have to say. It is not at all clear what the appropriate means of communication *is* for authority. On the one hand, authorities need to analyze situations and advise people with great clarity; on the other hand, they betray the elusiveness of the good they are representing if they imply that everything ethical is clear to them.

This problem is exacerbated by the fact that in ethics direct speech sometimes defeats its own purpose. Kierkegaard, arguing for "indirect communication" in religion and ethics, pointed out that if your object is to get someone to take on a commitment or responsibility for himself or herself, it will detract from that end if the person accepts the commitment only because you say so. Similarly, if you are trying to show someone how to express heartfelt love or contrition, it will do no good if the person merely parrots words or tokens that you recommend. And if you want to express your own inner commitments, simply describing them will not necessarily be enough. Always on the lookout for self-interested motivations behind what people say, your listeners may remain skeptical, however sincere you try to sound, unless they see your commitments demonstrated in your life as well as your words. Sometimes the best way to show that something is important is not to say that it is important; acting toward it, playing down the importance of other things, speaking around it, or simply a silence born of the inadequacy of words may be more eloquent.[21] Furthermore, those who judge with deep accuracy may not be able to say fully how they do so even if they want to; a love and respect for details is often something deeply and pretheoretically bred into people, something that is only diminished by attempts to analyze or systematize it. We therefore seek the ring of truth not only in the speech of our candidates for authority but in their entire way of life. Practical faith is demonstrated in practice. We can see a person's passion for the good only in a thoroughgoing commitment to it, and we can see the almost inchoate knowledge that goes into good judgment only in the way in which a person negotiates around her own difficulties.

We also need to look behind words to determine that our candidates for authority act and speak out of more than a blind commitment to a tradition (the difference between trust and blind trust is crucial here). We feel more comfortable about a person who can become uncertain to the point of anxiety about a dilemma, who can grieve to the point of his own embarrassment at suffering or dehumanization, or who can wonder whether his most deeply held beliefs are misguided, than one who has a conventionally or systematically correct answer for every situation. We even wait for the occasion on which a potential authority will make a claim—perhaps reluctantly, disturbed by its implications—wildly out of synch with his tradition, not because we disbelieve in the tradition or delight in iconoclasm, but because we need to know that his loyalty is not to a specific way of life per se but to the good for which it stands. Even those who bind way of life and ultimate good tightly together, such as Orthodox Jews and Muslims, want to know that a person speaking for the tradition is not citing bits of it randomly but interpreting it in accordance with some general view of what it is about—albeit one that may be borrowed, in the first instance, from the tradition itself. Even they, looking for an authority, wait for the moment of passion to break through the idols of current interpretation, not because they want to overthrow that interpretation but because the possibility of such a break gives evidence that the process of interpretation points to something beyond itself—and thus gives it the capability of being "true" (only where falsehood is possible does the notion of truth have a place). Authorities must see themselves as speaking for a true good, whether as specified in traditions or insofar as it transcends and defines those traditions, not for anyone's feelings or interests or for a merely arbitrary set of conventions.

Of course, no one will display perfect concern for truth, perfect sensitivity to the demands of judgment, perfect decency, and a perfect understanding of interests and a tradition. The ideal is there to give us criteria by which we can conceive the type of moral authority; to identify tokens of that type, we need to look for approximations to those criteria. We will surely make some mistakes in such identifications and find that some whom we have correctly identified will later let us down. Failures like this do not invalidate the possibility of moral authority, any more than corrupt or foolish scientists invalidate the possibility of learning from science. Furthermore, people may be authorities to greater and lesser degrees. To offer decent and intelligent advice, not everyone need be an Aristotle; to teach us moral possibilities we have never before considered, not everyone need be a Gandhi. We place trust in many different people—different amounts of trust, qualified a bit here and reserved a bit there, and all with an expectation that the people we trust also trust one another, in some sort of vague hierarchy. As long as we recognize that the position we occupy, as agents, prevents us from being able to see everything we need to know for our actions, we know that we must make room for authority in some part of our everyday ethical lives; it does not follow that we must be able to pick out the people who will fill that place with perfect accuracy and clarity.

Thus when people have the virtues of authority, they differ from experts in that what they tell us is not something we, without those virtues, could find out for ourselves by reading what they read, observing what they observe, or combining any such factual knowledge with an algorithm they might teach us. Their words are not a shortcut to a truth we could derive from our own resources, but stand in for the absolute truth itself, for that aspect of truth by which it surprises us. For all this, however, they do not speak for an intrinsically mysterious truth or use mysteries to attain their wisdom. They are simply alive to many social and natural particulars, feeling them intensely, absorbing them, and at the same time struggling to make a general sense of them and to bring that sense under ethical scrutiny. If they succeed, they may not know quite what they are doing. An unarticulated sense for particulars, and for how to interpret them, must precede interpretation if one is not to be overburdened "conceptually" (to use Kant's language), if one is not to be a walking theory trying to impose itself on the world.[22] So their inarticulable sensitivities to particulars is one thing that places the wisdom of authorities beyond their listeners' reach; another is simply that they must sit and think, about the good and about the nature of the world, much more, and harder, than most agents can afford to do.

By standing somewhat outside the values, institutions, and interests that provide the terms by which we act, by examining those terms more deeply and more passionately than the rest of us do, and by, in particular, reflecting on how to bring the details of those paths together with some overall shape or idea, authorities are in a position to see more of what we truly want and what, were our life more fully played out, we might recognize as what we *ought* to want, than we can ourselves. They can therefore tell us something that, if we trust them and act on it, we will recognize as right, but to which they cannot, from our present position, bring us by argument. A person disposed to anger accepts on authority, against all his practices and principles, a discipline of flattering everyone for a week; to his amazement he finds that he thereby maintains both control over his anger and his self-respect.[23] This is speaking truth without persuasion: it is not that there are no arguments for the claim in question, but that *you*, in your present position, would not be convinced by those arguments, and to reach a position from which you would be convinced, you must first accept and act on the claim in faith. If the counsel is good, you may, with the interests you have after you have acted on it, see it as what you ought to have believed from the beginning, but you will also know why you would not then have been able to see that. Authorities, where they exist, do not reveal extraordinary truths, in principle obscure, but bypass the routes of persuasion to show you a quite ordinary piece of truth you would otherwise have overlooked.

AUTHORITY AND FREEDOM

It follows, quite to the contrary of what was believed in officially authoritarian societies, that blind obedience is not the appropriate relationship to authority. If authorities are essentially teachers, then authority and power ought not to be identified, and trust in authority ought not to be based on ignorance, superstition, or fear. On all these points the Enlightenment critique of authority was absolutely correct. Human beings may need trust and guidance to lead a coherent and decent ethical life, but they also, and to exactly the same degree, need freedom and responsibility. What the Enlightenment missed was only that freedom and responsibility, far from being incompatible with authority, necessitate and are necessitated by it. Authorities provide the terms by which ethical claims can have a sense, and if one does not place a certain amount of unargued trust in some authority, one will have no ethical terms with which even to criticize. Once the terms are given, however, they are there to be wrestled with, doubted, challenged, and changed—if only to produce new terms that will have at least a talking point with the old ones.

Those who learn from authority *must* wrestle with it, and those learn most who wrestle hardest. Aquinas never seems more independent of Augustine and Aristotle than when he thinks he has most satisfactorily reconciled them.[24] The Freudian critic Harold Bloom has pointed out the paradox that writers find their own voices only by struggling to the death with their literary fathers,[25] and the same is all the more true in ethics. Bloom makes this a psychological matter, out of which the individual may find a sort of literary equivalent to maturity; again, I think the Freudian approach gets the real nature of "father"hood backward. You need to go beyond your biological, literary, and ethical fathers not (just) because they are psychological hindrances to your independence, but because their function is to teach you a truth that by its nature goes beyond anything they can embody. If the terms they are giving you are to be ways of reaching truth, then they must get you to understand that what they are teaching comes from beyond them as well as beyond you, that it is not merely their invention, the product of their private desires or fantasies. And if they are giving you terms for a truth that is always partially obscured, they must communicate the obscurity of that truth together with its terms, the limitations they themselves face in trying to grasp it. Thus, when they perform their role well, it is essential that you are able to go beyond them, and those parents who understand their role deeply will rejoice when their children demonstrate that capacity. The more deeply you understand the truth for which you need authorities, the more you will be able to conquer your authorities, to correct them or turn their words to new purposes. But it is the mark of the very deepest understanding to refrain from such revision except when you feel that the truth for which the authorities themselves stood absolutely demands it—and even in that case to clothe the revision, as much as possible, in terms your authorities would have accepted.

Blind obedience to authority is thus a sign of a weak or limited understanding of what the authority has to teach, and, in general, faith or trust should not be blind. Blind trust does have a place in the ethical life, but only where understanding, for one reason or another, needs to be limited. The person who goes to the priest or rabbi for a definitive decision on a difficult matter may have no time to think it out for herself or may not have had the time in the past to examine her ethical tradition deeply enough that she can now make her decision wisely. And the time that could have been used for such ethical investigations may well have gone instead into extremely worthwhile occupations: we noted before the frequent incompatibility of reflecting on an ethical life and living one. So a division of labor between agent and authority is no more unreasonable than any other division of labor, even though one cost of it is the need, at times, for blind trust. But we should not forget that this is a cost, and the agent who does not have the time fully to understand, to appropriate for him or herself, the words of an authority ought to feel a little uncomfortable about being in such a position and to hope there will someday come a time to remedy this reflective inadequacy. Blindness creates a distance, not a greater closeness, between authorities and those who consult them. Authorities draw their greatest and proper strength from a sincere attempt to aim at truth, and therefore from the correspondent understanding of their words by those who consult them. Hence the hold of authorities is greatest over those who struggle hardest to understand them correctly, although freedom comes also with that struggle of interpretation, and in an authoritative society those are most free who submit most deeply to the terms the authorities provide.

So blind faith is not the point of an authoritative society, and a society that tries to enforce such blindness has misunderstood, and will corrupt, the very structures of authority. When a regime squelches humor and irony, diverse interpretations, and challenging and skeptical questions, then people come to doubt that the supposed authorities have confidence in their ability to speak for truth. If power has to replace wisdom as the means by which authorities provide guidance, then surely it must be because their words will not stand up against any thoughtful interpretation of the tradition, or against the demand for disinterestedness. In the furor over Martin Scorsese's film *The Last Temptation of Christ* and Salman Rushdie's novel *The Satanic Verses* (both of which were, as it happens, deep and respectful attempts to come to grips with the very notion of religious authority), one saw the weakness, not the strength, of Christian and Muslim fundamentalists. The Inquisition, the Wars of Religion, and the nationalist and Communist dictatorships of this century similarly reveal not the height but a loss of authority. On a lesser level, one sees this every day in attempts by ultraorthodox Christians, Muslims, and Jews to keep their children away from all the secular knowledge with which contemporary religion must come to terms. Rich traditions of laughter and doubt flourished, at the best of times, alongside authorities, and when that balance is lost, authorities cease to speak for us, rather than merely to us. They also lose the sense they themselves need to have that they are responsible to a truth beyond themselves, and not voices, like God's, that can create the moral and natural world by fiat. The alternative to recognizing authority is to lose the possibility of thoroughgoing reflection about interests: evaluation of desires becomes limited, ultimately, to evaluation of their effectiveness at attaining their own ends (and authority is de facto given, in that case, into the hands of blind impulse and/or blind social conformity). But the identification of authority with power transforms a learning process into a form of manipulation. Authority and freedom go together; only where they coexist is thoughtful ethics possible.

AUTHORITATIVE TEXTS

So far we have spoken about authority as if it were always instantiated by persons. But one can learn through trust rather than reason from a text, an event, or even an earlier stage of one's own personality, as well as from another human being. The notion of authority itself is simply the radical denial of egalitarianism in the process of reflection: the denial that all moments, places, and positions have equal access to the truth, or that their inequality can always be compensated for in the long run. There are moments—of conflict, of failure, or of prolonged inaction—in which one is able to perceive something about one's own or another's interests, about the interlocking of interests and values, or about their application to the natural and social world, to which one is blind in the normal course of events. These moments may be enshrined in texts—an *Isaiah,* a *Quran,* a *Faust* cannot be written in just any circumstances; they may be the occasion for one person to speak authoritatively to another; they may issue in a work of art or a political act; or they may be preserved as a resolution or a sharp and passionate memory within one individual mind. I recall, perhaps, that at one point I had good reasons for committing myself to asceticism or political liberalism without recalling exactly what those reasons were, and unless and until I am able to remember and review them, I submit myself to the authority of what I regard as my then superior clearheadedness. This is probably the limiting case of authority: the notion that individuals may have authority over themselves threatens to break down the distinction, essential to authority, between bearer and receiver of truth. Traditional texts, on the other hand, are as much a paradigm vehicle for authority as the individuals of wise judgment who speak for them.

Consider the analogy between traditional texts and authoritative people. When I find a recommendation of drug legalization in Aquinas, of abortion in Kant, of toleration of cultural difference in the sixteenth-century monk Francesco de Vitoria, I may well be more impressed and moved than if I found a similar argument in the writings of my contemporaries. Why? Well, first, because I have reason to trust my impression that the text is imbued with a thoughtful and wise interpretation of the good. Of course, the words of my contemporaries, or even my own thought, may be similarly imbued, but the fact that a text predates the idols of current controversy and that it has maintained its influence over the centuries testifies to its ability to transcend local interests and prejudices. Just as some people are in a better position to understand and judge an action than the actors themselves, so some historical periods may be better situated for the understanding and judgment of a later period than the inhabitants of that period itself—either because the events of those periods (e.g., fifth-century Athens) dislocate people radically enough to unsettle values and modes of interpretation that had hardened into idols, or because they witness the founding of projects (e.g., the American republic) that later generations merely live out.

This brings us to the second reason for which we may turn to Aquinas or Kant or Francesco de Vitoria to illuminate current issues. From our point of view, Kant is a fairly disinterested commentator on abortion— debate over it did not rage in his time—as Aquinas is on drug legalization, and Vitoria, if not without his own interests in cultural difference and toleration, is at least removed from ours. At the same time, a view embedded in the past of our tradition, whether itself shaped by different interests or not, is likely to have had a deep influence on the interests that have come to shape us. So the texts of our tradition stand in a relationship of disinterested engagement vis-à-vis our own concerns.

I can therefore explore who I am and what I want at least as much in such texts as in the words of authoritative contemporaries. And when I sit down to rummage through eighteenth-century or late medieval writings, I may well find that an idea or mode of expression removes me from my own context, begins new trains of thought, and refines and deepens my judgment better than anything I can gather from straight introspection or conversation with my contemporaries. The more deeply I understand and submit to their terms, indeed, the less I may need to turn to human authorities around me; I have, after all, gone to the source of much of what goes into authoritative wisdom. But there is a catch in turning to texts for authority. To determine what they have to say, both in themselves and in application to a current situation, I need to interpret them, and in the course of interpretation I may, if I am not careful, make them say whatever I want them to say. In the very process of coming to "speak" to me, they can lose their relative disinterestedness. If they are to serve as a corrective to interested choice rather than an excuse for it, I must therefore filter my reading of them through authoritative interpreters. And interpreters of texts acquire authority by bringing their readings into as much coherence as possible with those of other authoritative interpreters. Authoritative texts are thus inseparable from a tradition of reading, while that tradition in turn depends on the presence, in every generation, of authoritative readers.

When surveying the function of authority earlier in this chapter, I took it more or less for granted that an authority will speak for a tradition. I am now in a position to say something stronger. Only by expounding, if not a written text or set of texts, at least some set of beliefs and stories passed down orally from generation to generation, can a person claiming authority force humility, disinterestedness, and sensitivity to the range and depth of her society's conception of the good, on her own judgment. Only by submitting to authority can one achieve authority, and that means, among contemporaries in the same social setting, submitting to the texts of preceding generations. Neither here nor anywhere else should such submission be blind, and walking the line between blindly pious and irresponsible interpretation of texts is again a matter of judgment, but authorities who judge out of their own personal insights alone open the way for their wisdom to become narrow, manipulative, or out of touch with the projects of their society. Indeed, one way by which listeners keep their own trust in authority from blindness is by correcting authorities against the tradition for which they speak. At the same time, one of the things we value about traditions is the fact that they provide terms by which personal authorities can give us guidance.

It follows, as suggested earlier, that tradition and authority are inextricably bound together. It follows also, as also suggested earlier, that the tradition that speaks to each individual is authoritatively given to that individual. Although any tradition may have something worthwhile to say to me—sometimes precisely because of its distance from the interests that inform my own—the one in which I have been raised will normally engage with my interests and problems much more deeply than any other. To recognize this, moreover, is to humble myself to my context and limitations, in the way that alone enables tradition and authority to speak to me at all. Contrary to what early theorists of culture supposed, there is no natural connection, no tie of "blood" or inheritance of acquired characteristics, that binds individuals to the culture in which they are raised; there are merely the relations of upbringing itself, and the consequences, for action and morality, of those relations. But that is enough, from the moral point of view, to establish a tie of supreme importance.

We now have reason to revoke Descartes's banishment of the fathers from the province of reason. For ethical purposes at least, both the terms our parents provide us with (tradition) and the mode by which they provide them (authority) are crucial to the very process by which we can reflect on those terms. Authority and tradition, on the one hand, and argument and criticism, on the other, are not separable in practical reason. We saw this two-sidedness in the fifth antinomy of Chapter 2, and that bifurcation of thought underlies the splits we have since examined in living out and evaluating interests, accepting authority and acting freely, and negotiating between specific and general interpretations of traditional texts. In each case, reflective judgment is all that can bring the two sides together. So one conclusion of what we have seen so far is that authoritative traditions are ethical constructs, and as such have built into them the two-sidedness of practical reason and the incompleteness and uncertainty that that two-sidedness brings in its train. As we shall see in the next chapter, these considerations were ignored when authoritative traditions were transformed into "cultures" and "nations" at the end of the eighteenth century. By restoring them to their proper place, we may be able to make good some of the failings, especially the moral failings, of ethnology and nationalism.

5. From Traditions to "Cultures"

The invention of "culture," in its modern sense, begins in a most unlikely place. In the midst of the most rationalist of all Enlightenment philosophies, the philosophy that above all insists that everything is accessible to reason, there occurs the following passage:

> But, you object, perhaps it is ordained from all eternity that I will sin. Find your own answer. Perhaps it has not been. Now then, without asking for what you are unable to know and in regard to which you can have no light, act according to your duty and your knowledge.[1]

Leibniz, who more than anyone else represented natural religion, who contended, contra Newton, that there was no room for anything inexplicable in science, here comes startlingly close to the presuppositions for tradition and authority. The individual cannot have enough knowledge to determine the relation of his own nature to the circumstances of his actions. Part of the knowledge going into his action should therefore be an awareness of his own ignorance, and he should act according to "duty" as well as knowledge. The separation of the two terms makes clear that "duty," in this instance (as in the ordinary use of the term), refers to something at least in part given, rather than rationally determined. The distinction between knowledge *tout simple* and knowledge for an individual, the recognition that individuals will not have adequate knowledge for the purposes of their action, and the notion that something must therefore be added to knowledge as a practical guide are all present, if only in embryo, in these words of Leibniz.

Both the style—the direct command, separating individual readers from the "universal person" for whom Leibniz generally writes—and the content are somewhat surprising, but they do not contradict any of Leibniz's central principles. Although he believes every contingent claim to be explicable in terms of a chain of sufficient reasons, that chain is supposed to be infinite, so absolute knowledge of contingencies is reserved to God. Indeed, for Leibniz as for Spinoza, individual human beings are defined as individual (specific, determinate) *by* the limitations on their knowledge; without such limitations, they would be indistinguishable from the whole. Leibniz's individuals—monads—are perspectives on the absolute universe, but the very notion of a perspective, for him, entails the presence of some confusion, and various perspectives are distinguished from one another by the different mistakes or degrees of ignorance each contains. Monads are constituted by an infinite set of relations by which they reflect and express the entire world, but they each perceive clearly only a finite part of those infinite relations, and it is that finitude that comprises both their distinctiveness and their potential for error.[2]

This is not the aspect of Leibniz that is usually stressed. In contrast with and in polemic against his contemporaries, he believed that reason and nature take priority over faith and revelation, a claim more striking than any hint he may have left to the effect that attempts to ground morality on knowledge alone might be hubristic. But among Leibniz's few devoted readers in the late eighteenth century, two, the playwright Gotthold Lessing and the philosopher of history J. G. von Herder, took up the hint in very important ways. Lessing used the limitations on empirical knowledge to develop a theory of history that introduced, for the first time in the modern philosophy of religion, a distinction between literal (historical) and moral or religious truth;[3] he also suggested, in *Nathan the Wise* and *The Education of the Human Race*, that all historical religions be seen as Leibnizian monads, partially but never fully correct perspectives on an absolute truth. Herder used Leibniz's account of human limitations to argue that we each individually depend on the group to which we belong for much of our thought, and that those groups all grasp a piece of the universal truth but each grasps only a piece. Both Lessing and Herder looked to a Leibnizian universal harmony as a product of the interaction of human groups, but the important point of their positions for our purposes is that they saw intrinsic value in the workings of these separate groups at all. The individual self-sufficiency of the Enlightenment began to make room for such distinctly anti-individualist doctrines as nationalism and cultural determinism.

That individual minds are limited, in their clear perception, to "those things which are nearest or greatest in relation to each [of them]"[4] suggested to Lessing an explanation of why the truths of natural or rational religion had to be revealed via the "positive" or historical religions: truth must speak to that which is "nearest" to the mind receiving it, so only in the form of stories of revelation could moral truths make sense to the human race at the time those stories were accepted. Like other eighteenth-century thinkers, Lessing picked out a rational standard of moral conduct as the core of truth in every religion, but unlike his contemporaries, at least in his later and more sophisticated writings, he did not feel that what covered and conveyed that kernel of truth could or should be simply discarded. As Henry Allison has pointed out, Lessing's suggestion that the literal falsehood of revealed histories does not prevent them from containing a core of moral truth is an original and important contribution to the philosophy of religion.[5]

But Lessing has something even more original to offer. For all that he shared the belief of his time in a rational and absolute moral standard—the standard of "humanity," which for him was summed up in the words, "Little children, love one another"— Lessing left considerable indication that he positively respected, rather than merely tolerated, the historical form of religious revelation. Compare the position of his immediate predecessor Reimarus, one of whose "major arguments against the acceptance of any historical religion was that an individual's beliefs are largely the product of ingrained childhood prejudices,"[6] with the words of Nathan, the hero of Lessing's 1779 play *Nathan the Wise:* "History must be accepted wholly upon faith . . . [and surely we rest this faith on those] who from our childhood gave us proofs of love. . . . How can I trust my fathers less than you trust yours?"[7] The idea is the same but the tone markedly different. Where Reimarus condemns faith in one's parents as a form of prejudice and superstition, Lessing praises it on ethical grounds. Is this a mere disguise for his true beliefs? Perhaps, but I suggest not, since it fits in extremely well with a preference he shows elsewhere for oral rather than written transmission of truth and for the personal education we receive in childhood over the impersonal productions of scholars. In his youth, he wrote a broad and rather simplistic attack on all written doctrines, beginning with Plato's, for corrupting the morally improving method of the oral teacher Socrates.[8] In "On the Proof of the Spirit and of Power," a late (1777) writing, and its companion piece, "The Testament of John," he recommends the apocryphal last words of John over the Gospel of John, and it seems no accident that those words were passed on orally. "Must everything be a book, then?" Lessing asks his interlocutor in "The Testament of John," and hints slyly, in the ensuing exchange, that it is better to recount the Testament "out of [one's] head" than to look it up in a written source: "Do you prefer what has been carefully prepared? . . . It is quite certain that John's address was never that. For it always came straight from the heart."[9] Finally, in his 1778 "Necessary Answer to a Very Unnecessary Question," he points out that a set of oral principles, the *regula fidei*, preceded the books of the New Testament, and that it was considered an offense "for the laity of the first Church to put more trust in the written words of an apostle than in the living word of their bishop."[10]

So when, elsewhere in *Nathan the Wise*, Recha, the virtuous daughter of the virtuous Nathan, tells us that her "father loves . . . too little that cold book-learning which impresses on the mind just lifeless symbols," when she says she has gathered what she knows "only . . . from listening to him. And in most cases I could tell you still how, where, and why he taught it,"[11] it is not unreasonable to suppose that Lessing is making a far from casual case for the necessity of loving, parental teaching to the transmission of moral truth.[12] The stories of Recha's father make his teaching interesting; the particular circumstances of his teaching show where and how it is to be applied; and the personal concern and devotion with which it is imbued make it possible for Recha to grasp emotionally what "Little children, love one another" is supposed to mean. For ethical reasons, Lessing hints that the mode in which historical religions are passed down, the faith in one's parents they demand, is not merely compatible with but essential to the moral teaching at their core.

Lessing did not explicitly say this,[13] and there is enough indication, in the *Education of the Human Race,* that he ultimately dreamed of a purely rational, nonhistorical religion for one to conclude that the historical theory of morals I have attributed to him is but an idea he toyed with. But his concern with education, with how truths, especially moral truths, are communicated, his recognition that rationality cannot alone either convey moral teaching or explain why myths and stories matter to people, and his attempt, almost mystically (in the spirit of Leibniz's almost mystical belief in the Principle of Variety), to find something of value in all products of human history are characteristic of a move at the end of the Enlightenment to back away from the original Enlightenment hope of banishing everything not explicitly rational from human thought and action. This move took a number of forms, including the development of romanticism in art and literature, of "common sense" philosophy, and of a mostly unfortunate tendency, in practice as well as literature, to represent "reason" as the enemy of "passion" and champion the cause of the latter. Lessing has little to do with any of this. He represents a fourth, smaller but ultimately more significant, response to the Enlightenment's limitations: an insistence that the reason of an individual must be understood in a wider, social context, and that the *way* individuals learn from society is as important to knowledge and action as *what* they learn.

Lessing reflected on this subject in terms of religion, but we need to remember that "religion," for him and his contemporaries, was not a set of dogmas and rituals, but the presuppositions and prescriptions of a communal way of living—such that "natural religion" was simply rational morality. This is actually a very old way of using the word, common in the pre-Christian era,[14] but it points in a direction by which "nation" and "culture" could come to take over the place of "religion." For those for whom natural religion went morally bankrupt in the French Revolution, while return to historical religion still threatened to bring back all the superstitions and irrational doctrines that the Enlightenment had worked so hard to discredit, "nation," "folk," and eventually "culture" became first

the preferred and then the sole terms for socially shared ways of life ("religion" then reverted to designating one aspect of those ways of life). And
with "nation," "culture," and especially "folk," we come to Herder, who
began with the same Leibnizian premises as Lessing and reached many of
the same conclusions about social versus individual thought and about the
relativism of historical truth to those who receive it. But while Lessing's
ideas have been taken up by a handful of theologians, Herder's influence
has extended to everyone since his time who has practiced nationalism or
studied cultural anthropology.[15]

Practically no society has been unaware of the fact that human groups
in different places have different tastes, manners, beliefs, and morals, and
the eighteenth century was, if anything, more aware of this fact than most,
but such differences have generally been counted either as of little importance or as mistakes—bad behavior and false beliefs—incurred as a result
of isolation, or corrupt and tyrannical leaders, having prevented a people
from achieving civilization. Anything human beings in a civilized society
knew or did, human beings in other societies could, if properly taught, be
persuaded of as well; attaining the best in human knowledge and action
was a matter of "culturing" one's reason. Reason could be "cultured" or
"cultivated" much in the way that land could, and it would then similarly
move from wild barrenness to ordered fertility; "culture," as a noun, was
how one described the result of this transition. We still use the word this
way, as a synonym, now often ironic, for erudition. Today, however, we
also speak of "cultures," in the plural, by which we mean social structures
of action and thought that not only differ from place to place but are so
comprehensive that the very notion of "bad behavior and false beliefs,"
and, correspondingly, of "the best in human knowledge and action," must
be understood as, to some large degree or other, relative to these structures. What an individual can and should attain, and can or should be persuaded of, is supposed to depend at least as much on the culture to which
he or she belongs as on his or her personal capacities. This view, without
which neither the modern doctrines of cultural relativism and nationalism
nor the modern notions of "culture" and "nation" would be possible, is
the discovery or invention of Johann Gottfried von Herder.[16]

Herder did not use the word "culture" to designate his thought-
determining social structures—the term was first employed, in this sense,

by Gustav Klemm in 1843—but instead of taking the essential unit of humanity to be the individual, as Leibniz and Kant had, he traced all human activity and significance to the *Volk*, as in *Volkslied* ("folk song"), a word he coined.[17] He construed these *Völker* strictly on the basis of Leibniz's monadology. Each *Volk* is supposed to constitute a coherent and unique perspective on the world—"singular, wonderful, inexplicable, ineradicable"—with its own internal principle.[18] None grasps the absolute truth, and all are necessary for human history to reveal anything close to the absolute truth: "No one lives in his own period only; he builds on what has gone before and lays a foundation for what comes after. . . . History may not manifestly be revealed as the theatre of a divine purpose on earth . . . for we may not be able to espy its final end. But it may conceivably offer us glimpses of a divine theatre through the openings and ruins of individual scenes."[19] Each society, on Herder's account, has something on the order of a group "mind," and individual minds can only be understood only via their relation to that mind, to the internal principle of the group:

> The ideas of every indigenous nation are . . . confined to its own region: if it profess to understand words expressing things utterly foreign to it, we have reason to remain long in doubt of this understanding. . . . [One can] compose a catechism of [the Greenlanders'] theologico-natural philosophy, showing, that they can neither answer nor comprehend European questions, otherwise than according to the circle of their own conceptions.[20]

One consequence Herder drew from the monadic nature of a *Volk* was thus that we must understand each *Volk* in its own terms; another was that no human being, in the West or anywhere else, will have any real life unless he or she draws it from the energizing principle of his or her particular *Volk:* "It will remain eternally true that if we have no *Volk*, we shall have no public, no nationality, no literature of our own which shall live and work in us. Unless our literature is founded on our *Volk*, we shall write eternally for closet sages and disgusting critics out of whose mouths and stomachs we shall get back what we have given."[21]

The influence of these ideas can hardly be overestimated. Herder is one of the main inspirations for nineteenth-century nationalism, and his use of Leibniz's monadology recurs with eerie consistency in nationalist rhetoric down to the present day, despite the fact that many of the speakers have doubtless never read either his writings or Leibniz's. Fichte, who still allowed for a distinction between individual and group freedom, at the same time insisted that "only when each people, left to itself, develops and forms itself in accordance with its own peculiar quality . . . does the manifestation of divinity appear in its true mirror."[22] The leading Danish nationalist of the 1830s and 1840s, Bishop Grundtvig, spoke of peoples as having a "hidden but active life-force"; Johann Bluntschli, in Switzerland, declared the "national spirit (*Volksgeist*) and . . . national will (*Volkeswille*)" to be "something more than the mere sum of the spirit and will of the individuals composing the nation."[23] The Frenchman Ernst Renan called the nation "a soul, a spiritual principle," while Mazzini declared that "God has divided the human race into masses . . . evidently distinct; each with a separate tone of thought, and a separate part to fulfill."[24] A 1951 article on culture as a political matter remarks that it is "the human right of every people to reveal its soul, to express itself freely."[25]

In anthropology, Herder's ideas strongly influenced Adolf Bastian, a nineteenth-century traveler who is now generally acknowledged to be the founder of ethnology and who, in particular, had a considerable impact on the young Franz Boas.[26] Boas was the first ethnographer to insist on learning the language of the peoples he studied, rather than relying on translators or pidgin English, and in this and many other ways he brought the notion that one needs to see cultures in their own terms and immerse oneself within them to the practice of cultural anthropology. Boas is also said to be the first to use the concept of "pattern" to describe cultures, and as one of his most famous students elaborated it, a cultural "pattern" is a clear descendant of the Leibnizian monad: "A culture, like an individual, is a more or less consistent pattern of thought and action. . . . [It] is not merely the sum of all its parts, but the result of an unique arrangement and interrelation of the parts that has brought about a new entity."[27] Through Boas's many American students—including Ruth Benedict, Margaret Mead, and Robert Lowie—Herder's views have spread through ethnology as widely and as anonymously as they have through nationalism.[28]

One face of both ethnology and nationalism has always been a moral one.[29] Gustav Klemm spoke for many nationalists when he hoped that nations would supplant "priestly dominion." Ever since the French Revolution, nationalism has attempted to replace the moral function of traditional religions, employing vigorously antireligious rhetoric while trying to take over institutions that have previously been religiously controlled. The French Revolution itself, for all its appeals to the Enlightenment, is often considered the watershed of nationalism because the fervor, the rituals, and the violence by which it moved from reason, as a mode of debate and discovery, to what it explicitly called the "Religion of Reason" also served to transform its cause from the promotion of universal human rights to an exaltation of the specifically French people and their new history and politics. One of the few consistencies across nationalisms since that time is that they have always been movements of passion rather than reason, expressed in a preference for violence, or at least the threat of violence, over the cool processes of judicial, legislative, or diplomatic change. Hegel, in the *Philosophy of Right*, analyzes nationalism as part of a wider philosophical movement championing emotion against reason. I believe he is exactly right on this. Nationalism flared up in the late eighteenth and early nineteenth centuries in large part as a response to the failure of the "science of morals" to stand in for the day-to-day practical function that historical religions had once performed. By speaking to the emotions rather than reason, and by drawing on folk myths and customs, it tried to address the specific, given nature of human beings in the way I have argued traditions do, and by capturing educational systems, enforcing movement discipline, and aiming at the individual's subordination to a powerful state, it hoped to guide and shape individuals, as authorities had once done. None of this was formulated in terms of an explicit defense of tradition and authority, but, if my analysis of the role of tradition and authority is correct, the methods of nationalism, and its historical placement as a reaction to the Enlightenment's critique of myths and nonrational means of influence, indicate that it was trying to fill those significant gaps in Enlightenment moral theory. By substituting violence for the persuasive power of authority, however, it was led to cruelty and corruption.

As for ethnology, it began as a part of the nationalist project. Herder, the brothers Grimm, and Klemm all analyzed the nature and collected the products of the German *Volk* in order to provide, in Herder's words, a "public," a "nationality," a "literature of our own which shall live and work in us." From Herder's day throughout the nineteenth century, the collection of "folklore," "folktales" and "folk songs" was always meant to provide the basis for a turn away from liberal, universal principles in the practice of religion, art, politics, and everyday life.[30] And when this heritage was cast off, and ethnology became a haven for those who wanted more to expose what was valuable and exciting in other peoples than to solidify and exalt their own, one moral strain in Herder's legacy was simply exchanged for another. For while Herder's immediate successors may have been concerned only with the development of the German people, Herder himself preached the freeing and revitalization of all *Völker*. Practically, this meant that he collected and studied more than simply German folk materials. Theoretically, it meant that he envisioned the highest good as a product of the free development of and interaction among all *Völker* in the world. So when Margaret Mead recommends that Americans learn from the folkways of Samoa, when Melville Herskovits tells us that "the greatest contribution of anthropology" is to nourish "a willingness to recognize the values that are to be found in the most diverse ways of life," when Clifford Geertz seeks by means of the study of culture to clarify and widen our ethical imagination, they are all looking as much back to Herder's hopes for the rebirth of folk traditions as the provincial nationalists they would decry as "ethnocentric."[31]

Like nationalists, moreover, anthropologists have offered a substitute for authority as well as for tradition. Cultural determinism, the dogma that most ethnologists have espoused since Boas, maintains that biological necessity will keep people in the moral ways of their culture regardless of what their reason tells them. Where nationalists wield physical force to do the work of authority, ethnologists allow a biological force to do that work by itself, but in both cases a naturalistic replacement is found for the "trust" or "faith" that goes beyond reason. In this respect, nationalists and ethnologists are heirs to the Enlightenment as well as critics of it. They are critics of the Enlightenment insofar as they feel that reason, at least as universally and scientifically construed, is inadequate to explain or justify what structures and informs everyday lives, but heirs to the Enlightenment insofar as they embrace its naturalism and its rejection of the notion that the influence of childhood could ever be a source of *justifications* for action. The only alternatives to reason they know of, again like their Enlightenment forebears, are emotion and force—and the two are not sharply distinguished since the influence of emotion is understood to be an irrational force—so they either declare that our ethical lives are in fact run by such a force or they ensure that they will be so run.

Of course, this in turn destroys the moral basis of their projects: neither the threat of physical force nor the assertion of biological force gives one any *justification* for considering a way of acting intrinsically worthwhile. Instead, when presented as the ground for ethics, such forces suggest merely that there is no ground for ethics. In actual practice, before and after every spurt of nationalist or culturally relativist fervor, people have been repulsed by the ethical claims involved rather than drawn toward them. Ethnology, as a moral project, has generally tended to inspire skepticism and apathy, not a revival of the power of traditions. Nationalism has an almost unremittingly violent and ugly history, for all that it remains a powerful force throughout Asia, Africa, and now Eastern Europe.

Perhaps it would be best, then, to avoid the moral face of ethnology and nationalism altogether. They do not regard themselves, after all, in a primarily moral light. Ethnology takes itself to be a mode of observing and analyzing a scientific given ("ethnocentrism" is supposed to be a scientific and not merely a moral failing): there are cultures in the world, and this is how to study them. Nationalism similarly presents itself as a political response to a brute fact: people are naturally divided into nations, so there will be war and misery until each of those nations has a state. And ethnology has indeed issued in richer and more accurate accounts of other societies than existed before the word "culture" was introduced, while nationalism has, although much more erratically, issued in some sensible solutions to political problems (in nineteenth-century Germany, Italy, and Greece, at least; whether it has had so much as a single real success in the twentieth century, history has yet to show). But it is not clear that their central terms are really factual ones. To see this, we need to consider the problems plaguing attempts to define those terms.

DEFINING "CULTURES"

The general form of these problems is as follows: People who live together in a society may well not share beliefs and habits, while people who share beliefs and habits may yet live far apart from one another. Moreover, people may share beliefs and habits in politics and science but not religion and art, or in any of a number of other ways ally their ideas and activities with different, sometimes conflicting, social groupings. It follows that those who want to find a level of social structure that guides or determines its individual constituents' whole thought and practice inevitably wind up torn: first, between the materialist extreme of deriving norms purely from the behavior of the society with which individuals come into daily contact and the idealist extreme of deriving behavior purely from formal statements of socially shared belief, and second, among the claims to priority of geographical, linguistic, and historical definitions of society, and political, religious, and ethical divisions of belief. Is "Western Europe" too large to be a culture or nation? Are the Southern Baptists or the Libertarians too small or too narrowly defined? Are the Huguenots as French as their Catholic counterparts, and if so, are they French first or Huguenot first? Are German Czechs properly German or Czech? And if all these larger and smaller divisions can be called "cultures" or "nations," those terms will end up too vague to do any substantive work. This dilemma is not accidental: if social structures do indeed shape all our thought, including, if not science itself, at least the uses of science, then the very process of seeking them should itself be informed by such a structure, and in that case there is no neutral answer to the question of what constitutes that structure. The question goes too deep in that case, is too fundamental, to be a task for science. Science cannot, as Kant showed, investigate its own limits without running into contradictions.

In practice, the question, What is a culture (nation)? gets answered from several different points of view. Scientists collecting data for theories of human interaction do not need a final, settled definition of the term; a rough guide is sufficient to motivate and give some direction to their speculations or gathering of evidence. A final categorization can take place once the evidence is in or the theory built. Representatives of social institutions have a markedly lesser ability to tolerate vagueness and ambiguity. Elected officials and school administrators, bank managers and union leaders, curators and social workers face problems involving cultures ranging from settling disputes over hiring to accommodating bilingualism or religious differences in a school or arts program. They have to make *decisions* about cultures, and they need some firm line on what to count as a culture, so that their decisions will have the justice of clarity and consistency, so that they can resolve in advance as many difficulties as they can possibly anticipate, and so that their decisions will cohere with the other decisions of their institution and the society it serves. The individual agent, finally, also needs some sharp definition of "culture," although she needs to determine more what to count as her *own* culture than what to count as culture in general. All the well-worked-out definitions and empirical evidence in the world are of no use to her if they pretend to show that her beliefs and attitudes are expressed by a group product that she does not recognize as expressing her at all. One criterion of a successful theory of culture, for her, is that she be able to say, "That is *my* culture!" of some application of the theory. On the other hand, she usually takes some interest in what one might call the "external" view of what to consider her culture. We all know of cases in which individuals insist that they have nothing Italian about them when all their tastes, habits, and friends are Italian, or that they are English when they are only Anglophiles, and if we resemble these individuals, we generally want to know about it. So the distinction between defining "culture" in general and defining one's own culture is not one to which we can adhere strictly.

Consider, in this light, the history of the word "culture." The modern, anthropological use of the term was introduced into English by E. B. Tylor in his 1871 book *Primitive Culture*. Tylor's definition of the word, in the first sentence of the book, served as the only definition in use for the next thirty years and has dominated most discussions of the word ever since: "Culture . . . is that complex whole which includes knowledge, belief, art, morals, law, custom and any other capabilities and habits acquired by man as a member of society."[32] In the twentieth century, there have been fierce tussles over the word, and, according to Alfred L. Kroeber and Clyde Kluckhohn's *Culture: A Critical Review of Concepts and Definitions,* still the controlling text on the subject,[33] more than a hundred and sixty definitions were proposed for it between 1920 and 1950. Many of them share Tylor's inclination to assemble a lot of different things without explaining why they belong together and to leave the term "society" without a clear referent, although they usually describe something close to what I have called an "authoritative tradition": a socially established network of beliefs, institutions, and practices, handed down from the past, which shapes individual thoughts and lives.[34] Two excellent examples are Edward Sapir's 1921 comment that culture consists in "the socially inherited assemblage of practices and beliefs that determines the texture of our lives," and Clifford Geertz's 1966 definition of the term as "an historically transmitted pattern of meaning embodied in symbols, a system of inherited conceptions expressed in symbolic forms by means of which men communicate, perpetuate, and develop their knowledge and attitudes toward life."[35]

On the other hand, the definitions are so varied and in so much conflict with one another that some lack even these properties. Many talk about artifacts and patterns of behavior to the exclusion of beliefs ("The sum total of the possessions and the patterned ways of behavior which have become part of the heritage of a group"),[36] and some allow for or explicitly include the products of highly transitory groups. When writers, like many functionalists, want to let the word cover "everything . . . artificial, useful and social" that meets our biological or socioeconomic needs,[37] they leave little room for a distinction between the activities and beliefs of a group of people who happen to wind up on a desert island together and the more fundamental activities and beliefs of the societies in which such desert islanders grew up. Clyde Kluckhohn and W. H. Kelly, in 1945, push this problem to its limits when they recommend "speak[ing] of the culture of cliques and of relatively impermanent social units such as, for example, members of summer camps."[38] They prefer to restrict only the term "society" to more permanent and distinctive groups, and that term is normally used in social science to isolate groups by geographical, political, or economic criteria rather than by beliefs.

The most common criterion for distinguishing cultures is language. Indeed, before the word "culture" came to designate the ways of life of different peoples, Herder and others who felt that such ways of life played an important role in shaping thought appealed to language as the hallmark and source of differences in thought.[39] Many of the enumerative definitions that Kroeber and Kluckhohn present include language in their list of cultural products. Clark Wissler, in 1920, puts language with marriage and art in his examples of the "social activities" with which he wants to identify culture.[40] Ernst Cassirer equates culture with "language, myth, art, religion, [and] science."[41] More to our point, since lists give no priority to language among cultural products, is D. M. Taylor's description of language as "the vehicle of culture" and C. F. Voegelin's claim that "it is relatively easy to . . . define linguistics without reference to culture . . . ; it is much more difficult to . . . define culture . . . without reference to language."[42]

On the other hand, H. Hoijer notes that people "sharing substantially the same culture" may speak different languages, while "peoples whose languages are related may have very different cultures."[43] Franz Boas adds that although cultures shape languages, it is highly unlikely that "morphological traits of [a] language" have any significant impact on the nature of its speakers' culture.[44] People are certainly more likely to develop shared beliefs and interests when they speak the same language, but one should not dismiss too readily the possibility of a culture among people with different languages, nor assume that shared language guarantees shared culture. The Jews, who for the past two thousand years have tended to share only a poorly spoken second tongue, have still managed in that period to share more beliefs and goals with one another than with the societies among which they have lived. Similarly, although linguistic difference remains very important to the various groups in India and Indonesia, the possession of shared second languages (Hindi and English in the first case, "Bahasa Indonesia" in the second), together with the desire of most of the inhabitants to live in an independent and relatively powerful political unit, has led those groups to seek and in part to find a common culture. The various linguistic groups in Switzerland have worked toward a comparable goal for much longer and with considerable success.

That linguistic unity is not even a sufficient condition for harmony of beliefs and interests is demonstrated by the importance of religious differences, from the fervent but peaceful disagreements among fundamentalists, mainstream believers, and secularists in the United States, to the violent conflicts of Catholics and Protestants in Northern Ireland. Here, as in the complementary case of the unity among Diaspora Jews, the possession and use in education of certain texts, and certain traditions of interpreting those texts, play a greater role than the mere language in which the texts are read and taught. Diaspora Jews are held together by their educational emphasis on the Hebrew Bible and its rabbinic commentaries; Catholics by the Latin Bible, the Church Fathers, and Aquinas; Southern Baptists by the English Bible and a tradition of preaching; and American secularists by the Constitution, the writings of its authors and their philosophical contemporaries, and the tradition of science and philosophy of science in the modern academy. In the last two examples, I have included preaching and academic teaching as a mode of producing shared texts: insofar as ideas can be conveyed in verbal expressions so similar to one another that one preacher or professor or congregant or student can predict fairly exactly what will be said in another church or school, "texts" need not be strictly limited to the written word. We can in this way allow that nonliterate societies may also pass down texts, in the form of an oral tradition of proverbs, stories, codes of law, and so on.

With this broader definition of the word "text," we might try using it instead of language as the prime cultural determinant. By means of shared texts, groups pass down interests and ideas, rules and models. Groups trying to maintain a shared culture in spite of linguistic difference, moreover, or wanting to separate themselves from the community with which they share a language, generally combine and dissent by means of an attachment to some text or set of texts. The unifying texts for the Swiss may be a body of positive law, while the separatist Biafrans share stories of past glory and recent oppression, but insofar as these groups become and remain a people at all, they must pass some tales down to their children.

There remains the question of what *kinds* of shared texts have decisive influence in establishing and shaping a cultural group. We surely do not want to say that any shared history, for instance, establishes a separate culture. If all and only the people of Astoria, Queens, discuss and recall some crime or scandal in their neighborhood, that does not turn them into a culture. Nor need every political division and subdivision in the world (Biafrans, Nigerians, Tamils, Indians, Iraqis, Arabs) reflect a complete, or single, cultural group. Instead, some texts have an insignificant effect on the shaping of beliefs and ideals, while others are overwhelmingly important, and the relative strength of different kinds of texts varies from occasion to occasion. Thus on one occasion an epic, on another a religious writing, and on a third a code of law will have decisive impact on the formation of a culture. In addition, individuals tend to be shaped by several different texts and traditions of texts, and peoples tend correspondingly to overlap in various ways. An agent may be pulled in one direction by a strict Catholic Sunday school, in another direction by a family that reveres the tradition of liberalism associated with the Bill of Rights, and in a third direction by teachers and peers with a fondness for Zen Buddhist literature. At least three sets of texts, at least three cultures, can in this way converge in a single individual.

These considerations do not make texts, and the single language in which a given text is usually conveyed, useless as a distinguishing mark of culture, but they do mean that one cannot entirely solve the problem of identification by pointing to that mark. Cultures usually revolve around a few shared texts; languages are usually identified with certain texts, and texts with certain languages; hence shared language coupled with shared texts remains an excellent means of picking out most cultural groups in the world, as well as most of their members. But there are some hard cases in which this mark identifies too many or too few groups, and many hard cases, especially in the diverse and highly interactive communities of the West, in which it sifts out three or four groups with which an individual may identify but says nothing about how to select further among these three or four.

For that further selection, we need to work out hierarchies among texts, which is one of the motivations for nationalism, especially among those who do not want to turn back to religion as the source of such hierarchies.

In order to base a state on a cultural group, nationalism has had to try to establish a decisive hierarchy of cultural allegiances and to impose its answer on each individual, within the group it selects, by means of a political structure and a body of positive law. How successful has it been?

INVENTING "NATIONS"

In the terms of a familiar distinction in jurisprudence, the history of nationalism follows a progression from "found" to "made" nations. For Herder and his contemporaries, nations were to be found in the natural divisions of the human race, ordained by God and endowed each with its own character, the purity and inviolability of which its citizens had a duty to preserve.[45] Herder's "national soul"—corresponding, as we have seen, to the Leibnizian monad—maintains the identity of a culture through all its changes and interactions, and this national soul deserves independence for the same reason that individual souls deserve freedom: because the only morally healthy condition for a soul (mind, spirit, etc.), according to the weird marriage of Kant's ethics and romantic expressivism that dominated post-Kantian philosophy, is one in which it develops according to its own, "internal" laws.[46] Thus Herder, who wanted all nations to live in freedom; thus Fichte, who was passionately dedicated to specifically German unity and independence; and thus Schleiermacher, who attributed to each nation a different historical task.[47]

When these thinkers descended from their mystical visions to real historical or political projects, they had to find concrete determinations for their "natural divisions of the human race." For the most part they opted for language as the distinguishing characteristic of these divisions, but that brought its own problems. Language was viewed as the concrete expression of mental life, the means by which "man becomes conscious of his personality,"[48] and it was more likely to serve as a repository for group experiences than the individualist mental structures Kant had identified as "categories." On the other hand, as was already known in the eighteenth century, languages tend to borrow from one another, even to form curious hybrids. In addition, many people learn more than one language and may wind up speaking or writing in a language other than their native one. Fichte tried to prove that the presence of foreign words obscures a native speaker's own grasp on what he means,[49] and others embarked on a search, via such studies of folk speech and literature as the work of the brothers Grimm, for the original, primitive languages of the world, hoping that these would reveal the true nations.[50] As nationalism developed through the nineteenth century, language moved from its pride of place as *the* distinguishing mark of a nation to a position as one of a set of criteria, which also included race, history, and religion. The interdependence of this set helped to determine, among other things, which languages were to count as pure and proper expressions of a nation and which speakers of a language were to count as appropriate shapers and representatives of its use. According to Charles Maurras, no Jew could properly speak French.[51]

If the fall from a simple, linguistic criterion into a babble of overlapping and conflicting ones looks familiar from my discussion of culture, that is because the theories of nations and of cultures arose at much the same time and for similar and closely interwoven reasons. In Germany, where both theories have their roots, the word *Volk* was often used for either "nation" or "culture," and both *Kultur* and *Nation* were seen—by Kant and Fichte, respectively—as a context for the full flowering of (individual) freedom.[52] Herder, moreover, is claimed as a major precursor by both nationalists and anthropologists. Herder's search for the essence of each culture (*Volksgeist*) turned into the search of Adolf Bastian for essential "folk thoughts" (*Völkergedanken*); Herder's notion of each ethnic group as almost a Leibnizian monad, unique and irreducible, is echoed not only in Bastian but throughout anthropological work.[53] The identification of these groups was a crucial starting point for nationalist polemics, while the project of nationalism helped, as we saw earlier, to inspire much comparative linguistics and study of folk literature. Finally, in a symbiosis that provoked discomfort and self-examination right through the 1970s, anthropologists have been associated throughout their history with the service of those European powers who simultaneously represent one expression of nationalism and have attempted to contain or squelch other such expressions.[54]

It should not surprise us, then, that the indeterminacy we encountered in the concept of "culture" reappears in the concept of "nation." Every nationalist movement has found itself beset by sub- and supernationalisms: groups that defy the linguistic, historical, or religious self-definition of a particular nation (such as the Armenians, the Kurds, the German Czechs, or the Muslim Indians), and groups that would dissolve that nation into a larger whole (such as the Pan-Slavs or Pan-Arabs). Among Third World states that have arisen out of a nationalist revolution, says Geertz, "nationalisms within nationalisms" constitute a major threat to the "national identity in whose name the revolution was made."[55] He points out that most "Tamils, Karens, Brahmins, Malays, Sikhs, Ibos, Muslims, Chinese, Nilotes, Bengalis or Ashantis found it a good deal easier to grasp the idea that they were not Englishmen than that they were Indians, Burmese, Malayans, Ghanaians, Pakistanis, Nigerians or Sudanese."[56] As Geertz's list of ethnic groups indicates, part of the problem lies in the fact that nations, like cultures, are unable to decide whether they ought to be religiously, linguistically, racially, or historically based. The conflicts between Pan-Arabism and Pan-Islamism, between Hindu, Muslim, or Sikh "fanatics" and the idea of India, or among Malays, Indians, and Chinese in today's Malaysia demonstrate dramatically the absence of a definitive criterion for nationhood.

One might suppose, as Herder presumably would have, that this problem could be solved by granting a state to every self-declared national group. Given the economic and military need, however, for a state to attain a certain minimal size, one stark statistic will deal the deathblow to this hope: while up to the sixteenth century the longest list of the world's peoples contained 177 separate groups, an early twentieth-century count yielded 650 "primitive societies," and a 1931 estimate offered us "12,000 tribes, language groups, nations, clans and other social divisions."[57] Twelve thousand nation-states is a prospect that would probably give pause even to Herder's contemporaries.

Hence the move, within nationalist movements as well as theoretical studies, to a view of nations as "made" rather than "found." As the revolution approached in most of the Third World, says Geertz, it was assumed that "the nationalists would make the state and the state would make the nation."[58] By appealing to loose and selective readings of the traditions of the dominant ethnic group(s), while instituting a common language and a common body of law, the new states tried to mold their disparate peoples into a political unity, somewhat distinct in its character and history from other such unities in the world and thereby worthy of the title "nation." Nationalism in this sense "consists in defining, or trying to define, a collective subject to whom the actions of the state can be internally connected, in creating, or trying to create, an experiential 'we' from whose will the activities of government seem spontaneously to flow."[59]

Like found nationalism, made nationalism draws on an analogy between the cultural group and the individual human being. Geertz's remark above about the collective subject bears an uncanny resemblance to Bernard Williams's definition of an individual agent's integrity: "His actions and his decisions have to be seen as the actions and decisions which flow from the projects and attitudes with which he is most closely identified."[60] Geertz makes this comparison explicit in a later article: "[A state's] acts must seem continuous with the selves of those whose state it pretends it is . . . This is not a mere question of consensus. A man does not have to agree with his government's acts to see himself as embodied in them any more than he has to approve of his own acts to acknowledge that he has, alas, himself performed them. It is a question of immediacy, of experiencing what the state 'does' as proceeding naturally from a familiar and intelligible 'we.'"[61]

Unlike the found nationalist, however, what the made nationalist finds fascinating about individual human beings is not their uniqueness but their indeterminacy and (concomitant) capacity for self-creation. Here the made nationalist can take Hegel as a forebear, although in the context of his own time Hegel belonged in the antinationalist camp.[62] The very first definition of "personality" in the *Philosophy of Right* compares individuals and nations but warns that neither one has any personality until it achieves self-knowledge.[63] This is a theme that runs throughout the work. Nations constitute the "ethical substance" of a state, but not until a state has shaped it does that substance attain "a universal and universally valid embodiment in laws, i.e., in determinate thoughts," and the "recognition from others" that comes with such a determinate form.[64] For Hegel, a nation is not naturally or divinely ordained as a "division of the human race" from the beginning of historical time; instead, it develops from "a family, a horde, a clan, a multitude, etc." toward a specific and unified "mind" that it achieves only in the state.[65] By means of a political structure and a body of positive laws, the state forms an explicit and rational order out of the chaotic, nonrational, and conflicting traditions of the families, hordes, clans, etc., that make it up. This account retains hints of a one-nation-one-state view in its appeal to preexisting, identifiable (if vague and chaotic) ethical substances, but the decisive move in the creation of a nation is clearly the establishment of the state. We can easily see that establishment as a way of grafting a decision procedure onto the competing ethical claims of the various candidates for the status of "culture." That is, in Hegel's picture— and the one favored by many, if not all, modern nationalist states—we settle the conflicts among social norms via positive law (enforced, political, state law, as opposed to "moral" or "natural" law): by fiat, in effect, and that fiat, that body of enforced law, forges a unified social group out of the originally conflicting ones.

The advantage of this approach is that it does in fact, in many cases and for many purposes, settle disputes over what should determine a culture. The disadvantage is that positive law seems a most inappropriate medium for the final determination of a set of beliefs and practices. States inevitably have jurisdiction over more than one reasonable candidate for a cultural group, in this world of twelve thousand such groups, and laws tend to be made by means of a compromise among "interest groups," which include but are not limited to cultures, rather than as an expression of any one of these groups' norms. Furthermore, in a democracy, legislators but imperfectly represent their constituencies, while even intelligent and benevolent autocrats but imperfectly understand their people's traditions and how best to implement them. As a result, positive law always constitutes at best a good stab at defining the interests and beliefs of the people it is supposed to rule. It usually is, and always ought to be, corrigible, and to keep it that way one needs to maintain a distinction between culture and nation, or nation and state, precisely so that each culture/nation can correct the state representing it. People want to keep the legal stabs at expressing their values open to later, better attempts at such expression and to attempts at expressing changes in those values. And if the law is widely inconsonant with their norms, they want to have an ethical option of dissenting from or even disobeying such law: hence the ethical traditions of civil disobedience and revolution. Moreover, precisely because positive law intrinsically entails the use of force, and force may be an ineffective, inappropriate, or dangerous way of winning people over to an ethical position, practically every legal system ignores vast areas of ethical life. For all these reasons, while positive law forms *an* expression and determinant of most systems having reason to call themselves a "culture," people need not, and generally do not want to, regard it as the overriding, the final, arbiter of who belongs to their culture and what it has to say.[66]

In sum, the central terms of ethnology and nationalism tend to have either one vague meaning or two or more sharp but conflicting ones. It is perhaps not unreasonable to see this problem as a shadow of our fifth and Kant's third antinomy. If societies flow from a united, thinking "collective subject," resembling the morally responsible self of an individual, that subject will never be determined absolutely within the bounds of the thought for which it is itself responsible; if they do not have such a unified source, science will find only piecemeal and provisional social determinants of individual thought. For the purposes of action, we attribute to our societies, as to our individual selves, some specific identity, but that attribution is only a posit *for* the purposes of action. That is, any conception of "cultures" and "nations" as distinct and coherent, like any such conception of our individual selves, is a moral construct.

CULTURES/NATIONS AS MORAL POSITS

To appreciate the significance of this claim, we must return to the philosophy of Herder. The key problem with Herder's account of culture lies in his appropriation of the Leibnizian notion that each monad has a unique and irreducible internal principle. Much of Leibniz is surprisingly congenial to a theory of group minds. Leibniz describes the monad as a simple, a process of perception, a set of relations among everything in the universe, and an expression of those relations[67]—and *as simple* it must be all these things at once. Hence its perception is irreducible; it perceives the relations it has, and the relations it has determine its perception; and the way it perceives and the way it expresses its relations must be closely related, if not identical. It follows that for Leibniz, as for Spinoza, much mental activity need not be explicitly conscious. Insofar as my bodily size, shape, position, and reactions depend on relations with all other bodies in the universe, their particular configuration expresses something about all those other bodies, and insofar as I am aware, on any level at all, of my bodily characteristics,[68] I am also aware, to some degree or other, of the entire universe: "Although each created monad represents the whole universe, it represents more distinctly the body which specially pertains to it. . . . And as this body expresses all the universe through the interconnection of all matter in the plenum, the soul also represents the whole universe in representing this body."[69] The weathering of a stone, let alone the capacities of a heat-seeking missile, might belong on Leibniz's continuum of mind, so placing the interactions and institutions of a group on it is none too difficult.[70] Unlike the Cartesian conception of mind, more common in the history of philosophy, in which the capacity for introspection, or at least for "felt" sensation, is essential to having a mind, Leibniz's monads fit anything that can be said to have a unified and distinctive set of relations, and mode of expressing relations, with the other objects of the universe.[71]

The difficulty is to determine what marks groups as unified and distinctive. According to Leibniz, the principle of sufficient reason guarantees that there can be no two similar monads, and the nature of a simple substance entails that whatever makes one monad differ from another must be internal to the workings of all its thought and experience: "The natural changes of the Monad come from an internal principle, because an external cause can have no influence upon its inner being." Leibniz draws from this the consequence that monads have no direct influence on or knowledge of one another; as he memorably puts it, they are "windowless."[72]

To make use of these metaphysical principles in the empirical study of groups is deeply problematic. The internal principle is supposed to be something that cannot be identified empirically, since it precedes and structures all empirical data, and in any case one monad is not supposed to be able to perceive the internal principle of another. For Herder, the various groups in the world interact, striving with one another in a sort of Heraclitean flux.[73] So far he is actually rather similar to Leibniz. A similar echo of Heraclitus makes an appearance, as characteristic of the realm of matter, in *Monadology* §71: "All bodies are in a state of flux like rivers, and the parts are continually entering in or passing out." But participation in flux, for Leibniz, is characteristic *only* of matter, while Herder wants each group to have access to other group *minds*. We "must enter the spirit of a nation," he says, "before [we] can share even one of its thoughts or deeds."[74] That the nation has a "spirit" essential to its thoughts and deeds recalls the internal principle of Leibnizian monads. That we can enter it, on the other hand, implies that group monads are not windowless. The *Volksgeist* serves as an antechamber, not a barrier, to cross-cultural understanding.

Herder never resolved the ambiguity over whether groups are essentially self-contained and therefore incomprehensible to one another, or essentially comprehensible to one another and therefore not self-contained, and confusion about how, if at all, Leibniz's "internal principle" is to be conceived in empirical accounts of group thought has remained to the present day. If a group's internal principle is something metaphysical, then it may well be important, and definitive of the group, but it can have nothing to do with the empirical world, which means that neither science nor politics need pay any attention to it. Metaphysical principles will neither show up in anthropological studies nor be affected by political actions, whether nationalist or antinationalist.[75] If, on the other hand, internal principles are something natural, it is hard to see why they too should not participate in the flux embracing all natural things. A group may be unique insofar as it occupies one particular position in history, but it surely has a past in a larger, or several smaller, wholes, a present that includes friendly and not so friendly exchanges of ideas, practices, and goods with its neighbors, and a future in which it may blend or divide into some other identity or set of identities.

Nationalists have tended to waver between demanding political expression for metaphysical distinctions and trying to turn natural differences into something fixed and unchangeable. The consequence of the first has been confusion, a politics that, since it cannot appeal to reason, has had to make use of deception and violence. The consequence of the second has taken the specific forms of racism—the doctrine that moral differences among human beings are carried down, with strict biological determination, in "the blood," and outrageous distortion of history. Such distortion is found in myths that a contemporary people is the direct and sole descendant of a successful people in the ancient world (that the present-day Germans are descendants of the Greeks, that the Russians or Slavs are the heirs to the Byzantine Empire), that some group or another (the Aryans, the Arabs, the Africans) has produced all the important achievements of humanity, or that intermingling of groups has historically brought about dire effects.[76] Attempts to defend these notions have resulted, of course, in great evils and in terrible science; nationalism has probably provided the largest educated audience for wildly irresponsible and dishonest scientific claims since modern empirical methods took over from alchemy and astrology in the seventeenth century.

I suggest that a way to avoid some of these consequences, while holding onto the advantages of Herder's approach to human groups, is to interpret the "internal principle" in moral terms. There are hints of such an interpretation already in Leibniz and Herder. Leibniz attributes the "natural changes of the Monad" to its internal principle, while Herder describes the *Volksgeist* as a source of energy or vitality (an "energizing principle"): for both, it is clearly a spring for action.[77] But they may have overlooked the significance of this point because they regarded metaphysics, not moral thought, as the main methodological alternative to empiricism.[78] It took Kant to transform practical reason into a distinctive mode of thought that complements and transcends empirical investigation. Today metaphysics has been more or less discredited, in part because of Kant, while the distinction between thought apart from action and thought in the course of action retains its force.

Suppose, therefore, that we view cultural or national uniqueness as a moral posit, rather than a metaphysical or scientific one. Then, to begin with, we must recall that for the purposes of morality we rely on one side of an antinomy, such that the uniqueness of cultures, while a necessary presupposition of their moral function, need not be maintained from the speculative point of view. As Kant has shown, in order to act we need to presuppose that each of us has a unified self capable of free action, and (although Kant did not say this) in the context of each specific action we need to presuppose that our unified selves have specific characteristics from which specific decisions can flow. It may well be true, as Herder recognized, that we also need to presuppose a unified "group self," with specific characteristics, against which our individual acts can be judged and individual selves defined. *But it does not follow, any more for the group than for the individual, that the unified self can be identified scientifically,* or that the transcendental supposition that such a thing exists ought to affect biological, psychological, and sociological attempts to construe selves in terms of their genetic and environmental influences. For the purposes of science, and of political decisions based on scientific results, we need to recognize that cultures may, as every evidence indicates they do, imitate one another and blend with one another; that individuals may belong to several cultures at once, without giving any one a clear priority over the others; that the word "culture," as a general term for the social products of the human mind, may have several different, even incompatible, scientific uses; and that some of those uses may have little to do with the decisions of the people labeled by it. That cultures are distinctive and crucial for decisions about how to live is a view we take up when, and only when, we regard them as social interpretations of the good.

On this view, the distinguishing mark of cultures, the instantiation of Leibniz's "internal principle," will be their authoritative traditions. Paradigmatically, a culture, as a unique and energizing force in the individual lives of some society, will comprise an oral or written text, passed down and interpreted from generation to generation, which explains and mandates a distinctive set of actions. As we saw in Chapter 3, each tradition constitutes a limited view of the good[79] and stands in a relation to other traditions simultaneously of recognizing them as also views of the good and of claiming superiority for its own view. Since the groups are formed by denying the adequacy of one another's views, they will naturally tend to multiply into the greatest possible variety of different views. Exactly as Herder says, then, "the human species is such a copious scheme . . . that

. . . its great and numerous capacities could not appear on our planet otherwise than *divided among millions.* Every thing has been born, that could be born upon it; and every thing has maintained itself, that could acquire a state of permanence according to the laws of Nature."[80] And since the absolute good can reasonably be construed as the limit of this variety of finite views of the good, we can even make sense of Herder's claim that universal harmony is at least a potential goal of the interaction of cultures, that moral equilibrium arises only through the "wild confusion" of cultures contending with one another, denying one another's adequacy.[81] But where Herder, starting from Leibniz, founders on the limitations of metaphysics, we begin with the resources of Kant and Kierkegaard—intellectual descendants of Lessing—who transformed the certainties of metaphysics into precisely what we are *least* certain of, into the project of the moral life rather than the result of the intellectual one. Recasting Herder's views in these terms, we can hope to make them more plausible and less dangerous.

One might object that many of the groups we might pretheoretically want to call distinct cultures—Serbs, Australians, Irish or African Americans—lack either a traditional text or a set of authorities. Here the paradigmatic nature of the definition comes into play. Not everything claiming the title "culture" deserves that name, and having a paradigm for what a culture looks like can help us explain why some groups have trouble maintaining a cultural identity. If, paradigmatically, a culture comprises an interweaving of traditional text, authority, and practice, then something that lacks one of these three constituents may more or less resemble a culture without quite succeeding in being one. In many cases, a shared history and social structure take the place of the traditional text, but the fact that the history is not transmitted in a clear and consistent way weakens the culture's capacity to define and mandate practices. In other cases, the shared practices are so clear and distinctive that a text could be read off from them (think of the strict French customs about when and how to eat), but in fact there is no such text. Again, something will be missing: there may be no problem determining what the practices are, but there will be a question as to why they should be considered important. To lack a story is to lack a rationale, and without a rationale a culture cannot maintain its grip. Finally, in many places authority has decayed, as a result of Enlightenment (modernist) influences, or oppression by another group, or communal dispersion. Here it is very difficult to renew the application, and especially to preserve the power, of a group's practices, and there is little reason to expect the group to survive over time.

Thus, far from being a drawback, the fact that some groups do not quite fit the definition of culture in terms of tradition and authority points up a strength of that definition: it can diagnose weaknesses in groups that want to preserve a cultural identity and indicate ways in which those weaknesses might be overcome. There are groups, too temporary or heterogeneous to have any distinct and continuing identity, that misunderstand the term "culture" or manipulate it for political purposes. There are also more and less cohesive cultures, cultures with greater and lesser senses of the nature and/or importance of their identity, cultures that are succeeding and cultures that are failing to claim the allegiance of their societies, cultures that are enabling their followers to flourish and cultures that are encouraging unhappiness, illness, moral weakness, or corruption. If culture is to play a significant role in the explanation and justification of action, we must be able to make these kinds of discriminations and determine, and sometimes judge, the relative place of different cultures in the lives of the agents they guide.

ADVANTAGES OF A MORAL VIEW OF CULTURE

Both for the paradigm and for the less-than-paradigm cases, we reap several advantages by adopting a moral approach to the uniqueness of cultures.

(1) We can abandon the mythmaking (in the sense here of lying and exaggerating, not in the sense of telling interesting stories about the world) that has plagued nationalism and ethnic identity movements. Using science to prove that cultures are distinctive and morally significant is a confusion that leads to corrupt science; insisting that morality accept the scientific views and uses of culture is equally a confusion and equally corrupting of morals. For the purposes of science, cultures can be admitted

to be a blur, a flux of mutual influence and interaction. Anything essentially unique about them lies not in their racial makeup or in any empirical element of their texts, customs, or history, but in the way they appear, as moral conceptions, in the practical reason of their adherents.

(2) The view of culture I am offering is not deterministic, and it leaves room for criticism of the culture, both by insiders and by outsiders. One way in which the science of culture has corrupted the ethics of culture is by tying the individual too tightly to his or her social origins. If I am but a puppet or epiphenomenon of a group mind, what I do individually can hardly be of great significance, even to me. On the account presented here, cultures provide a set of terms for, not the whole content of, their members' actions, and the force they exert is not of a kind to overwhelm, or make pointless, individual reason. In these respects the view I am offering resembles Clifford Geertz's interpretive theory of cultures, although on my account culture is an interpretation of something beyond itself, not merely the unending process of interpretation itself.[82] Seeing cultures as conceptions *of the good* opens up a space between the interpretation and what it is an interpretation of, such that it makes sense that an individual in the midst of a culture could condemn it for "going wrong." On Geertz's view, it is not clear what there might be to go wrong about. Claiming that one's culture has gone wrong would seem to be just one play or ploy in the ongoing play of meaning, a part of the way meaning works. But this not only removes all force from the critic's objections; it misconstrues the whole relationship between the critic and his or her opponents. Although the terms of their debate will have to be set by the culture itself, both defender and critic of a culture feel that what is at stake lies beyond those terms, and on the approach I am recommending that feeling is not in any way a delusion. Both cross-cultural judgment and intracultural dissent may be understood as attempts to interpret or correct a culture by means of its own commitment to a higher but elusive good. We will explore this possibility in detail in Chapters 6 and 7.

(3) Tradition and authority are fairly clear, if not strictly empirical, marks by which to distinguish cultures and to show how and why a culture's distinctiveness can matter. As long as the unique "internal principle" remains vague, and vaguely mystical, it spawns embarrassing when

not dangerous attempts to overturn all the enlightened, liberal achievements of a culture in favor of folktales and folk practices (think of the anti-intellectualism of the Nazis, of the tribal dictators in 1970s Africa, of Muslim fundamentalists in Iran and Jewish fundamentalists in Israel) or to "purify" cultures of human beings said to be tainting its essence. We now have a straightforward way of determining where distinctiveness lies in a culture and why it is important—and we can see that that distinctiveness is in conflict neither with a group's more cosmopolitan achievements nor with the presence of foreigners in its midst.

We can also see that there is no need for a culture to be absolutist in the sense that its representatives or leaders brook no dissent. I argued in Chapter 4 that freedom goes together with authority, is indeed part of the process of interpretation making authority possible. It follows that cultures, if they are indeed authoritative traditions, are shaped by individual choices even as those choices are also shaped by cultures. This conclusion has ramifications both for politics and for the theory of culture. For politics, it means that the attempt, common if not ubiquitous in nationalist movements, to enforce cultural unity is as misguided as it is oppressive; cultures can flourish amid fervent, even bitter, disagreements over their nature. For theory, it means that the question of whether a culture is to be centered on a religion, a history, a language, or a political structure, on a tradition, a set of authorities, or a set of practices, will be settled in large part by the individuals who constitute it, and will be settled—can only be settled—at and for a given time, and with the recognition that, like other aspects of the interpretation of culture, it might be renegotiated and settled differently in the future. On the account I have given of the moral point of view, it is unnecessary for a culture to have a single, fixed view of itself. The nature of action demands that we reach a decisive conclusion about issues bearing on our action, but the fifth antinomy suggests that such conclusions, while final in the sense of having an endpoint, are not final in the sense of being absolute (the endpoint is not the sum of the infinite series that establishes contingent truths). Ethical conclusions, while fixed at each moment of action, can always be opened up again. So when we draw on our culture in deciding how to act, we need some clear idea of who and what is in it and of what it has to say, but we can remain aware that the absolute truth on these questions eludes us every time, and we can be open to including different people or ideas in, or revising our interpretations of, our culture whenever the heat of action subsides to make room for new reflection.

(4) *Because* it is not absolutist, this moral view of culture can say something useful about the characteristic modern condition of agents with multiple cultural allegiances. I, the author of this book, am, among other things, a Jew, an American, a child of immigrants from Germany, and a nominal British citizen. I have strong attachments to norms derived from the mostly Christian writings in which I was educated, from the political liberalism common among my friends and relatives, from the romanticism of the operas my parents love, from the rich law and ritual of the Jewish tradition, and from the elegance and elitism of the British literature that I grew up reading. On the whole, these cultures share a great deal with one another (not surprisingly, since their histories have overlapped for many years), but sometimes they conflict, producing in me mixed emotions—as when, looking in India at monuments to the British Empire, I was filled simultaneously with romantic pride and liberal shame—or even mixed directives—as when my "Christian" inclinations toward valuing absolute love lead me to believe I should immediately and entirely forgive someone, while my Jewish inclinations toward tempering mercy with justice tell me that forgiveness is not always respect. But such conflicts need not interfere with my general sense that I am guided by my cultures in my actions, and I need not even determine finally which of my cultures is to predominate. My list of cultures, while long, is not infinitely long; the cultures on the whole cohere; and on the whole I do have a pretty clear sense of which takes precedence over which (liberal over romantic, Jewish over Christian, to a lesser extent American over British). That there are hard cases where two of my cultures claim me almost equally means that culture, as an ethical guide, is not complete, does not guide all my actions. It does not mean that the appeal to culture is incoherent or useless.

This account fits what the contemporary literature likes to call "the moral facts." Most people, at least in cultures that have mingled freely with other cultures, can tell a similar story to my own. Most still feel that they are a product of a definite list and mix of cultures.[83] Most have a pretty firm sense of which among their sets of norms generally take precedence over which others. And most feel that they encounter hard cases in which they do not know quite what to do, which of their cultures and cultural norms to favor. But this incompleteness only adds plausibility to the ethical claims of culture: it is one of the essential features of ethical life that we run into situations where there is no clear right decision, and where we may not determine what to count even as the *best* decision, if we ever do, until after we have had to take some action in the midst of confusion.[84]

One way the individual agent may settle the priority of the various cultures claiming her is by making choices, especially sets or series of choices, aligning herself with one culture (or one subset of her cultures) more than with others, or interpreting and reinterpreting the claims of her various cultures so as to make the choices they mandate increasingly compatible. A welcome consequence of this possibility is that agents define their cultural alignments more clearly and more thoughtfully as their lives progress. In this way, they may come to face fewer and fewer cultural dilemmas, although perhaps at no point do dilemmas disappear. In this way, also, especially insofar as they harmonize and reinterpret what they perceive of their competing cultures, agents can help reconcile the various group views and groups that conflict in their neighborhoods or even in the inter-national (inter-cultural) arena.[85]

We now have a full-fledged case for splintering ethics into specific communities, traditions, and networks of authority. That case is itself universalistic, in the sense that it mandates not just of our own, Western culture, but of any group wanting to claim the moral legitimacy conferred by the word "culture," that it have some sort of central text, some set of authorities, some recognition that its text and practices aim at a wider good at which other cultures may also aim, and some recognition of the fact that the relationship of moral authority entails a free apprehension and interpretation of moral truth on the part of those subject to authority. In some form or another, these conditions are generally present in all cultures. Differences then rest principally in the specific details of practice entailed by the texts and histories of interpretation in each community and in the specific way that the general conditions of culture are conceived: how authority and tradition are described and justified, what amount and kind of freedom is considered necessary, what specific attitude, theoretically and practically, is prescribed toward other communities. It is here that the contemporary debates in Western culture between authoritarian and libertarian, traditionalist and rationalist, universalist and relativist have their place. The question is not, Should we spread our own ethical beliefs or tolerate those of others? or Should we adhere to authorities and traditions or criticize them in the name of freedom and reason? Rather, we need to ask *which* views we ought to propagate universally and how, when and how we need to be tolerant, and where and how we ought to criticize our own beliefs or make room for such criticism by others. To these issues, at least in general outline, I now turn.

6. Beyond Cultures (I): Judging Others

If the notion of culture is essentially open, even divided, there will necessarily be openness and division in the attitudes one culture has toward another. As we renegotiate who exactly belongs to our own culture, so we renegotiate who counts as an outsider; as we reinterpret what our culture has to say, so we reinterpret, inter alia, what it has to say about other cultures. And as we lean, within our own community, now more on the fundamental or natural conditions that define any ethic, now more on the particularities of our own traditional story, so we tend to be more demanding or more tolerant in our judgments of other cultures. It is not surprising, then, that each culture tends to contain both universalist and relativist strains, held together by a variety of complex strategies, depending on the experience and self-conception of the society at any given time. In the light of the atrocious history of our attempt to spread Christianity and capitalism over the world, of an anthropology and biology that no longer sees other cultures and races as more primitive versions of our own, and of a crisis within our own values in which we may well wonder whether the advances we have made in scientific knowledge and philosophical thought have anything other than means of destruction to offer us, we in the West have today a number of motivations for respecting other peoples' ways of life and evaluating them according to the standards of their own culture. We also have ethical reasons, however, for the opposite position—that there are absolute standards to which all human beings should be held—and both positions may legitimately claim to represent our desire to deal with our fellow rational creatures in respect and charity.

The universalist position enables us to condemn Nazism, to represent principles of racial, religious, and sexual equality in our dealings with other peoples, and to provide a solid foundation for the value of human interaction. The relativist position keeps us clear of the twin dangers of allowing our local traditions to stand in for the supposed universal standards and positing such standards while remaining so agnostic as to what they might be that we have no means of ethical judgment at all, even for our local context.

Between universalism and relativism, between authority and reason, between a culture as a unified moral self and cultures as impermanent nodes in the flux of universal human interaction, between the specific way of life that we know we should not impose on anyone else and the general conditions which that way of life and all others ought to meet, there lies nothing but judgment. It is judgment that brings theory into practice, and it is on the grounds of the judgments it provokes and shapes that a moral theory is itself judged. I discussed judgment earlier, in connection with authority, but I want to say a little more about how exactly it can add to theory.

JUDGMENT AGAIN

Judgment is the meeting place of the general and the specific. There can be no adequate theory of judgment—we would need judgments, independent of the theory, to determine how good any theory of judgment itself was when applied in particular cases. Yet we know, from daily life and from the practice of common law, not only that there are good and bad judges, but that one can learn to judge well, at least from practice and an acquaintance with many different specific cases.[1] According to Aristotle, judgment (*phronesis*), like perception, is concerned with the particular and learned by experience and example.[2] Since the kind of knowledge we need for our daily decisions always comes down to a judgment or set of judgments, a person lacking in *phronesis* will be renowned, like Anaxagoras or Thales, for not knowing how to get around in daily life.[3]

There is nothing absolute about a judgment: its very form reeks of limitation, finitude, "situatedness." It betrays on its face its need to be interwoven with other judgments; it cannot help revealing its lack of self-sufficiency, as well as its birth in particular situations, in the mouth of particular speakers, and in the service of particular actions. "Reagan was a terrible president." "That's a car (for the purposes of Regulation XIII)." In each case, there is an explicit reference to a particular and an explicit or implicit use of a general term. To know what the particular is, one needs much other knowledge, general and particular. To understand how the standard for the general term works, one needs a sense of what it is for and of how it has worked in other specific cases. For both these reasons, individual judgments are always incomplete.[4] Individual judgments are interwoven with other judgments: I know that that's a car (for the purposes of Regulation XIII), because I know how else that regulation has been applied.

Authority is essential to the process of judging,[5] and judgment is the characteristic expression of authority. In Anglo-American common law, and to some extent in all law courts, authority rests heavily on the practice of judging, in the form of precedent.[6] At the same time, judgments can themselves be authoritative for future judgments—especially, again, in common law. And despite their indeterminacy when taken singly, judgments can come together to form a distinct *way*, an authoritative tradition, of judging: English law differs from American law, and an appropriate decision in a British law court may be inappropriate in an American one. Judges are supposed to learn from the precedents of their own system and follow them, and particular judges may fail or succeed at this.[7] Common law judgment is thus the paradigm example of speaking in a specific situation, out of a specific tradition, to an audience that cannot make up its mind on its own: it is the paradigm of authoritative speech. And if the judgment is produced by a community that makes reference in its decisions to a central story, and a story about the good, then it will also be the paradigm expression of what we have been calling an authoritative ethical tradition, or "culture."

It follows that if one culture wants to influence the practices of another, it had better do so in the terms of the other culture's history of judgment.

Rather than seek some absolutely universal standard against which all cultures can be judged, we ought to seek, in cultures whose practices we would like to see changed, analogs to the elements of our own language and practices that we would want to recommend instead. Not only is this theoretically consistent with the view that ethical discussion is always grounded in a specific culture, but it has the practical advantage of making us see ourselves, and present ourselves to others, more humbly, as more an equal in discussion, than if we claim to be representing the "absolute right." The acknowledgment that our attachment to a particular ethical belief—such as equality between the sexes or the right to due process— has the same local, "tribalist" basis as the practices we are criticizing forces us to respect, and work through, the local traditions of the people we want to influence, rather than permitting us to direct them toward some "higher," transcultural standard on which we are supposed to have a better purchase than they do.

We may therefore perform cross-cultural judgment by assuming that the notion of a higher good to which all ethical systems must be responsible has some specific realization within each culture, and by seeking to find, in each culture, parallels to the specific shape it takes in our own. Within our own culture, there are standards that we consider peculiarly appropriate for our own society and standards that we believe all people ought to share. By looking at the universal standards we come up with and the way in which we draw the distinction between universal and local standards, we have a model for how to discern similar standards and similar distinctions in other cultures. And if we can successfully persuade the authorities and/or members of those cultures that a similar notion of universality exists within their system, we will have a successful cross-cultural judgment. What is important here is that we never go strictly *outside* either our own or the other culture: rather, we seek universal principles within both cultures' traditional terms. We thus maintain throughout the assumption that the general good cannot be expressed in a language of its own, but we also maintain, in the very process of trying to achieve agreement with the other culture, a presupposition that there must be some notion of ethical rightness transcending all specific ethical languages.

DIALOGUE ACROSS CULTURES:
EXONERATING SALMAN RUSHDIE

To make the implications of this approach clear, consider an example of how it might work in practice. In 1989 the Ayatollah Khomeini decreed a death sentence on Salman Rushdie for the offensiveness to Islam of his book *The Satanic Verses*. Iran was roundly condemned in the West as barbaric, along with all Muslims who supported this move. How dare they declare death sentences on Western citizens? And how narrow-minded they must be not to respect the freedom of speech! A minority, finding this response culturally insensitive, pointed out that under Islamic law the death sentence could be fully justified: *as* Muslims, Khomeini and his supporters had done nothing wrong. How dare we impose our culture's standards on them!

Neither of these attitudes takes Islam to be a conception of the good. The first rejects it in favor of what is supposed to be a higher standard of behavior; the second, by refusing to apply any standard to Muslim behavior except internal ones, reduces it to a pointless code, void of interest or meaning to those not already immersed in it. Neither attitude, moreover, requires a deep enough engagement with Islam to determine whether Khomeini's interpretation of it has to be accepted as correct.

What an alternative attitude might look like, I can indicate by means of an anecdote. Shortly after the Rushdie affair broke, I was at a dinner with several Muslim professors. Virtually all agreed that Khomeini's action could be justified and were outraged at the reaction it had evoked in the West. Yet during an extended conversation in which I tried to defend the book to one of the most traditional of these scholars, two interesting things happened. In the first place, the informal setting of the conversation, and the fact that I was arguing for the book's intrinsic value rather than merely for the principle of free speech, allowed my dinner companion to entertain the possibility, after a while, of reading the book himself. I bring this up to suggest that the context of intercultural exchange may be as important as its substance. (A point not unrelated to the priority of judgment over theory.) In the second place, however, I learned that there might be a basis in Islamic legal thought for Rushdie's exoneration—even if his book was irredeemably offensive. That basis is an odd and at first sight quite unappealing one: namely, the determination that Rushdie is insane. The insane cannot be regarded as heretical under Islamic law. The professor I was talking to did not offer this consideration as if he thought that Rushdie really was insane; he offered it as a legal fiction by which Rushdie might be extricated from his predicament without bringing down the entire structure of laws against heresy in Islam.

It is the role of such legal fictions that interests me here. A legal fiction need not be a revelation that a code of behavior is hypocritical or morally empty. Rather, legal fictions arise as means by which traditional practices can adjust themselves to new situations in a humane and fair way without losing their coherence (either with one another or with their history). Thus Jews stretched their legal resources to develop some way to keep fires going on the Sabbath once they moved north from the Mediterranean coast and began to experience the cold of northern European winters.[8] Thus Islamic law has developed complex mechanisms to bypass its own stringent conditions on what can count as legitimate court testimony.[9] Law is malleable even when it appears most fixed: where necessary, new resources can practically always be found to adapt a legal system to serious demands of justice or pragmatism. And, in order to affect the system, those demands do not have to be formulated as another system, a *code* of humanity and fairness such as the Universal Declaration of Human Rights.

Now whether the Islamic category of "insanity" could legitimately be extended to include the kind of modern heresy that Rushdie represents, I do not know. Possibly the "insane" have traditionally been regarded as confused, and one could argue that Rushdie's lack of faith, or revised faith, in his religious tradition expresses a relevantly similar type of confusion. It should certainly be possible to draw some distinction between the heretic who deliberately intends to slander or reject Islam and someone who, like Rushdie, is earnestly trying to reconceive it (whether successfully or not, in the eyes of traditional authorities). My point is not that this option would necessarily help matters but that it went unexplored. I relate it by means of anecdote precisely because I learned of it only by means of the personal, oral encounter I have described. I have never seen any reference to it in writings on the Rushdie affair. This suggests that most people involved were unaware of it, or dismissed it all too quickly as irrelevant, or felt that the true issue was and ought to be only the general principle—either the universalist general principle (freedom of speech) or the relativist one (cultural integrity).

Imagine if, instead of voicing these general principles, the British Foreign Office or U.S. State Department, or the Catholic church or British Chief Rabbinate had sent a delegation of scholars of Islamic law to try to persuade Khomeini and his courts that Rushdie could be exculpated within the terms of Islam.[10] How might this work? Well, I have chosen the "insanity" defense as a possibility because I know—from conversations of a kind that I could again relate only anecdotally, of the kind that I am suggesting is crucial to healthy cross-cultural judgments—that something much like it is precisely what is used today to prevent the enforcement of laws against heresy in traditional Judaism. A Jewish heretic (*apikoros*) is in theory subject to severe punishment, but there is a rabbinic principle that an ignoramus (*am haaretz*) cannot be a heretic—he or she knows too little to defy Judaism intelligently—and rabbis of the past century or so have assumed that *all* Jews nowadays, including themselves, are ignoramuses. If I were arguing with fellow observant Jews who claimed to have spotted a "heretic," I would cite this line of reasoning; I would know how to set it in a wider context of discussions of *apikorsim* and *amei haaretz* and of general concerns for tolerance and communal harmony in Talmudic and post-Talmudic sources;[11] and I would also know, from experience of such conversations, which particular sources and modes of argument were likely to be most persuasive.

To do the same with Islamic law, one would have to know it practically as well as a Muslim cleric does. The representatives of the West we are imagining might offer passages from the Quran and the Hadith to support the claim that Rushdie could be considered insane; the Islamic authorities might reject their interpretation of those passages or accept the interpretations but put forward other texts, more important or numerous, that undermine the thrust of their claim; the Westerners would then have to know enough about the tradition to be able to draw on other texts or switch the grounds of their defense from insanity to some other category that might work better. They would have to have thought long and hard about just why we in the West value freedom of artistic expression—that, and why we believe it to further the search for truth, including the truth about religion and God—as well as about how this value might have a parallel in Islam. To develop such a parallel, in direct dialogue with Islamic religious leaders, the Westerners would have to have a thorough knowledge of Islamic law, if they were not to be laughed away as frauds; a sincere respect for it, if their presence was not to be more offensive than a blanket condemnation would have been; and an open and wide imagination capable of exploring many different avenues of interpretation, if the dialogue was to get anywhere.

We do not, as far as I know, have people capable of such a dialogue in our state departments and major religious seminaries. Scholars of Islam are kept in specialized academic departments, while diplomats are not expected to be versed in religious scholarship. When the academics and the politicians meet, it is only so that one can give the other advice on manipulation: "What do Muslims want? How can we get them to do what *we* want?" The idea that cultural and religious scholarship should be intrinsic to intercultural and international relations is alien to our dominant political philosophies, which have been shaped by the Enlightenment view that there is no room for reason within traditions, or traditions within moral reasoning.

Of course, there are drawbacks to the procedure I am recommending. Suppose, in the first place, we succeed. We might reasonably wonder what we have accomplished if we manage to persuade Muslim clerics that Rushdie is insane. How can we regard this as a triumph of "the right to free speech"? Is it not rather a capitulation to a division (true believers/heretics) that we consider abhorrent in principle? This only goes to show that as we try to give our moral concerns some voice in the contemporary Islamic tradition, we must also try to translate the terms of Islam back into our own voice. Again, let me draw on the analogous scenario in the Jewish tradition. To call modern skeptics and nonbelievers "ignoramuses"—is that not a ruse? An insult? An utterly insensitive attitude toward the general human right, even responsibility, to question? We can certainly read it this way, but we can also read it in other ways: saying that we moderns are all "fools" might, for instance, also be much like what Beckett means by calling the modern world "absurd." Hebrew distinguishes sharply among words denoting intellectual achievement, and it is quite possible in it to suggest that one can possess great cleverness or scientific understanding (*da'at*) even while lacking wisdom (*chokhmah*); surely it is the absence of the latter, not the former, that marks an *am haaretz*. That is, it is indeed our ignorance that demands the possibility of questioning, revising, even deriding religious traditions, but that ignorance is a direct consequence of our scientific achievements, not a result of laziness or blindness—a *loss* of knowledge, not an abandonment of it. And this ignorance has redeeming features, even apart from its technological results: it has driven out much moral hypocrisy, opened up remarkable new paths of human thought and expression, and, when taken seriously, taught us all a deep humility. I see no reason why "insanity," if it does indeed work in the Islamic tradition as ignorance does in the Jewish one, cannot be built into a similar story. We moderns are all mad, in the sense of "confused" or "lost." The post-Enlightenment world is one of disorder, one that lacks moral and spiritual guidance, even if that disorder has had some splendid results.

Of course, Muslim "insanity" would in this case be something of a metaphor, as is Jewish "ignorance" on my reading—a metaphor for a condition of humanity—but so what? What a tradition means depends on the way it is actually interpreted and applied. That is often a matter of extending the meanings of earlier terms and bits of text. What starts as a metaphor, if it passes into ordinary usage, may thus become the dominant meaning of a term.[12] In our hypothetical dialogue, we are asking Muslims to see the toleration of free speech as a metaphor. So to see the "human right" to question traditions, of which the West is so proud, as metaphorically contained in some of traditional Islam's and Judaism's more insulting terms need not, I think, distort either those terms or the Western ideal. Rather, it may shed a dislocating, poetically intriguing light on both.

The more serious drawback to my suggestion is that it may fail. Dialogue would continue only as long as the Western representatives demonstrated a deep knowledge both of Islamic sources and of how they are used today—as long as they could speak with an authentically Muslim voice. But this means that they could not simply sit with fellow academics in a

Western university until they found a passage in Muslim literature that looked acceptable to them. They would have to be able to make their interpretations stick in actual dialogue with people who maintain and represent the tradition today. And that entails that they could not know in advance whether their interpretations would work. If a dialogue had been set up in 1989, Khomeini's courts might well have stood firm in their judgment.

But the failure of any one such dialogue, even one involving something as serious as Rushdie's death sentence, ought not stop us from pursuing this approach in general. Consider its advantages. In the first place, when it succeeds, each group greatly deepens its appreciation of the other tradition. If we in the West can understand the logic of Islamic laws against heresy well enough to persuade Islamic courts that Rushdie ought not be brought under those laws, we will surely have to understand the point of the laws well enough to see what counterparts they have among our own values and practices. And if we can see the notion of "insanity" do the work of exculpating modern questioners of religion, we will surely gain a much deeper insight into the nature of Islamic law, and the way in which it struggles toward the same good at which we ourselves aim, than if we merely condemn—*or* excuse—the system a priori.

In the second place, if there were an ongoing dialogue between Western scholars and Islamic authorities, aimed normally at concrete problems but attempting, even in the absence of concrete problems, to clarify the ways of Islam to the West and the ways of the West to Islam, then, even if the discussions were in some particular case to fail, there would be a series of intercultural judgments that *could themselves constitute a text* for the moral practices pertaining to the intersection between the two cultures. Successful judgments, whether in law or in moral practice more generally, can set precedents for future judgments, and if a series of both successful and unsuccessful judgments, together with the histories leading up to and resulting from them, was widely publicized and discussed, representatives of two conflicting cultures would have something to refer to besides their own traditions and the thin universals that are supposed to be transcultural. The procedure I am recommending thus works through text and tradition in several ways: it demands that each culture find its own terms in the other culture and the other culture's terms in its own, while simultaneously creating a text and a tradition out of the cross-cultural judgments themselves.

The principles we in the modern West want especially to find in other cultures—having abandoned, for the most part, organized political efforts to promote a particular religion—are those we call "human rights," and what I am proposing might be called, in analogy with a position in mathematics, a constructivist approach to human rights. Philosophers of mathematics have generally been divided between Platonists, who believe that numbers and geometric shapes are real entities that mathematical statements try to describe, and conventionalists, who believe that numbers and geometric shapes are fictions and that mathematical statements are made true by according with certain conventions (the rules of the game we call "mathematics"). A minority has held an intermediate position known as "constructivism": mathematical objects *come into existence* as a result of our making mathematical statements. Analogously, to those who say either that human rights are objectively "out there" or that they are mere figments of certain conventions, I want to suggest that they come into existence as real universal principles precisely insofar as we build a network of cross-cultural judgments making them a part of each culture's discussion and practice. Mathematical objects may not exist independently of the process of mathematical construction, but insofar as they are needed to make sense of that process, they do indeed exist; similarly, perhaps, human rights come into existence insofar as they are needed to make sense of ethical dialogue across cultures. In Chapter 3 I supposed that the good might be a project whose completion is infinitely deferred, but bringing traditions about the good closer together was a part of that project, and bringing them to some agreement at least on what constitutes respect and degradation of humanity seems an essential condition for the achievement of any ultimate good, whether full cultural convergence belongs to that achievement or not.

REACHING FOR CONSENSUS

Something along these lines has been proposed before. In 1977 the neo-conservative sociologist Peter Berger, responding, at least implicitly, to President Carter's belief in basing United States foreign policy on the promotion of human rights throughout the world, recommended that we draw a sharp distinction between some human rights and others, and promote only those rights on which we could establish some sort of intercultural consensus. Berger claimed that while many non-Western nations find incomprehensible such principles as freedom of the press, economic equality, and women's rights, a wide consensus exists across cultures against genocide, torture, enslavement, the forced separation of families, and the desecration of religious and ethnic symbols. He supported this claim by showing how we might make use of several non-Western countries' own traditions to censure their governments' acts:

> When we condemn the horrors inflicted on the people of Cambodia by [the Pol Pot] government, we need not do so by reference to Western values alone. Cambodia is a Buddhist country, and it is Buddhism that has as its highest moral tenet the "respect for all sentient beings." Similarly, the atrocities inflicted on the Chinese people in the course of various Maoist experiments, such as the physical extermination of entire classes of the population or the separation of children from their parents, are not just violations of Western notions of morality . . . ; rather, they are violations of the entire corpus of ethics of the Chinese tradition, which holds, among other things, that government should be "human-hearted" and that "filial piety" is one of the highest human goods. And if we pass moral judgment on a Muslim ruler . . . for acts of cruelty, we may do so, not alone in the name of the Judeo-Christian tradition, but in the name of the ethical core of Islam itself: every call to prayer, from every minaret from the Maghreb to Java, begins with an invocation of God who is *al-rahman al-rahim,* whose nature is to be compassionate and who has compassion, and who commands men to be compassionate also.[13]

I want very much to endorse the general outlines of this approach. We ought indeed to find some limited standard of behavior to expect of other cultures, and we ought to determine that standard by seeking actual consensus with the cultures we want to judge rather than philosophically deriving a set of rules to which, in principle, they should all conform. But Berger himself seems insufficiently aware of the difference between seeking consensus and proving universal principles. He offers his proposed distinction between sets of rights as an attempt to provide a basis for "universally relevant moral judgments," to delineate those rights "that pertain to the human condition as such."[14] The fact that there is a consensus on certain rights would not prove that those rights pertain to the universal human condition, however, even if the consensus were universal. All human beings could be *wrong* about what they take to be morally correct; all human beings have, in the past, hunted witches and kept slaves. More important, Berger does not claim that the consensus against genocide, slavery, and the like is in fact universal; he says only that it "emerges from all the *major* world cultures" (emphasis mine). From here to universal legitimacy is a large step, in moral judgment. To reach a true consensus, every party to that consensus must agree. We are not dealing with a scientific generalization, in which the background rules of the discipline allow for an inference from a majority of actual cases to all possible cases, or with a political decision in a democracy, in which the population of a country unanimously agrees, at least implicitly, to abide by the vote of the majority. A consensus on fundamental moral principles will necessarily reach too deep for us to be able to presuppose agreement on the relevance of empirical science or democratic politics to the establishment of that consensus.

Finally, Berger moves much too fast from the Buddhist "respect for all sentient beings," Confucian "human-heartedness," and Muslim belief in "compassion," to condemnations of Cambodian, Chinese, and Muslim rulers. It is worthwhile seeing what happens when we slow down his inferences. From "respect for all sentient beings," "human-heartedness," or "compassion," there may yet be room for atrocities if (1) the victims are not considered sentient, human, or the kind of human deserving of or needing compassion, (2) death, torture, expulsion, or slavery is considered to be for the victims' good, a high mode of respect, or a form of compassionate treatment, or (3) death, torture, expulsion, or slavery is considered a regrettable necessity, an unavoidable violation of respect and compassion in the service of some higher or more final good. To argue against these moves in particular cases, we would need to know a lot more detail about the Buddhist, Confucian, or Muslim traditions, as well as about just how those traditions fare today among those we take to be their adherents.

But getting dragged into the arguments of the other culture is exactly the advantage of Berger's approach. We then have to make our case from *inside*, from the specific examples and argumentative strategies that the culture itself uses in everyday moral debate. We will need to study the other culture's language, literature, religion, politics, and history in great depth, and in the process of doing so will display more respect for it than we could with a thousand gestures of relativism. And although this display may be, at first, mostly just that, a display, over the course of time we will undoubtedly find things we really do admire about the other culture, and things we could not have anticipated finding, whether we came into the original dialogue as relativists or universalists.

STUDIES IN CROSS-CULTURAL JUDGMENT

The pressing question is whether this approach would actually work. *Are* there in fact tolerant strains interlaced with the evangelical and imperialist strains of Western Christianity? Are there really notions of universal humanity in small tribes? I shall try to answer these questions with case studies, showing how both toleration and universalism may exist where one would least expect to find them. To begin with, let us treat the moral tradition with which we are most familiar as itself a cultural artifact.

Christian Toleration

At least since Thomas Aquinas, Catholic philosophy of law has recognized a distinction between divine and natural law. Natural law is accessible through reason; divine law only through revelation. It might be just as true that all people ought to accept Christ as that they ought to refrain

from murder, but they are not responsible for fulfilling the former obligation unless and until it is revealed to them, by a specific person or text, at
a specific moment in history. The obligation not to murder, on the other
hand, is incumbent on all reasoning creatures, regardless of experience and
place in history. Of course, these two kinds of law are ultimately unified in
what Aquinas calls the "eternal law," but the eternal law is identical with
the "divine nature or essence" itself and is therefore unknowable to all but
"the blessed who see God in His essence."[15] For ordinary human purposes,
the univocal core of all law is unavailable and the laws that concern us are
of two clearly different kinds.

This distinction has important practical implications. According to the
Catholic Church, natural law, the law that is rationally accessible to all, can
in principle be imposed on those who violate it; divine law, which is accessible through faith alone, can only be preached. Francesco de Vitoria, a
sixteenth-century Thomist whose series of lectures on how the Spaniards
ought to treat their new acquaintances in the Americas is among the
founding documents of international law, insisted that the Amerindians
could not be coerced to accept Christian doctrine, that indeed they ought
not believe in Christianity unless it was preached to them with "demon-
strable and reasonable arguments, . . . accompanied by an upright life,
well-ordered according to the law of nature [in the preacher]."[16] More radically, followers of Thomas have been loath to impose even natural law
universally. The same principle that links persuadability and coercion with
respect to the precepts of faith has been brought to draw a distinction
between universal and nonuniversal natural law. For Thomas, the aspect
of natural law that all human beings share is simply a very general notion
of the good, while the specific conclusions of practical reason do not have
"the same truth and rectitude among all men": "hence arises the diversity
of positive laws among various people."[17] In practice this provides grounds
for Vitoria, and, following him, all early theorists of international law, to
bar the imposition of most Western moral standards on non-Western
peoples. Vitoria says that "Christian princes can not, even by the authori-
zation of the Pope, restrain the Indians from sins against the law of nature
or punish them because of those sins."[18] Why not? Because it is not the

business of Christians to judge those who cannot be persuaded they are doing wrong:

> Coercion . . . is not lawful for fornication; therefore not for the other sins which are contrary to the law of nature. The antecedent is clear from I *Corinthians*, ch. 5: "I wrote to you in an epistle not to company with fornicators," and . . . lower down: "For what have I to do to judge them also that are without?" Whereon St. Thomas says: "The prelates have received power over those only who have submitted themselves to the faith." Hence it clearly appears that St. Paul declares it not his business to pronounce judgment on unbelievers and fornicators and idolaters. So also it is not every sin against the law of nature that can be clearly shown to be such, at any rate to every one.[19]

The law of nature, in the sense in which it includes all that Christians believe to be moral, does not win explicit assent from everyone. And where it fails of explicit assent, we do not have a right to impute implicit assent:

> What is it that [is supposed to constitute the Indians'] profession of the law of nature? If it is mere knowledge, they do not know it all; if it is a mere willingness to observe the law of nature, then the retort is that they are also willing to observe the whole divine law; for, if they knew that the law of Christ was divine, they would be willing to observe it. Therefore, they make no more a profession of the law of nature than they make of the law of Christ. Further, we certainly possess clearer proofs whereby to demonstrate that the law of Christ is from God and is true than to demonstrate that fornication is wrong or that other things which are also forbidden by natural law are to be shunned.[20]

In principle, it may be possible to derive any moral precept from reason alone, but in practice, says Vitoria, some people are unable to carry out the derivations, and where they have not carried out a particular derivation, we have no right to assume they "profess" the standard in question. There is, as Hugo Grotius, Vitoria's great successor in the development of international law, was to say, such a thing as "invincible ignorance" of the natural law: "As . . . in matters of civil law, ignorance is deemed an excuse, so with respect to the law of nature, wherever infirmity of understanding forms an invincible obstruction to the knowledge of its rules, such infirmity may be allowed as a vindication."[21]

Grotius here follows the Thomist tradition quite closely. Aquinas writes that a thing can be self-evident in two ways, "in itself" and "in relation to us,"[22] and if a particular mathematical proposition is not self-evident to one of us despite being self-evident in itself, then all the more so particular moral conclusions, which depend for their truth on historical circumstance, need not be universally known even if they are self-evident in principle. Grotius uses exactly this analogy to argue that we need not assume particular evils to be universally obvious:

> [We must make] an accurate distinction between general principles [of the law of nature], such as the duty of living according to the dictates of reason, and those of a more particular though not less obvious meaning; as the duty of forbearing to take what belongs to another. To which many truths may be added though not quite so easy of apprehension: among which may be named the cruelty of that kind of punishment, which consists in revenge, delighting in the pain of another. This is a method of proof similar to that which occurs in mathematics, the process of which rises from self-evident truths to demonstrations, the latter of which, though not intelligible to all alike, upon due examination obtain assent.[23]

These are elaborate contortions, these attempts by figures as important as Aquinas, Vitoria, and Grotius, to find excuses for crimes that are supposed to be self-evidently wrong. "Self-evidence," like "reason" and "natural law" itself, are generally taken by twentieth-century writers to be moral foundations that, if they succeed at all, will guarantee the universal applicability of the morality they establish. We would expect to find appeals to the self-evidence or naturalness of a moral precept going together with claims that anyone violating the precept is doing what he must know himself to be evil, as today appeals to the supposedly self-evident wrong of homosexuality or abortion go together with precisely such claims. But Aquinas, Vitoria, and Grotius go to great lengths to *avoid* such conclusions.[24] Just when the Church had a full-fledged, nonscripturally based

philosophy on which to ground its moral claims, it also developed doctrines designed to block the application of that philosophy to peoples outside the scriptural fold. And in the practice of its legal judgment it used
those doctrines to prevent itself from justifying the coercive imposition of
its own law on Jews, pagan Slavs, Saracens, and Amerindians.[25] None of
this is to deny that atrocities against such peoples occurred. Amerindians
were plundered, raped, and murdered, despite the admonitions of Vitoria;
Jews and Muslims were killed in Crusades. But the *standards* of the
Church, on the whole, recognized that these acts were wrong, and those
standards survived the people who failed to honor them, to become the
basis for such things as the placement of national self-determination at the
foundations of international law.

Double Standards

Cultures throughout the world draw distinctions between laws that
apply to their own members and laws that apply to all human beings, and
what falls in the latter category tends to be roughly similar all over. Jews
distinguish between 613 commandments incumbent on their fellow Jews,
from observing the Sabbath to separating meat from milk, and seven commandments incumbent on "the children of Noah": to establish courts of
justice, and to avoid blasphemy, idolatry, incest, murder, robbery, and
eating flesh cut from a living animal.[26] Muslims demand that non-Muslims
who live in their lands (1) avow monotheism, (2) not harm a Muslim or
offend against Muslim practices or interests, (3) not intermarry with Muslims, and (4) not practice usury.[27] The imagined world ruler in Buddhist
thought would demand of all human beings only the five moral precepts
of the Buddhist layman: (1) to "slay no living thing," (2) not to "take that
which has not been given," (3) to act rightly "touching bodily desires,"
(4) to "speak no lie," and (5) to "drink no maddening drink."[28] And Max
Gluckman reports that the Lozi tribe in southern Africa distinguish between their specific laws and more general "laws of humankind," the latter
including laws against adultery, incest, theft, assault, murder, and perhaps
beer drinking.[29]

We may call each of these distinctions a "double standard" if we like, the people concerned demanding and expecting less of those outside their communities than they do of themselves. Double standards can of course bring contempt for the outsiders, but by limiting a group's demands enough that outsiders can reasonably accept them without renouncing their own way of life, such divisions can also make coexistence between cultures easier than do single sets of principles. Our Western interest in the essential equality of all individuals inclines us to reject double standards as hypocritical or demeaning, but we then wind up having either to impose our entire ethic on unwilling peoples or to refrain from enforcing any ethical principles, and ethically justifying any use of force. If we could couch our demands for others in an explicit double standard, we might recognize them as, like the oddly assorted demands of the Jews, Muslims, Buddhists, and Lozi, at least in part an expression of ethical norms that are simply very important to us, not a rational consequence of some universally evident principle. People are more humble when they talk from a double standard, less prone to the philosopher's error of assuming one can ensure agreement by concocting arguments to which others "must" assent.

The "quirks" on the lists I have given—not eating flesh from a living animal, not practicing usury, avoiding alcohol—are thus reminders that the lists are not mere derivations from some universally self-evident standard of right action. Rather, they are arrived at in utterly different ways. Jews derive them from a moment in their sacred history in which God is supposed to have established a covenant with the descendants of Noah; Buddhists imagine them as the structure of a worldwide Buddhist state; the Muslim code represents the terms of a cease-fire with members of the non-Muslim world (*dar al-Harb*) with which Islam is technically at war; and the Lozi seem to have developed their "laws of nations" as a means of preserving peace among the various tribes whose legal disputes they have occasion to adjudicate. We may find these different roads irrelevant to the conception of humanity at which they arrive, and the differences among the laws themselves frustrating: we are inclined to suppose that natural law, the law of reason, will guide everyone to the same intercultural standard, and a more sensible standard at that. But taking seriously the notion that our own moral code is also a local, "tribalist" one entails understanding the ways in which it too is quirky, and indeed the idea that there are human rights to such things as freedom of speech, equality between the sexes, or sexual preference look extremely odd to non-Western peoples. If we want to persuade others of them, we had better recognize at the beginning that they belong with a particular story—the very notion of moral guidance by reason alone belongs with a particular story—just as other "laws of humankind" do, and that to a great extent only those who accept the story will accept the principles.

The many similarities among the lists we have considered, on the other hand, provide empirical evidence that we can find some general consensus across cultures on the moral questions that most concern us.[30] There are even more similarities if we look a little beyond the lists. Jews, for instance, have a tradition that they may *enforce* only the prohibitions of idolatry, adultery, and murder among non-Jews. The Lozi are not terribly serious about enforcing their law against beer drinking, and they seem not to include it among the laws that ought to be obvious even to complete foreigners such as whites.[31] I suspect we might find similar patterns among (what seem to us) the quirky laws of Buddhism and Islam. In addition, there are striking parallels across cultures in what we in the West call "international law" (the *ius gentium*) and among notions of what, in general, constitutes a human being. On the first point, consider the fact that Vitoria, Grotius, Muslim law, and the Lozi kuta all place the sanctity of emissaries among the most important principles of the laws of war.[32] On the second, consider the following parallel, between spokespeople for cultures so widely separated by time, place, and culture that there can be no suspicion of mutual influence:

> Once . . . kuta men began to discuss whether the Bushmen who live in Western Barotseland were human beings. MUNONO held they were not for they neither cultivated nor kept cattle. As soon as I described Bushman marriage and exogamic taboos, and funeral rites, he said: "They are indeed men, with laws of humankind." Similarly, when this point was discussed in the Palace at Lialui, King Imwiko said: "They are men. Once in Liuwa I shot a giraffe. The Bushmen came and hovered on the edge of the bush. We offered them meat: they came running, crouched before us as chiefs, cut

up the meat and cooked it for us. They know kingship, and so they are of human kind."[33]

[The Indians] are not of unsound mind, but have, according to their kind, the use of reason. This is clear, because there is a certain method in their affairs, for they have polities which are orderly arranged and they have definite marriage and magistrates, overlords, laws, and workshops, and a system of exchange, all of which call for the use of reason; they also have a kind of religion.[34]

Human beings tend in general to recognize one another as kin, by their shared rituals if by nothing else. We should wonder at this fact, not take it for granted—the history of racist doctrine in the West over the past two centuries alone teaches us that this tendency can be overridden—but at the same time it does give us reason to think that some kind of world consensus about how, minimally, all human beings ought to be treated is achievable. We have empirical evidence, if not a transcendental proof, that cultural relativism in ethics need not force anyone to stand idly by while foreign peoples perform torture and genocide.[35]

In addition to the rather skimpy sampling of brute facts I have offered, moreover, there are some general, although still empirical, reasons why we might expect that cultures contain within themselves rules for dealing with outsiders humanely. First, practically every society needs to trade with people beyond its borders and practically every society is near enough to another human group to fear the possibility of attack. To avoid being attacked and to secure trade against injustices that might lead to war, societies need to agree on some standards of decency and justice. Furthermore, once trade links are established, contact with other peoples often spurs a group to impress its new neighbors with the virtue of its way of life. Once a culture mingles seriously with another culture, especially if it loses members to that other culture, a justification for its way of life in terms of a good beyond both cultures becomes more than a theoretical necessity.

Now these empirical considerations *about* moral discourse lie outside the actual realm *of* moral discourse. It is obvious that the widespread belief in protection of emissaries may be a product of the need to develop acceptable laws of war and peace, but that need does not suffice as a *reason* for any group to adopt this principle that has not already done so. Between empirical facts and moral reasons there is a gulf fixed. Most human groups tend to seek peace with other human groups because they value their security or survival, but it does not follow that one *ought* to value security, or even survival, or value it in this or that particular case, or at any price, or at the price that most groups are willing to pay. So at no point can we in the West legitimately say, "You must agree to such and such because everyone else does," although if we encounter groups who are simply uncertain of *how* to deal peacefully with outsiders, we might propose the principles we find elsewhere as a model for them to work with.[36] Rather, the empirical evidence that human groups recognize one another as deserving respect provides encouragement to those who want to rely on the resources of culture as a basis for ethical discussion. As the specter of the irredeemably cruel and inhumane culture fades more and more from view, it becomes less frightening to give up on universalist moral theories and adopt a consensus approach to defining and instituting some conception of universal human rights.

What about Hitler?

What, now, about those hard exceptions? What happens when we come up against Nazi Germany, or the Ik of Uganda, or Pol Pot's Cambodia? What if there are tribes of convinced cannibals?

In the first place, we should remember that in many, perhaps most, cases our complaints are not with a society as a whole but with individual leaders, who may be just as hateful to their subjects as they are to outsiders. Idi Amin and Pol Pot are good examples of this: the numbers of their own people they had to kill is evidence enough that their policies were not supported by their societies. That there are terribly cruel individuals in a society, even that such people should come to be rulers, is not an argument against the society's culture. There are such individuals and have been such rulers in every society. Their existence and success represent a failure, not an absence, of the society's moral norms; the success is usually short-lived; and condemning it on universalist grounds is hardly likely either to offend the other society or to vitiate our own attempts to pursue cultural relativism.

The case is more difficult with someone like Hitler or a people like the Ik. A substantial portion of the German population voted for Hitler. It is no accident that he had to manipulate and eventually destroy the democratic process to achieve the power he really wanted, and one can argue that even those who voted for him in 1933 did not necessarily support the more horrifying parts of his program—perhaps they did not understand them or believed he would not perform them—but there is no getting around the fact that a sizable number of people did know about, enthusiastically support, and help to carry out the building and use of the death camps. As for the Ik, according to Colin Turnbull, virtually every member of the tribe finds death uninteresting, the suffering of children comical, and family and friendship meaningless. How can we avoid condemning these societies?

I do not think we can, but I want to draw a distinction between condemning a society and condemning a culture. The word "society" can describe a group of people at a given time; the word "culture," if we use it as I recommended in the previous chapter, must refer to a set of practices and beliefs that persists over several generations, else there is no room for the institution of a central story, a tradition of interpretation, and a mode of recognizing and consulting authorities. Every culture must be enacted by a society, of course, and every society will attempt to realize one or more cultures, but a society's representation of its culture at any given time is not the final word on what the culture really is. There is thus room for the notion that a society may *mis*represent its culture, as measured by the interpretations of its ancestors and descendants. There is room for the notion that a particular society may represent an aberration of its culture, even if the whole society participates in the pursuit of this aberration.

Obviously, identifying a society as an aberration of its own culture may well be simply patronizing. Who are we, outsiders that we are, to pretend to knowledge of another tradition intimate enough to say what is and is not a fair representation of it? We may also misuse the possibility of such an identification for crassly selfish ends. I offer therefore some conditions

171

for determining when the identification might be appropriate. We may regard an entire society as having distorted its own ethical tradition into an inhumane version of itself if

(1) we can see that the society has been subjected to external pressures threatening its very survival (members of any culture can lose their ability to concern themselves with ethical judgment when they live in fear of murder or starvation);

(2) we can locate a larger cultural structure, extending back before the pattern of actions we want to condemn, to which we can appeal as a more solid, long-term identification of the culture; and

(3) we can find clear signs, preferably independent of the practices to which we are objecting, that trust in the structure of authorities which normally carries the culture from one generation to the next has broken down.

All three of these conditions hold for Nazi Germany and for the Ik. The former went through a severe economic crisis; the latter through a (yet more severe) famine. Nazism was a short-lived phenomenon in a culture that had a long past of humanity and decency; the Ik, until their recent famine, had rich traditions of friendship, familial love, and generosity of feeling. Since the famine, the Ik have lost respect for all their own traditions and institutions; the way in which Nazism filled in for teachers and parents after a tremendous breakdown of traditional authority has been studied ad nauseam. I am inclined to believe that, since the condemnation of an entire society is such a very serious business, threatening the entire project of respecting other cultures, before we resort to it we ought to look for all three of these marks, with the same kind of healthy evidence of their presence that we have in the cases of the Nazis and the Ik.

Finally, what if we do encounter a culture that cannot be condemned for inhumanity in its own terms because it has no such terms, that simply contains nothing we can recognize as respect for humanity however we interpret it? This possibility may well be just a philosopher's example—I have never heard so much as a claim that such a culture actually exists—but for the sake of argument let us suppose it to be realized. What then? It seems to me we have two equally acceptable options. We can interfere with the culture, by force if necessary, in the name of "saving the innocent" (whether among its own members or among neighboring cultures it has been harming), or we can leave it alone in the name of maintaining respect for cultural integrity. The risks of the former option are fairly obvious. We set a dangerous precedent; we lead other cultures to look askance at our claims to uphold intercultural toleration; and, as surely as ambiguous choices and a bad reputation can bring a previously decent individual to feel that he might as well actually commit a crime, in both these ways we set ourselves up for more disingenuous interferences with other cultures in the future. The risk of the latter option is that we may lose faith in our own moral values. Even if the obnoxious tribe is so isolated that it brutalizes and degrades only its own members, for us to stand by and let the atrocities continue could shake our confidence that we really do value human life and dignity. To allow people to be brutalized and degraded is a severe violation of our own moral commitments, and when the atrocities we are allowing to go by are great enough, claims for the overriding importance of cultural self-determination or integrity look like a wretched subterfuge.[37] So we may be damned if we do and damned if we don't: *both* interfering *and* not interfering with the obnoxious practices of another culture can damage our moral self-confidence and weaken our ability to pursue our own values in the future.

The notion that we may interfere with a culture primarily to protect our own moral well-being is a dangerous one and needs to be hedged around with enough "ifs," "buts," and exceptions that it becomes, like the irredeemably obnoxious culture to which it would appropriately apply, more a philosopher's tale than a practical consideration. Nevertheless, I want to insist that it is precisely the right *sort* of justification to give if the tale of the obnoxious culture ever came true. After all, what is absolutely right, morally speaking, is not the question here. That question is unsettleable, if the account I have given of moral thought is correct. The question we need to answer is what our *conviction* of being right licenses us to do. And if the reasons we can show another culture have indeed given out, and if we can offer ourselves no more justification for not interfering than for interfering, then making open appeal to our local moral commitments is both a more human and a more easily backed-away-from approach than setting ourselves up as the avenging angels for the principles of universal morality. Bearing in mind that one's vision of universal humanity is locally shaped and colored should keep politicians and their constituents more wary of imposing that vision than the vain thought that one could sometime grasp, and enforce, moral claims whose self-evidence transcends all cultures.

There is even some reason to believe that this "tribalist" approach to the universal defense of human rights has roots in our tradition, that we in the West have not always seen ourselves as having self-evidence on our side. Vitoria's arguments that the Spaniards have a right to preach the Gospel peacefully, and that they have not only a right but an obligation to rescue innocent people from cannibalism and human sacrifice, depend essentially on quotations from the Bible:

I assert also that without the Pope's authority the Spaniards can stop all such nefarious usage [i.e., cannibalism and human sacrifice] among the aborigines, being entitled to rescue innocent people from an unjust death. This is proved by the fact that "God has laid a charge on every individual concerning his neighbor," and they are all our neighbors. . . . A further proof is given by *Proverbs*, ch. 24: "Deliver them that are drawn unto death, and forbear not to free those that are being dragged to destruction."

Christians have a right to preach and declare the Gospel in barbarian lands. This proposition is manifest from the passage: "Preach the Gospel to every creature," etc., and also, "The word of the Lord is not bound" (II *Timothy*, ch. 2). . . . [The Indians] are our neighbors, as said above: "Now the Lord has laid a command on everyone concerning his neighbor" (*Ecclesiasticus*, ch. 17). Therefore it concerns Christians to instruct those who are ignorant of these supremely important matters.[38]

The reliance on Scripture in these passages comes not from an incapacity for independent argument—Vitoria gives very good arguments on other subjects, including the impermissibility of spreading Christianity by force—or, as we have seen, from a belief that whether a person believes she is doing wrong or not is irrelevant to whether she is in fact doing wrong. On the basis of the connection between persuadability and coercion, Vitoria emphatically denies to the Spaniards any right to enforce prohibitions against such abominations (to sixteenth-century Christians) as adultery, homosexuality, and bestiality.[39] Only in the cases of the right to preach peacefully and the duty to prevent cannibalism and human sacrifice does he waive consideration of what the Indians might have to say against these precepts. Is it stretching the text to suggest that he waives his general "don't impose where you can't persuade" attitude in these cases because he believes that Christians who give up their mission to preach the Gospel and their commitment to relieving obvious human suffering could no longer be Christians? That even to spell out just *why* this mission is so important or just what "obvious" means here would betray the faith that must at some point precede reason in being a Christian? In the introduction to his lectures on the Indians, Vitoria remarks that moral discussion ought to concern only issues on which there is a legitimate doubt, and he intimates that the legitimacy of a doubt may vary with the community that is engaging in the discussion:

> We must bear in mind what Aristotle says (*Ethics,* bk. 3), namely, that just as there can be no questioning or deliberation about matters either impossible or necessary, so also there can be no moral investigation about those which are certainly and notoriously lawful and seemly, or, on the other hand, about those which are certainly and notoriously unlawful and unseemly. For no one can properly raise a question whether we ought to live a temperate and brave and upright life or a wicked and base life, nor whether we ought to commit adultery or perjury, or cherish our parents, and other matters of this kind. Certainly such discussion would not be Christian.[40]

Basing himself on Aristotle's claim that there is no deliberation over the impossible and the necessary, Vitoria extends this category to include acts "notoriously" right and wrong. What is "notorious"—obvious—belongs outside the limits of moral conversation. Here, presumably, further probing would only shake the faithful foundations from which any such discussion must begin. What is morally obvious is then supported by faith *rather than* reason, even though in general, moral beliefs should reflect a combination of both faith and reason. But there remains room for some subtle distinctions: it is obvious to a Christian that adultery is wrong but not that non-Christians are responsible for knowing that it is wrong, while it is obvious both that human sacrifice is wrong and that non-Christians are responsible for knowing that. It seems to be similarly obvious that preaching the Gospel is so important to the good of all humankind that the right to do so may be defended by force, even if acceptance of the Gospel may not itself be coerced.

A more dramatic way in which tribalism appears in our tradition's attitude toward other cultures is the fact that the doctrine of "humanitarian intervention" in international law has had a long history of being invoked particularly on behalf of Christian peoples oppressed by non-Christians. The *Vindiciae Contra Tyrannos* states this explicitly: "[Interference is justified] in behalf of neighboring peoples who are oppressed on account of adherence to the true religion or by any obvious tyranny."[41] Vitoria similarly gives us a special title to help Christian converts in pagan countries, "based not only on religion, but on human friendship and alliance, inasmuch as the native converts to Christianity have become friends and allies of Christians."[42] Lingering in these writings is the medieval concept of the Respublica Christiana, under which system Christians felt an obligation to other Christians everywhere, regardless of temporal lords. It has indeed been argued that international law developed under Grotius and his successors precisely to create "a surrogate for the religious community, which had been the foundation of political community in the medieval period."[43] For a long time, the international community that resulted, insofar as it existed at all, was merely a secularized version of the old religious community, explicitly "invoking Christianity as a basis of [its] unity" until the Ottoman Empire was admitted to the Concert of Europe in 1856.[44] And in almost every one of the major cases in which humanitarian intervention was invoked in the nineteenth century, Christian powers were coming to the defense of their own against the wrongdoing of infidels.[45]

This pattern may look merely hypocritical, but I suggest it is really an extension of the tendency of individuals, in everyday life, to come more fully and readily to the aid of their friends and family than of strangers. Christian powers, as Vitoria openly acknowledges, regard other Christian powers as friends—as Islamic nations (at least in principle) regard other Islamic nations, and as modern Israel regards Jews and Jewish communities elsewhere. Why should the nations of the post-Christian,

Enlightenment West not regard other adherents of the Enlightenment the same way? If we have to choose between a culture and the members of that culture who regard it as oppressive, surely we may prefer the latter simply because they are our friends. They are, as it were, "converts" to the Enlightenment story.

But this last move can be dangerous. If used to interfere with any practices less horrific than torture and murder, it can undermine the whole attitude of intercultural toleration I have been recommending. My point is not that we should adopt the same attitude toward "Enlightenment converts" as European powers of the Middle Ages took toward Christian converts, but that the attitude of those powers reveals that Western universalism has always had a tribalist streak. To that streak I recommend we return, emphasizing the local color in our visions for humanity rather than being embarrassed about it.

CHARITY AND RESPECT

We in the West have not adequately explored what can be gained from understanding ourselves, and that means both our Christian heritage and our secular "rights" theories, as a culture among other cultures in the world. Too often the West is condemned for being too universalistic or too relativistic. Or one or the other of these attitudes is defended as in fact correct. But the modern West, like other cultures, contains both universalist and relativist strands. *Of course* we believe our own way of life to be the best: otherwise we would not follow it. And of course we also try, and know we ought to try, to avoid imposing this way of life on others except in extreme cases: we recognize for others, as well as for ourselves, the need to come to ethical beliefs out of one's own conviction rather than by force. The antinomy that, in Chapter 2, we found to characterize moral thought necessitates some such division in our attitude toward our own ethos. Insofar as we believe it to be the best we could have, we must hold that belief for reasons we could present to anyone, but insofar as we recognize that the truth of this claim depends on an endless chain of argument, we cannot be so sure we have the right piece of that chain as to rule out, absolutely, alternative pieces as incorrect.

In concrete ethical language, we express this division as a conflict between charity and respect. When we seek the well-being of all individuals, the good as we construe it, then we are pursuing charity; we pursue universal charity, and sometimes we think we should universally pursue it. When we seek the freedom of all individuals, distancing ourselves from them enough to let them define what they construe as good (and for that they may have to appeal to their culture), then we are pursuing respect; we pursue universal respect, and sometimes we think we should universally pursue it. But it does not always cohere with charity.

The balance between these two ethical interests is elusive, and I have offered no reason to suppose there is a way to locate it theoretically. I do not think there is anything wrong with this theoretical omission: the balance between them should be found not by theory but by judgment. On this point, let me make two suggestions. First, it is helpful always to bear in mind that both our interest in caring for others *and* our interest in tolerating what they do are shaped by our own local tradition, our own beliefs and history. We may then return to sources in that tradition for the resolution of specific conflicts of interest. Just how far did this or that text or historical experience drive us toward charity or respect? Did its intention (if a text) or impact (if an experience) extend to the type of situation we face in this specific case, or should we turn here to a different influence, perhaps geared toward the other interest? We should practice these kinds of questions and interpretations, rather than the construction of theories intended to reconcile the two projects.

Second, conflicts between interests occur not as abstract arguments over respect versus charity, but in specific situations, and they therefore require a set of judgments rather than a theory. We are short today on universalist and antiuniversalist judgments, not on theory, although texts to inform and occasions to inspire such judgments abound. Perhaps we should think of ourselves as constituting a court of ethical common law, in which we do best to take each case of cross-cultural interaction on the model of cases and decisions that have gone before— precedents, and arguments over or reflections on those precedents. The advantage of judgment over theory is that it allows us to acknowledge the richness of concrete decisions; the disadvantage seems to be that we risk not knowing what to do in a situation, or at least not having a clear guide in advance to which all participants can adjust their decisions. This is a risk built into all practical thought, however, and approaches that appear to remove it turn out to be illusory. Abstract theories fail just as readily to tell us what to do in many situations, since they are open to widely conflicting interpretations. The success of common law courts, on the other hand, shows us that precedent can provide clear solutions and a standard for public guidance. We need not fear that replacing the Universal Declaration of Human Rights with a series of judgments will dilute or obscure the world's commitment to humanitarianism. On the contrary, such a replacement is likely to make that commitment stronger—by giving it richer, more specific, and deeper roots within each culture's own tradition.

7. Beyond Cultures (II): Judging Ourselves

Not coincidentally, the account I shall give of cultural self-criticism resembles the one I have given of cross-cultural judgment. Every culture has reason both to hold its local beliefs and habits immune from supposedly transcultural standards and to seek revision in the light of precisely such standards; many, if not all, cultures have built into themselves traditions corresponding to these two attitudes; and the balance between those traditions is better sought by looking to specific judgments and histories of judgment than by coming up with a general theory of when and how cultures ought to be willing to revise themselves. But this is too brief and too abstract. I shall spell out the arguments for each of these points a little, then look more closely at two ways in which cultural self-criticism has been envisioned in our own Western tradition.

The argument for a transcultural standard of goodness runs as follows: If a culture is immune to criticism in the light of some standard beyond itself, then as a whole it will inevitably appear pointless, a mere game one can play if one likes but for which there is no reason that one *ought* to play it. In the arguments I have offered for the ethical value of tradition and authority, it was understood that these institutions can provide conceptions of the good only if we presuppose a broader, more fundamental conception of goodness against which to judge them. That a tradition is a conception of a higher good means in part that individuals who disagree with the conception will probably leave or try radically to change the community upholding it. That authorities are interpreters of a higher good means that their hold on their listeners is contingent on those listeners' ability to challenge and revise their teaching. It follows that cultures, if they are indeed authoritative ethical traditions, must be understood against the background of some notion of the good and the right that lies beyond their borders. The contemporary British philosopher Simon Blackburn, criticizing the notion of basing moral judgments on social consensus, puts this point very well: "One of the essential possibilities for a moral thinker is that of self-criticism, and of the thought that our own culture and way of life leads us to corrupted judgment. . . . Moral judgments are not based on consensus in such a way that they cannot be turned on that consensus, and find it lacking."[1]

The argument *against* the notion of a transcultural standard for goodness is, however, equally cogent. If cultures provide us with our best guess at what the good looks like, what notion of goodness is left to us when we want to condemn our culture itself? One can switch from one culture to another, condemning Russia as insufficiently Greek, or Greece as insufficiently Russian, and changing one's habitation accordingly, but by itself such a conversion will be arbitrary and fail to provide any way of evaluating either culture's practices. Rather, it is just when one wants to criticize one's culture as failing to achieve the good at which it itself aims that one feels a need for a standard transcending all cultures, but it is just here, also, that it becomes quite unclear how such a standard might be formulated. We saw in Chapter 1 that universal ethical principles at best yield a vague and minimal notion of how to act. Reason is a notoriously inadequate guide to how we ought to live; feeling, a notoriously untrustworthy and, most of the time, culturally structured one. What other transcultural tools are there? Intuition? Revelation? These are dangerous waters . . .[2]

It should be said that the need for self-criticism can often be met without appealing to a transcultural standard. Cultures usually, and perhaps inevitably, have room within themselves for disagreement and change. In response to possible criticisms along the lines that Blackburn pursues, Sabina Lovibond defends a culturally based approach to ethics by pointing out that cultures are "imperfectly coherent" forms of life, comprised of "institutions which are dedicated to incompatible (or dubiously compatible) ends," and from which "there can arise . . . competing habits of judging and reasoning."[3] Individuals in a given culture may proclaim the merits of some of these ends over the others, or they may promote the "habits of judging and reasoning" of one institution against what they take to be the corrupt practice and discussion of others. Thus the civil rights movement and its opponents, abortion activists on both sides, vegetarians and hunters, businesspeople and environmentalists have appealed to strains that conflict but coexist in the American tradition, urging that tradition to revise itself in such a way that the opposing strains are submerged or eliminated.

But this is only a first response to Blackburn. It is surely imaginable that every strand in a culture could approve of something abhorrent, that a single person "who dissents from the herd may yet be right."[4] A culture cannot maintain its claim to be directed toward the good unless it makes room for this possibility. Herein lies the legitimate kernel in our inclination to condemn cultures that are excessively closed ("authoritarian" as opposed to "authoritative"). How do we make sense of this inclination without positing a transcultural notion of the good? How, on the other hand, can we posit such a notion while continuing to insist that cultures supply the given of all ethical discourse?

I suggest that we must maintain the notion of a good beyond every strand of our culture, and we may suppose that successful criticisms of our culture are inspired by that notion, but we cannot formulate the notion into an alternative *system* that could take the place of our actual system for making day-to-day decisions. The notion of a highest good, far from being a hint to us that we ought to replace culturally bound codes with a universal way of determining everyday ethical behavior, stands precisely *outside* the ethics of the everyday. We will see that in fact it *must* stand outside the everyday, that it is in part defined by its contrast with normal, fixed patterns. How, then, can we look to this notion when we want to overhaul our ethical patterns, our normal business? In the paragraph with which I opened this chapter, I indicated that judgments and histories of judgment once again provide the best middle course between two opposing impulses. I will say a little more about this at the end of the chapter. In the meantime,

I would like, as in the previous chapter, to clarify by means of case studies what it looks like when a culture makes room for a notion of the good that transcends itself.

STUDIES IN CULTURAL SELF-CRITICISM

State-of-Nature Theory

The notion that political theory ought to begin from an imagined "state of nature" is a seventeenth- and eighteenth-century descendant of the main Western expression for a higher moral standard against which local customs ought to be measured: natural law. Natural law has acquired a bad reputation as a means by which the West tries to make its own customs universally applicable, but, as we saw in last chapter's discussion of Thomas, Vitoria, and Grotius, this reputation is mostly undeserved. Natural law has in fact played a number of roles, from serving as a legal device by which Roman courts interpreted the unfamiliar situations brought to them by members of non-Roman communities, to providing a justification for political institutions, in the Middle Ages, by which absolute rulers could be held responsible for violating moral standards.[5] In both these cases, it was more a way by which Western culture could stretch or protect its own legal and political imagination than a means of spreading that culture to peoples who did not want it. The same is true of the third major incarnation of natural law, as the foundation of "state of nature" theory, in which it gave birth to the notion of "natural rights," today called "human rights," which has helped set limits on what the increasingly powerful modern state can do to its citizens.[6] All states, the promoters of this theory said, must at least meet the needs that human beings would have had in a state of nature, and they held it to be "self-evident" that in a state of nature human beings would need life, liberty, and means by which to pursue happiness. States that fail to protect these "human rights" are illegitimate, and states with a healthy respect for human rights will keep themselves from encroaching on certain realms of their citizens' actions.

We have here, I think, an unquestionably *useful* doctrine. That does not mean we can make very good sense of how it works. It is hard to conceive how there might be any self-evident ethical truths or why one should learn ethics from what people might do in a state of nature. So what exactly can we suppose the highly intelligent and decent people who invoked the "state of nature" meant by that phrase? What did they imagine when they used it? How did it help their thinking, or make their thinking persuasive to others?

I believe the primary value of imagining human beings in a "natural" condition, whether one means by that an ideal condition or merely one without social conventions, is negative: it helps strip us of the automatic assumption that a particular institution or custom, code of manners or canon of literature is necessary, indispensable, has been around forever, and will be around for ever. It reminds us, standing in a city street or looking around at a cocktail party, that human beings can live very differently, and forces us to consider which, if any, of our ordinary habits and practices we really cannot give up. If you knew that only thereby could we save the planet or solve the problem of homelessness, would you agree to the removal of all cars and telephones? Would you agree to the end of all advanced technology? To anarchy? A totalitarian state? The abolition of marriage? Of all sexual activity? A flurry of such questions pushes you to take a stand on what all human beings minimally need—food, shelter, means of procreation, perhaps security from one another, love, justice, even education—and once you take *that* stand, it is easier to conceive, on a less radical level, how particular institutions that thwart rather than meet human needs might be changed or abolished. The angle at which we look at our world from an imagined stripped-down version of it superbly enables us to see even our most deeply entrenched social conventions as arbitrary, humanly created, and susceptible of change by humans.

This is the angle that state-of-nature theory helps us achieve, and without it many pernicious institutions and practices, passed down authoritatively with the rest of our tradition but no longer serving any decent purpose, would have gone unchallenged. By describing a state of nature, Locke and Rousseau showed us what we could be and how we fail in what we are. When Montaigne says that "lying, treason, deceit, greed, envy, slander and forgiveness" are unknown among the (supposedly apolitical and acultural) Amerindians, when Rousseau tells us that civil society brings depravity, selfishness, greed, jealousy, "crimes, wars, murders, . . . miseries and horrors," they do not pretend to be invoking a transcendental or purely natural standard of judgment.[7] Rather, they are condemning their society, in comparison with an imagined natural state, according to standards drawn from its own moral tradition. If we recognize what we would be independent of society, we need not hold, as the naive state-of-nature theorist might, that that state necessarily provides all standards for ethical judgment. Nor need we hold—and Rousseau does not—that we should return to the state of nature, merely that we should correct our society by it.[8] Rousseau's and Montaigne's states of nature were appealing in their time precisely as an alternative to the cruelties and absurdities of "civilized" Europe, as a haven where an individual might breathe free from all the petty dishonesty, fear, and spite involved in trying to live up to the norms that his fellow Genevans and Parisians wanted to impose on him. And their writings remain appealing because the possibility of removing oneself radically from one's social norms must always be presupposed in ethical reflection. Minimally, we want to be sure we are *able* to see our conventions as evil or absurd even if, finally, we decide to return to them. We want to see ourselves as able to assent to or dissent from our norms, as having, at least in imagination, a possible exit from the conventions around us.

What I do not concede to state-of-nature theorists is that this exit can serve as a basis for ordinary judgment in ethics. It makes no sense at all as a *source* of ordinary norms. Montaigne and Rousseau not only take critical distance from the absurdities and cruelties of our societies, but provide, in their "natural" condition, a superb metaphor for what constitutes critical distance; they do not, however—and Rousseau, at least, does not intend to—offer us a spring from which ordinary ethical judgment can be drawn.

To see why it is a mistake to suppose that the natural law position will suffice by itself for the construction of an ethical system, consider one of the sources of Enlightenment state-of-nature theory. In an otherwise largely quirky and shrilly dogmatic book on the Catholic sources of international law, E. B. F. Midgley makes the intriguing suggestion that the "state of nature" owes its origin to the theological hypothesis known as the *natura pura.* The *natura pura* ("state of pure nature") imagines what man might have been like without either corruption or grace, precisely as a way of clarifying what the fall (man's free, or arbitrary, act of pride) and salvation (God's free, or arbitrary, act of love) amount to. Part of conceiving that condition, says Midgley, involves bracketing out divine law; the Enlightenment error is to suppose that we can equally well imagine a condition without *human* law.[9] Man's "purely natural" end may well require living in society, with laws and authorities, even if it can be imagined to exclude a dependence on God. Midgley is far too ready to attribute every failing in modern political theory to Protestant deviations from Catholic orthodoxy, but his claims here receive support from no less and no less different an authority than Leo Strauss: "The state of nature became an essential topic of political philosophy only with Hobbes. . . . Prior to him, the term 'state of nature' was at home in Christian theology. The state of nature was distinguished especially from the state of grace, and it was subdivided into the state of pure nature and the state of fallen nature. Hobbes dropped the subdivision and replaced the state of grace by the state of civil society."[10]

I want to suggest this theological history as a source for the theoretical conception of the state of nature and keep that conception separate from a more empirical one with which it is frequently confused. Hobbes himself wavers uncertainly between theoretical construct and empirical claim. On the one hand, he derives the state of nature in tight argument from the presumption of human equality, while on the other he rebuffs suggestions that "there was never such a time, nor condition . . . as this."[11] Confusion about whether the state of nature is a transcendental or empirical supposition continues among Hobbes's successors, as we might expect. What we might not expect, but turns out to be of supreme if little-noticed importance for the future of the doctrine, is that as it gets further away in time from its theological origin, the language in which it appears evokes that origin more and more strongly. Pufendorf calls the state of nature a condition "as we may conceive man to be placed in by his bare nativity, abstracting from all rules or institutions, whether of human invention or of the inspiration or revelation of heaven"[12]—a virtual phrase-by-phrase translation of the abstraction from the fall ("human invention") and grace ("revelation of heaven"). Rousseau, the supposed high priest of empirical primitivism and an acknowledged precursor of anthropology,[13] not only makes a famous comment about "setting all the facts aside, for they do not affect the question," but goes on to an explicit invocation of the religious tradition about states of nature: "Religion commands us to believe that since God Himself took men out of the state of nature immediately after the creation, they are unequal because He wanted them to be so; but it does not forbid us to form conjectures, drawn solely from the nature of man and the beings surrounding him, about what the human race might have become if it had remained abandoned to itself."[14] Rousseau influenced Kant, especially as regards human equality (the key characteristic shared by states of nature in Hobbes, Locke, and Rousseau), and Kant clarified and justified the empirical/transcendental distinction in such a way that ethical and political theory could comfortably return to a purely transcendental form. Which the state of nature proceeded to do, in Kant's own political writing and especially in the work of his recent follower and interpreter John Rawls.

Now the transcendental ("pure") state of nature—human being "strip[ped] . . . of all the supernatural gifts he could have received and of all the artificial faculties he could only have acquired by long progress"— shares a curious feature with its theological ancestor.[15] The theological hypothesis asks what the end/telos/good for man would be even if there were no God. But it asks this question of a faithful audience, in the service of issues that will interest only the faithful, and it is surely looking not for what people would *consider* their end (they could be wrong), but for what would *in fact* be that end, as it were in the eyes of God. The hypothesis therefore comes very close to asking, What would be good in the eyes of God, even if there were no God? Very close—but it is not quite that circular, for the Scholastics recognized a distinction between what we know "naturally," through our "understanding," through the "book of nature," etc., and what we know only by revelation. They can thus be seen as inquiring what our (God-implanted) understanding tells us to seek as opposed to what we learn by revelation. There remains an implicit reference to God, however, for which reason both orthodox and heterodox Catholics have at times condemned the doctrine of pure nature as useless: for the believer, no fully intelligible human nature can be imagined independent of God.[16]

The secular version of this problem I can best put by way of Rawls's original position. In the original position we suspend our particular interests, empirical beliefs about ourselves, and conception of the Good and try to determine a fair distribution of primary goods, defined as those things "that every rational man is presumed to want," that "normally have a use whatever a person's rational plan of life," that "it is supposed a rational man wants whatever else he wants."[17] Rawls believes we would decide, in this original position, for a "maximin" distribution of these goods, such that the worst-off individuals have as much of them as possible. The obvious question is, *Are* there any things we can see as good regardless of our conception of the good? Do we know anything we want if we do not know what we want above all? Again, the obvious paradox is too crude. Rawls posits that any pursuit of any good would have to take the form of a "rational plan of life," and surely this, at least, must be true of whatever we could recognize as a "pursuit" or a "good." Someone who sought wealth, fame, a forum for his or her ideas, or peace for all humankind by sitting at home and wishing very hard for it could not rationally be regarded as in "pursuit"; someone apparently aiming at his or her own long- and short-term misery and degradation could hardly be said to be seeking a "good."

But it still seems readily possible that people might rationally regard Rawls's primary social goods—"rights and liberties, opportunities and powers, income and wealth"[18]—as including too little or too much. Too little, because they may regard the nonrational norms or institutions of their social or religious traditions as good in themselves, to be considered equally with individual freedom and welfare in any principle of social good. Too much, because in the light of their social or religious traditions they may consider such things as individual freedom or wealth absolute evils, or legitimate only insofar as they are subordinated to other projects. A person whose conception of the good turned out to be a very traditional, caste-affirming version of Hinduism might feel that the maximin distribution of social goods he agreed to behind the veil of ignorance was a mistake (even for the otherwise worst off, since their spiritual health would have been aided by having fewer social goods). Yet it does not seem impossible to pursue a "rational plan of life" in the service of traditional Hinduism.[19]

Ultimately, then, Rawls's view suffers from just what plagued the theological *natura pura:* a blindness to the possibility that arbitrariness (the need/desire for grace or the need/desire for particular traditions) may be built into human nature, not supervenient on it. The notion of pure or essential nature relies too much on the rational, and the rational tells us simultaneously less than the truth—that the shared, nonarbitrary ("unrevealed") interests of human beings are fundamental to ethics—and more: that those interests should override any socially conditioned or arbitrary interests with which they conflict. As rational argument cannot found the commitment we have to any specific way of thinking and living, so it cannot provide the whole content of anything we could count as essential human nature. That does not deprive it of its value for clarifying our cultural procedures and for reminding us of our basic biological and social needs, once our ultimate purposes are established elsewhere.

The Via Negativa

Natural law is supposed to be worked into the texture of any ethical system's normal practice. Those who criticize their culture for not living up to the demands of natural law are saying that the culture is not living up to minimal standards of decency that it itself and all other cultures normally recognize. But sometimes a critic wants to raise his or her culture to a level of practice or belief it has never yet attained. Models of such critics might include Socrates, Jesus of Nazareth, or Gandhi. One might say that the notion of the highest good is divided into a "good that everyone ought to perceive" and a "good to which our own highest efforts ought to be directed." I think most cultures do in fact divide what they perceive or understand of the good beyond themselves into these minimal and maximal notions. The minimal notion tends to include the humanitarian standards of state-of-nature theorists, to which each culture both holds up the others and struggles not to fall below itself. The maximal notion may justify the culture's belief in progress, if it has one, or at least explain how it can legitimately take on shapes that it has not had before. If a culture's way of life is supposed to constitute its best approximation at what is demanded by the good, any change in that way of life (the adoption of kingship, say, or of a university system, or of a new attitude toward sexuality) can only represent a deterioration unless it is possible that the highest good can somehow appear independently of the culture's normal habits and beliefs and itself help the culture find a better approximation of it. The maximal notion of the good also tends to be the one against which individuals convert from one culture to another. Discovering that your parents and teachers are cruel or corrupt will usually lead you (if you do not despair of all ethical systems) to emphasize the universalist aspect of ethics, the standards of humanitarianism, rather than to convert to another culture. Deciding that your parents' and teachers' way of life is somehow empty— "good enough as far as it goes but it doesn't go very far"—is more commonly a prelude to seeking some more adequate realization of the good. But you could hardly embark on such a search at all if the story and tradition in which you were raised did not itself contain some maximal notion of a good beyond itself against which you could judge it to be wanting.

Now, on the conception of moral argument this book has pursued, the terms we offer to justify and explain our decisions inevitably regress to a socially shared story and the authoritative judgments that story has inspired. Someone who wants to talk about a good beyond any of his society's conventions has therefore no ground on which to make his case. Recognizing this, the dissenter may, as Socrates, Jesus, and Gandhi often did, avoid giving grounds for what he says—speak ironically, obscurely, or not at all. He lays claim to a source of moral truth that, if it is to be perceived at all, can be perceived only groundlessly; his claims are groundless not because they are empty or false, but because, if true, they reveal a truth that underlies all our ways of giving grounds (and may therefore rewrite those ways).

Here we come upon a very difficult philosophical idea, with an ancient and complex history: the idea of the truth that transcends all reasons. One of the oldest ways of talking about the highest good is precisely to insist that the good cannot be spoken of. In religious thought, this is called "negative theology" or the "negative way" (*via negativa*) to God: one approaches an adequate conception of God only by denying, of each given predicate, that it properly describes God. Among the prominent exponents of the *via negativa* are Moses Maimonides, in the Jewish tradition, and Pseudo-Dionysus, Meister Eckhart, and Nicholas of Cusa, in Christianity. The *via negativa* does not begin, however, as a strictly theological matter. It has roots at least as far back as the pagan Neoplatonist Plotinus, who, interpreting *The Republic* (correctly, I believe) to imply that the highest good must be described metaphorically, insisted that there are only indirect routes to that source of all value and being. His theological successors sometimes added a further twist. Not only do we need to use negative language to describe God, they said, but we need precisely to break ourselves of all positive language. We need to find the error in everything that seems to lead toward God, and we need to find the kernel of good in everything that seems to lead away from God. Only then can our mode of religious expression approximate the unbounded comprehensiveness of what we are trying to express. Meister Eckhart says we must free ourselves from all ideas whatsoever if God is to be born in our souls: "Where is [God's] word to be spoken? . . . In the purest element of the soul, in the soul's most exalted place, in the core, yes, in the essence of the soul. The central silence is there, where no creature may enter, nor any idea, and there the soul neither thinks nor acts, nor entertains any idea, either of itself or of anything else."[20]

Believers in this notion of the good tend to be iconoclasts in their relationship with their societies' normal ethical language and behavior. If there is an absolutely infinite good, a purpose to the universe or to our lives in the universe that extends beyond every finite interpretation of itself, then every finite view of the good is inadequate, and when taken *as* adequate is false. So those transfixed by the infinity of the good often take it as their mission to attack the ideals and patterns—the "idols" or "icons"—that their societies take for granted. The Greek Cynics performed such outrageous acts as public masturbation to point up the emptiness of a life governed by an unquestioned adherence to social conventions.[21] Meister Eckhart, like Jewish mystics after him, suggested that to reach God one must get beyond the very idea of "God"; he also came near enough to violating the norms of Christian dogma to be put on trial for heresy. Early

Christians, heretics like the medieval Albigensians, followers of the Jewish mystic Joseph Frank, and those who believed that the 1960s youth culture offered a means of spiritual redemption took up radically antinomian attitudes toward both positive law and the normal conventions governing such practices as sex and marriage, in order to break through what they saw as the spiritually confining way of life around them. Kierkegaard, who belongs firmly in this tradition, wrote an *Attack on Christendom* and, in his personal life, broke off his engagement mainly out of the fear that a normal path of life would distract him from the absurd commitment—"criterionless choice"—that he felt God demands of us. And Gandhi brought religious silence, ritual defiance of laws, and a willingness to accept suffering into the practice of politics because he felt that what he had to say could be communicated only outside the normal political forums of discussion.

For all the interest of these people in breaking radically free of conventional approaches to the good, their own approaches share such deep similarities in language and manner as almost to constitute a new set of conventions. In the first place, with the exception of Gandhi they all stand firmly outside politics, in the sense both that they preach ideals for individual lives rather than social change and that the way they speak, the way they illustrate the power of their ideals, tends to be utterly nonpolitical. None of the Cynics' impolite gestures would help an assembly decide a single issue, while Jesus' parables about poverty could hardly enable a polis to develop a welfare policy. And Gandhi's political means are notable for the way they bypass the normal routes of politics, precisely because Gandhi was trying to make the conviction of the individual, rather than of either the majority or a minority group, politically significant.

In the second place, they all tend to recognize that the voice they are trying to hear, the voice by which a Being that breaks all bounds might communicate with individuals, must ultimately be a silent one—the "still, small voice" that Elijah hears in the wilderness. Compare:

> What should a man do to secure and deserve the occurrence and perfection of this birth in his soul? Should he co-operate by imagining and thinking about God, or should he keep quiet, be silent and at peace, so that God may

speak and act through him? Should he do nothing but wait until God does act? . . . [Good and perfect] persons know that the best life and the loftiest is to be silent and to let God speak and act through one. (Eckhart, *A Modern Translation:* 98)

The tragic hero who is the favorite of ethics is the purely human, and him I can understand, and all he does is in the light of the revealed. If I go further, then I stumble upon the paradox, either the divine or the demoniac, for silence is both. Silence is the snare of the demon, and the more one keeps silent, the more terrifying the demon becomes; but silence is also the mutual understanding between the Deity and the individual. (Kierkegaard, *Fear and Trembling:* 97)

A non-co-operationist strives to compel attention and to set an example . . . by his unobtrusive humility. He allows his solid action to speak for his creed. His strength lies in his reliance upon the correctness of his position. And the conviction of it grows most in his opponent when he least interposes his speech between his action and his opponent. Speech, especially when it is haughty, betrays want of confidence and it makes one's opponent sceptical about the reality of the act itself. (Gandhi, *Non-Violent Resistance:* 59)

Hannah Arendt, defining conscience as something quintessentially nonpolitical, says that it is a "soundless dialogue between me and myself," and she here echoes her teacher, Martin Heidegger, who was deeply influenced by Eckhart and Kierkegaard. Heidegger held that discourse, especially among the "they," the "marketplace" (polis), diminishes truth,[22] and the "call of conscience," the call to authenticity, comes in silence:

Losing itself in the publicness and the idle talk of the "they," [Dasein—human nature] *fails to hear* its own self in listening to the they-self. . . . If Dasein is to be able to get brought back from this lostness of failing to hear itself[,] . . . this listening-away to the ["they"] must get broken off . . . and [the] listening-away gets broken by the call [that] . . . arouses another kind of hearing which . . . has a character in every way opposite. . . . The call must do its calling without any hubbub and unambiguously, leaving no room for curiosity]. . . . *That which, by calling in this manner gives us to understand, is the conscience.*[23]

Finally, these thinkers tend either to recognize or, to their discredit, to demonstrate by their lives that a commitment to something beyond all conventional justification can lead just as readily to outstandingly evil as to outstandingly good behavior. If the ideal that one is following is truly independent of all finite ways of grasping the good, then it is a fortiori independent of the ordinary notions of "justice," "compassion," "humanity," and "decency." That means not that one must be indecent to follow such an ideal, but that it is hard to say why one should not be. Kierkegaard explicitly worries about this problem. In the quotation above, he remarks that silence is the mark both of the divine and of the demoniacal. He writes elsewhere that "the demoniacal has the same characteristic as the divine inasmuch as the individual can enter into an absolute relation to it. . . . It has therefore a certain resemblance which may deceive one."[24] Gandhi recommends nonviolence and the acceptance of suffering on oneself as the means of expressing the highest ideals, because he is well aware that beyond social justification the divine and the demoniacal can be easily confused.

More commonly, powerful visions of an ideal beyond conventional good and evil have been accompanied by a lack of interest in how those visions might translate into practice. Eckhart is careless, even contemptuous, of conventional religious acts when they come into conflict with his mystic vision.[25] The Jewish Kabbalists of the seventeenth century are notorious for encouraging, first, orgiastic and corrupt behavior, and then a cowardly betrayal of their people. And Heidegger has provided us with a remarkable example, in the twentieth century, of someone whose brilliance in appropriating Eckhart's ideas for secular purposes was matched only by the stupidity and arrogance with which he supported the Nazis and excused that support after the war.

It should be obvious from these cases alone that we do well to be wary of appeals to an ideal infinitely beyond all traditional standards, but we may learn from Heidegger, although he was too self-absorbed to apply this analysis to his own case, that such appeals not only generally are not a substitute for the ordinary resources of ethical discussion, but *necessarily cannot be* such a substitute. I have said that Heidegger provides a secular interpretation of Eckhart. That means in part that he avoids the word "God" and even the notion that the source of being to which he is gesturing deserves to be considered good. It means also that where Eckhart thinks human weakness prevents us from perceiving what is most important to us, Heidegger sees limitations on perceivability as built into the very notion of an ultimate source of what is important. Eckhart writes:

> What one grows to know and comes to love and remember, his soul follows after. Knowing this, our Lord hides himself from time to time, for the soul is an elemental form of the body, so that what once gains its attention holds it. If the soul were to know the goodness of God, as it is and without interruption, it would never turn away and therefore would never direct the body. . . . Since . . . the divine goodness is alien to this life and incompatible with it, faithful God veils it or reveals it when he will, or when he knows it will be most useful and best for you that he do so.[26]

Heidegger takes issue with Eckhart's claim that familiarity breeds eternal attention and concern. Rather, what is familiar fades from true understanding and commitment by its very familiarity: "Truth is never gathered from objects that are present and ordinary."[27] At any given moment we grasp "Being" in terms of some set of particulars. The appearance of truth, for Heidegger, is not a single event—or an eternal one—but must happen "always in some particular way." We focus on a particular interpretation of the world ("Forms," "atoms," "laws of nature," "frames of reference," "chaos"), on some particular objects more than others, on some particular activities and fields of thought more than others. Every time we choose such a focus, we do so because we think the particulars we have focused on so far have left something important out of our world: the unfamiliar rears up in the midst of our familiar ways of thinking and acting to force us to develop new patterns, focus on new particulars.[28] But these patterns will also become familiar, and when they do, when they dry up, once again, into mere present and ordinary patterns, their very familiarity will obscure important points, lead us into error or frustration or boredom, such that new particulars, including some of those that we buried in our last cultural revolution, will rear up to lead us to new visions and habits. Because the ultimate source of what matters makes sense only in terms of particular interpretations, it will always yield patterns of action and thought that can become so familiar as to lose all meaning or interest; but because particular interpretations must by definition always miss something of the whole they are interpreting, they can always be superseded by new visions and ways. And the ultimate *does* have to be grasped in particular ways if only because *we*, the human beings who seek it, are each particular, finite individuals who can attend to some things only by allowing others to return to obscurity: "Self-concealing, concealment, *lethe*, belongs to *a-letheia* ['dis-closure'], not just as an addition, not as shadow to light, but rather as the heart of *aletheia*."[29]

Heidegger uses this particularistic account of what he calls "Being" to claim that works of art, and especially poetry, are essential to what human beings consider truth, and that each age, each society, needs works of art, again and again, to open up its familiar patterns and lead it to new ones.[30] I think it applies equally well to the ethical theory of culture I have offered. If cultures provide particular interpretations of the good, precisely so that we, as particular beings, can do something with that intimidating notion, then they must always be open to the possibility that the particular factors they are emphasizing have blinded them to other particulars they ought to emphasize instead, to a renegotiation of what unfamiliar issues ought to be uncovered and what familiar ones might just as well be "thrust down."[31] Simply put: we cannot attend to everything at once; a story about the good is precisely a way of directing our attention to some things rather than others; but the limitations of such a direction always allow for the possibility that we will need to redirect ourselves in the future. But to say all this, although it presupposes that what matters about the universe infinitely eludes our grasp, is not to allow that our particular visions, our familiar patterns, are inessential to that ultimate value. On the contrary, there can be no unfamiliar without a familiar, no ultimate without limitations, no ultimate value without particular visions of it. We perceive "Being," as Heidegger would say, only by its contrast with beings. The absolutely infinite ideal, taken by itself, is a barely intelligible notion, and a mischievous one: it can inspire a Hitler or a Charles Manson as easily as a Baal Shem Tov or Francis of Assisi. As we saw in Chapter 3, we must posit that such an ideal exists, and we may posit that radical moral change in a culture—the changes, say, that brought Christianity out of Judaism or Buddhism out of Hinduism—or an individual conversion from one culture to another, takes place by means of a confrontation between the absolutely infinite ideal and one of its particular incarnations, but we cannot find for it, even as much as we could find for natural law, a language of its own.

The notion of such a confrontation, and the notion that a culture might change or an individual convert in the light of it, therefore belongs to ethical reflection as the antithesis that defines the limits of such reflection, not as itself a limit, an extreme, of such reflection as it normally takes place. In normal reflection we consider and debate ethical principles and judgments accepted in (some part of) our society, and we direct the deliberation according to stories and modes of justification similarly familiar to us. It is a familiar fact that these norms and modes sometimes fail a person or situation and that some people opt, in such circumstances, for a more or less mystical rejection of their old ways and an (equally mystical) acceptance of new ways or a new society, but we are not and cannot be familiar with why exactly they do so. Witnessing such moments of extra-ordinary change, we may be able to call them "conversion," or the "birth" of a new culture, but we cannot know what they consist in without converting or joining the new culture ourselves. By definition, the birth of new cultures, and conversion from one to another, take place outside, radically outside, our familiar moral norms and ways of arguing.[32]

CONCLUSIONS

Notions resembling the state of nature and the *via negativa* exist in many traditions. As long as they do exist, it is not hard to see how one can offer substantial moral criticism of one's own culture.[33] The idea that cultures provide our primary, even sole, means of conceiving the good therefore does not prevent us from trying to redirect that means or from converting away from it. Here again it is essential to the ethical view I am recommending that it embraces a paradox: in order to provide an adequate way toward the good, a culture must build into itself a language for how that way might be rejected. Language for the possibility that there is some kind of transcultural ethical ideal only strengthens the culture's ethical power, although it may be difficult to make sense of just what the ideal might look like independent of the culture's language for it.

I said in the beginning of this chapter that judgment can mediate between strands that encourage and strands that resist self-criticism in a culture, and this is indeed easy to do in the case of the state of nature, or indeed of any of the manifestations of natural law. We have observed that natural law, whether or not it can be well explained or defended, has served many useful purposes in the history of our culture. By looking at its history in detail, at just how it has been invoked and to what effect, where it succeeded, and at what went wrong when it failed, we can develop a set of precedents for good natural law judgments. The opponents of medieval tyranny, the founders of the American Republic, Thoreau, Gandhi, and Martin Luther King all provide rich material, in their lives as well as their writings, for such a history.

The elusive notion I have called "the absolutely infinite ideal," on the other hand, is much harder to place in a history. The most noble appeals to it have tended to share a respect for silence and a sort of deep, awestruck humility toward the world, but a notion that transcends any finite label or standard also transcends all manners of expression and indeed all instances in which its power has been expressed in the past. So a history showing that appeal to an absolutely infinite ideal has served human life best in such and such circumstances, or when accompanied by such and such personal qualities, is not sufficient reason for someone today who lays claim to prophecy, mystic vision, or the like to seek those circumstances or qualities. The absolutely infinite ideal transcends history along with everything else. This means that we can best regard it somewhat in the way I suggested we regard the irredeemably inhumane culture, and our irredeemably tribalist response to such a culture, in the last chapter: as a "philosopher's tale," a possibility that helps clarify a theoretical account of dissent from one's culture but that we need not expect to see realized.[34]

And with this suggestion I complete my description of how cultures can serve as ethical perspectives. If tradition and authority are essential to having and pursuing a specific view of how to live, if "culture"—despite the metaphysical and pseudoscientific connotations that have always surrounded it—was intended from its coinage to designate something much like an authoritative moral tradition, and if, finally, cultures can demonstrate how they are open enough to mutual toleration and self-correction that they can reasonably be seen as aiming at some good beyond themselves, then we can make good sense of an ethics based on appeals to culture. Cultures, we may then say, are prisms dividing the undistinguished light of the good into specific and colorful parts.

To lay out such an account was the main intent of this book, but to enrich the discussion a little and satisfy the curiosity of the reader, I want to close with a few words on an issue my project inevitably raises: just what, if anything, is *our*—Western—culture? Just what do we in the West, who develop culture into a matter for scientific investigation in large part to get away from its ethical demands on us, have left to trust as our authoritative tradition? The last chapter takes up this question.

8. Western Culture

It may look as if there is no Western culture, only a variety of religions and nationalisms *in* the West. Our stories are the stories of Christianity, Judaism, or Islam, of the German, Celtic, Serbian, or African American nations . . . These are, for many of us, the central stories. But most of us are Westerners whatever else we are, heirs to the peculiarly Western history of the Enlightenment, and some of us—a good many— are heirs to the Enlightenment first and foremost. What this means, in large part, is that we have tried to overcome, or at least weaken, our other cultural allegiances in the light of the Enlightenment critique of tradition and authority. The Enlightenment presented itself as an enemy of cultures, a destroyer of sacred stories and their authoritative interpreters. But it also produced a culture of its own, a distinctive Enlightenment culture, which bears much the same relation to its Christian past as Christianity does to the worlds of Greece and Judea. At least so I shall argue.

The paradox involved in such a claim may come out in the following anecdote. When I presented the project of this book to a group of academics, a literary theorist approved of the notion that ethical judgments depend on culture but then asked me, as if it were a matter of course, how I was going to deal with the sociological factors motivating cultural change. I said I wasn't going to deal with them at all, and the group looked shocked. I had offended against a dogma central to the culture of the Western academy—a Marxist dogma, in the sense in which Marxism is a sociological rather than political or economic doctrine.

It seems to me that my questioner missed the central point of this book: that, from the moral point of view, cultures provide the prism by which we interpret and try to guide our history and sociology, not the other way around. If we look at things the other way around, there must be some set of universal human interests, not of varying local stories and practices to which interests try to adjust, fundamentally directing our lives. The question I was asked urges us to step outside stories, to look beyond the interests cultures set for their members to some more basic set of interests motivating the people telling the stories. And it was asked—as, in my experience, it often is—by a person who considered herself a cultural relativist. I wondered why this kind of question seems so natural, and especially why those who profess the highest respect for culture fail to realize that their questions implicitly undermine the extent to which cultures *deserve* respect. This peculiar intellectual blindness bespeaks dogma, and it occurred to me that a set of interests, a story, a faith, lies behind the very attempt to stand outside stories. Can the old Marxist reduction of cultures to interests not be reversed on the Marxists? Surely the project of stepping out of moral stories is itself intended to serve a moral purpose: specifically, the purpose the Enlightenment thought it could achieve by overthrowing authority. But if Marxism has a specific moral purpose, on the account I have offered, we should expect to find a culture standing behind it.

One might suppose there could be no such thing as an Enlightenment culture, given that the cultures most familiar to us explicitly avow a commitment to some kind of God. I do not think this factor is all that important. All a story and set of customs needs in order to constitute an ethical way of life is the posit of some good beyond itself at which its efforts are aimed. Some religions mean little more than this by the word "God," and certainly this notion was more important to many citizens of ancient Athens and Rome than the pantheon of petty potentates officially regarded as deities. And the idea that there is some good at which to aim, some purpose to human life against which our more limited purposes, both as individuals and as a society, can be corrected, is not one the Enlightenment abandoned.

It did, however, conceive that purpose as rather less obscure, rather easier to understand, than other cultures had. This turns out to cause serious problems. I noted in passing, at the beginning of Chapter 3, that the Enlightenment conception of human goals was extremely naturalistic. From utilitarians to Marxists, there is agreement among the Enlightenment's moral heirs that people seek little more than health, happiness, and political freedom. One can tell a story around these goals and develop practices in pursuit of them, but it is not easy to pass a story and set of practices down authoritatively, from generation to generation, where there is no mystery that could possibly call for submission in trust or faith.

Still, insofar as the Enlightenment does have a story and set of distinctive practices, it constitutes at least a simulacrum of a culture. I think there are two Enlightenment stories, one more successful than the other. The first is a story about freedom, an eminently reasonable story that has yet proved impossible to work into a significant moral tradition. The second, about what is today called "diversity," is not nearly so reasonable but turns out to be a much more promising candidate for an Enlightenment faith. Let us pursue both of them some distance, using the analysis of tradition and authority we developed earlier.

FREEDOM

The story about freedom has issued in the American republic—its town meetings, proud individualism, and variety of "life-styles"—in the many constitutions that have tried to imitate the American one, in political forms ranging from civil disobedience to revolutionary reigns of terror, and in educational reform programs that have produced many Johnnys who can't read but also some remarkably imaginative and unstuffy writers, thinkers, and scientific investigators. These are its practices. As history, it regards the American Revolution as an unequivocal triumph, marred in its aftermath by the decision to retain slavery; the French Revolution as promise turned to tragedy; the 1848 uprisings as promise dashed by the never-to-be-underestimated forces of reaction; the 1917 revolution and the nationalist victories in Asia and Africa from 1947 until the late 1970s as triumphs again succeeded by tragedy and failure, but holding out the hope of future progress—which means future liberation. Its foundational heroes (Abraham, Moses) are Jefferson and Madison, Gandhi and Martin Luther King; its more troubled and mixed characters (Saul) include Robespierre and Lenin, Nyerere and Sukarno.[1] The common thread of its narrative is that freedom is always necessary but never easily or fully won: even when one supposes one has made the greatest strides, there remain hidden reactionary forces, waiting to work subtle or not-so-subtle forms of oppression into supposedly free states. Thus Marx told us that we need economic as well as political liberation; Freud, arguing that oppression may be found even in such preeminently "private" realms as sexuality and child raising, showed us how all human misery might be a consequence of lack of psychological freedom; and in the past twenty-five years followers of Marx and Freud have added various forms of sexual and racial oppression to the list of things from which we need freeing.

As the central story for a tradition, this is not a bad one. It has heroes and heroines to identify with, a host of specific incidents to use as paradigms for what one should and should not do, and a unifying theme that, like those of other cultures, rejects something about the social world that preceded it: in this case, the authority structures of Christianity. There is much for individuals to discuss and study, for a process of interpretation to latch on to, and indeed the freedom story has spawned novels and plays about individual liberation—from *A Doll's House* and *Huckleberry Finn* to *The Golden Notebook* and *Rubyfruit Jungle*—as well as legal systems, political theories, theologies, and artistic movements (twelve-tone music, the Bauhaus).

The problem comes when one asks what all this freedom is for. Freedom was once considered, and still seems, more a means to an end than an end in itself, even when construed so as to combine economic, psychological, racial, and sexual liberation. We rejoice as we watch dictatorships fall in Eastern Europe and the Soviet Union, but once those countries become more like ours, they will have to face the question we have yet to answer: What comes next?

Perhaps the sacred description of what comes next, for most followers of the freedom story until very recently, can be found in the early writings of Marx:

> As soon as the distribution of labour comes into being, each man has a particular, exclusive sphere of activity, which is forced upon him and from which he cannot escape. He is a hunter, a fisherman, a shepherd, or a critical

critic, and must remain so if he does not want to lose his means of livelihood; while in communist society, where nobody has one exclusive sphere of activity but each can become accomplished in any branch he wishes, society regulates the general production and thus makes it possible for me to do one thing today and another tomorrow, to hunt in the morning, fish in the afternoon, rear cattle in the evening, criticize after dinner, just as I have a mind, without ever becoming hunter, fisherman, shepherd or critic.[2]

The important point, looking at this passage today, is not just that every attempt to live out Marx's specific recommendations for how to get to his ideal has ended up as far away from it as one could possibly imagine, but that the ideal itself, which utilitarians, free market economists, social democrats, civil rights activists, modernists, and postmodernists all tend to share, is crucially flawed by the little phrase, "just as I have a mind." In Marx's ideal world there is nothing specifically to do; I can act on whatever desire occurs to me. The ideal remains a *means*, a framework for action, not an activity or condition worthwhile in itself.

Contrast a passage in the writings of Ovadiah Sforno, a fifteenth-century Jewish philosopher, commenting on the verse that describes humanity as made in the image of God:

The term *Elohim* used in a comparable sense . . . can be applied to every intelligent force . . . separated from matter which is perfect and in actuality and as such, is perforce everlasting. Therefore [this term] is used regarding God, the Blessed One, and His angels. . . . However, even though human reasoning functions without any material medium, expanding to the extrasensory and to a limited extent, even into the future, . . . before man contemplates and thinks deeply, lacking the perfection and completeness prepared for him, he cannot be called *Elohim*, but can only be called the *image of Elohim*—until he attains perfection. [This is] especially [so until he attains] the wisdom which brings [him] to the love and awe of God. Only then will he become one who is intellectually apprehensive in deed . . . ; perfect and separated from matter, resulting in immortality, existing even after the death of the body.[3]

Sforno, expressing here views typical of Jewish, Christian, and Muslim Aristotelians, tells us that through deep contemplation we can attain a condition beyond any the promptings of our material bodies might imagine for us. Indeed, we can reach the highest possible condition, the condition of the absolute that explains why every other condition seems to lack something. Here is intrinsically worthwhile activity with a vengeance, something that gives us all the reason in the world to humble ourselves and redirect our desires.

Not only is there no intrinsically worthwhile activity in the Enlightenment story, but it has trouble setting any limits at all on the desires appropriate for us. We saw in Chapter 2 that Enlightenment thinkers understood desires as quite independent of reason. David Hume, remember, said it is "not contrary to reason to prefer the destruction of the whole world to the scratching of my finger." What is missing in Enlightenment ethical theories can be traced to this conception of desire, and it was for this reason that I developed an alternative conception of desire (what I called "interests") before suggesting that submission in faith to traditions and authorities might open the way for rational reflection on, and redirection of, these desires. Enlightenment ethical theories, while they may tell us something about how we ought to pursue what we desire, have nothing to say to the person who wants to *change* his or her desires, to find something better to want. They have nothing to say to one whose desires as given lead to petty cruelty or dishonesty, drugs, degrading and meaningless sex, or an endless search for distractions, who is bored when her desires are satisfied and miserable when they are not.

Enlightenment thinkers, not in the least like this themselves, tended to suppose they did have answers for such people. Hardly a one explicitly said that freedom means acting on whatever desires one happens to be born with, and most believed there were better and worse desires, and standards by which to correct the worse ones.[4] This comes out in a number of ways. Freemasonry, the religion of choice for the Enlightened ones, offered a means by which even the "young, rich, intelligent, and well-educated" could find authorities to teach them how to live, as Tolstoy shows us brilliantly in the experience of Pierre Bezuhov.[5] Goethe ended the masterpiece that he developed over the whole course of his own explorations of life with Faust's discovery that living is worthwhile precisely when our desires stretch ever beyond the limited objects that they begin by aiming at.[6] On the political level, Rousseau, to whom Marx looked back, felt that human desires have been corrupted by society and can be made healthy again by social reform. True freedom, he thinks, will come about once interest groups are eliminated and everyone acts with the interests of all at heart. Madison and Jefferson shared this suspicion of special interests and hoped to educate citizens out of their natural inclinations toward selfishness. We need to have a civic sense, they believed, and not merely the desires we are born with, before we can be truly free. This emphasis on education was widely shared. Kant took it up as the means for developing what he called *Kultur*, the full flowering of all our virtues and capacities; *Kultur*, as opposed to the satisfaction of our given desires, he thought was true happiness. And Mill, while beginning from the explicit premise that the satisfaction of desire is indeed our purpose in life, thought that education could lead us to see that there are better and worse desires, and that the foundation of happiness, far from the fulfillment of desire, is "not to expect more from life than it is capable of bestowing."[7]

This Stoic element in a utilitarian definition of happiness may look odd to us, since it clashes starkly with the way utilitarianism and its Enlightenment kin have worked themselves out today. We are very optimistic about attaining whatever we set our hearts on. "You can have it all" has even been the slogan of a political movement. Myths of renunciation are considered a little disgusting. People change their jobs, divorce, leave their children—and "I just wasn't satisfied" is enough of an excuse to get heads to nod in sympathy. Most people in our society understand freedom to mean the ability to do what one wants and happiness to mean the attainment of what one wants. And overwhelmingly, this is translated in practice into lives filled by mind-numbing leisure activities, from beach vacations to television to drugs, not by the political discussion or endless education for which Madison and Kant had hoped. The texts that are most widely shared—popular novels, movies, and television shows—have a strong tendency to portray life as something in which dreams are usually fulfilled:

movie endings are changed when thought to be too unhappy,[8] and on tele-vision good characters always avoid severe disappointment by the end of a show. Although it is rarely brought in defense of popular movies and tele-vision, there is even a widespread political argument, in terms of the story of freedom, for affirming the desires people just happen to have. Standards for better and worse desires, we are told, are merely one of the tools by which whites, or males, or heterosexuals maintain their oppression of people unlike themselves: liberation requires the abandonment of such standards. And a good deal of evidence has in fact been uncovered that privileged people have used appeals to standards of desire to keep blacks, women, and other less privileged people out of jobs and positions of power. Those whose ethical bets are based on this particular fact regard more typical Enlightenment liberals as themselves agents of oppression.

To which the more typical liberals—heirs to Madison and Kant, Goethe and Mill—respond by pointing out that misuses of standards do not a case against such standards make, and that many nonprivileged people, including victims of oppression, appeal to standards of desire for their own purposes. The debate over this issue, however, rather misses the point. What contemporary radicals have brought out about the Enlighten-ment freedom story, albeit without recognizing that it ultimately under-mines both liberal and radical appeals to that story, is that nothing intrinsic to it prevents one from identifying freedom with "the ability to get what one wants." The confidence the Enlightenment places in science inclines it to take desires as the data, the given raw material, of human nature, and to try to develop some clear purpose for the human being out of those desires. That human purposes could be fundamentally obscure and that there could be standards for judging desire dependent on that obscurity are notions it finds both scientifically unsound and suggestive of the kinds of oppressive deception it saw in organized religion.[9] But without some such notion, no amount of talk about the general will, or *Kultur,* or eternal striving will convince people that they ought to have any purposes than the ones they already do have. And that means that the combination of complacency and despair, arrogant dogmatism and directionless searching, that characterizes so much current moral practice is unlikely to be helped, much less replaced, by anything that comes out of the Enlightenment's freedom story. Authoritative traditions can be made from a great many stories, but not from one opposed to their very foundation.

DIVERSITY

The other central theme of the Enlightenment, among some of its adherents at any rate, is a rejection of its Christian predecessor's universalism. Significant cultural differences can be based on little more than a shift of emphasis among interests or values everyone in principle shares. Who would deny the value of mercy? Who, the value of justice? But slight differences of emphasis between Christianity and Judaism on these matters make for great differences of story and community. Similarly, while all might agree that the purpose of our lives must be both highly articulated and somehow unified, Christianity emphasizes the unity of that purpose and the Enlightenment its diversity, whence follows a great deal of disagreement.

We hear a lot about cultural diversity today, and those who espouse it like to say that respect for it in the West is a result of non-Western influences and is a recent phenomenon. This is a rather surprising claim, for two reasons: first, because there is probably no society *outside* the West that is as interested in what other societies have to say, and second, because the value of diversity, far from being a fad of the past few decades, is a dogma of at least the past two centuries. Why and how to pursue diversity is a story that begins in the Enlightenment, and certain Enlightenment texts could serve quite literally as its Bible.

The believer turns to Bible or Quran and finds truth on every page— not only what she thinks she ought to believe but what she most emphatically *does* believe, sentences and stories that strike her as more profound and more profoundly right than anything she could say herself. We, cynically perhaps, suppose this is so only because the book has itself shaped her. She finds in it what she expects of truth because *it* has told her what to expect of truth. I suspect that, for many of those who scoff at such faithful readers, this cynicism falls away, and the wave of love and reverence that overcomes believers on opening their Bibles rushes in, when they encounter the following:

> In 1802 . . . [Herder] imagines a conversation between an Asian and a European: in the course of it the Asian (an Indian) says, '"Tell me, have you still not lost the habit of trying to convert to your faith peoples whose property you steal, whom you rob, enslave, murder, deprive of their land and their state, to whom your customs seem revolting? Supposing that one of them came to your country, and with an insolent air pronounced absurd all that is most sacred to you—your laws, your religion, your wisdom, your institutions, and so on, what would you do to such a man?" "Oh, but that is quite a different matter," replied the European, "we have power, ships, money, cannon, *culture*."' On this topic Herder remained uncompromising and passionate: '"Why are you pouring water over my head?" asked a dying slave of a Christian missionary. "So that you can go to Heaven." "I do not want to go to a heaven where there are white men," he replied, and turned on his side and died.'[10]

If one feels, reading this, "Here at last is a dead white male whose words still matter!" it is in large part because Herder himself created our current moral agenda: it is his issues we find important, his terms we use. I have already suggested, in Chapter 5, that Herder is the true founder of cultural relativism. He is more particularly the founder of that form of cultural relativism in which one not only tolerates the ways of other cultures but seeks in them something one feels is lacking in one's own culture. Isaiah Berlin, from whom the citation above is taken, writes that Herder's intellectual progeny

> in, let us say, England or America are to be found principally among those amateurs who became absorbed in the antiquities and forms of life (ancient and modern) of cultures other than their own, in Asia and Africa or the "backward" provinces of Europe or America, among professional amateurs and collectors of ancient song and poetry, among enthusiastic and sometimes sentimental devotees of more primitive forms of life in the Balkans or

among the Arabs; nostalgic travellers and exiles like Richard Burton, Doughty, Lafcadio Hearn, the English companions of Gandhi or Ibn Saud, cultural autonomists and unpolitical youth movements, as well as serious students and philosophers of language and society.[11]

Berlin could have added Walt Whitman or Whitman's admirer E. M. Forster, who was inspired to write by the travels in which he sought the *genius loci* of the places he visited and in whose novels Englishmen always learn to live more passionately as a result of an encounter with another culture.[12] Forster's *Passage to India* is said to have been influential in opening the eyes of many Britons to the inappropriateness of the British presence in India; it is today on a great many college reading lists as a seminal text in the critique of imperialism. When criticized, it is criticized for not being anti-imperialist enough. Students are encouraged to respect the workings, including the tribalist moral judgments, of other cultures, while questioning the workings, especially the tribalist moral judgments, of the West.

Such recent writers as Allan Bloom and Alasdair MacIntyre have seen in this attitude a sign that the West has abandoned its own traditions, and picked Nietzsche's scornful nihilism as the source of this abandonment. By tracing its genealogy to Herder instead, I allow for a different diagnosis of what it means. Herder, after all, is not in any sense a nihilist. An unsystematic thinker himself, he takes his metaphysical underpinnings from Leibniz, and Leibniz is about as optimistic as one can get about there being a structure and purpose to the world. But when Leibniz declared this world to be the best of all possible ones, he did *not* mean, as his more naive interpreters assumed, that this is the *happiest* of all possible worlds, only that it is and must be—because its Creator necessarily chooses it to be— the one that combines the greatest possible variety with the greatest possible order. Leibniz is known for his Principle of Variety, according to which God will necessarily create a world as full of different things as rationally possible, because there can be no sufficient reason for creating less than the most complete possible world and no sufficient reason for creating any two items of the complete world exactly alike. This doctrine is an interpretation of the maximal notion of the good I identified in the last chapter as the "absolutely infinite ideal," which has roots in the Western tradition as far back as Plato but runs against the current of that tradition insofar as it denies "that the good is one, while evil has many faces."[13] Berlin, whose words these are, calls Herder "an early and passionate champion of variety" against the monolithic tendencies of the West, but it is Leibniz who provided the groundwork of Herder's views, and Leibniz was drawing on an ancient and powerful, if minority, strand in Western thought. So Herder's "multiculturalism," far from representing a loss of faith in the West's beliefs and values, is in fact a direct outgrowth of Western theology. We must look outside our own culture, he says, indeed to all the cultures in the world, to determine how and why our life is valuable, but he says this because the good is revealed in that variety of views. And because he was looking to *all* cultures as a source of revelation, rather than to *other* cultures as a consequence of the bankruptcy of the West, Herder managed to be simultaneously a nationalist and a universalist, a promoter of German folk traditions and a denouncer of all European, including German, ethnocentrism.

We may thus explain the ambivalent attitudes of Herder's most faithful followers. T. E. Lawrence and E. M. Forster showed, in their personal manner, style of writing, and politics, as strong an attachment to their British heritage as to the cultures they wanted their fellow Britons to take more seriously. The lively excitement of such anthropologists as Margaret Mead and Clifford Geertz reflects their joy in discovering other cultures—a peculiarly Western joy—and bringing what they have learned to their Western home, not in having found some new culture to replace their Western one. No more do the West's many spiritual travelers, whether in the 1960s or the 1980s, and whether literally trekking through Asia or metaphorically exploring "non-Western" ways in New York and San Francisco, look to any particular other culture to adopt in place of the West. Rather, they like to sample a smorgasbord of alternative traditions, to find the best in every culture (except, sometimes, the one to which they were born), ideally to bring the best of all cultures together, and in this they pursue the peculiarly Western belief that the face of God is to be found in variety, that the good must be revealed in an infinite multiplicity if it is to be revealed at all.

I suggest that this is not only *an* important story of the West—and one that has had consequences for practice ranging from nationalism to tourism, and from the influence of non-Western art and music on expressionism and jazz to the influence of non-Western spirituality on New Age religion—but the most reasonable candidate for its moral faith. That does not mean that the story is itself reasonable, but the fact that its vision of the good is not fully clear or defensible is precisely what gives it an advantage, in the matter of faith, over the excessively rational story of freedom. At the same time, when interpreted sanely and humanely and not in the way nationalism has tended to favor, it is a story amenable to science, to the open political world to which science conduces, and to a world in which cultures live closer to one another than they have ever done before. Why these "external" factors should matter to a tradition's story, when, at the same time, it does better with a less rather than more reasonable central theme, are issues deserving our consideration.

Talk of a "reasonable" candidate for faith takes us back to a concern of Chapter 2: that ethical faith, although it must go beyond the demands of reason at some point, must also not conflict with them. A story about how to live may make claims about the ultimate nature and purpose of the world which cannot be scientifically proven, and any factual claims it makes may be open to a multitude of nonscientific interpretations, but people do want their factual and ethical views to cohere at least in a general way. If there is an objective good, a good whose claim on us we discover rather than invent, then the facts of the world cannot be irrelevant to what that good is; what ought to be must hang together with what is. Whenever an ethical system claims that we ought to do what we cannot do, or that the actions it recommends will have results they do not in fact have (world peace, the disappearance of economic or sexual jealousy), it loses plausibility; when it makes claims that reveal to us capacities we have or things we can achieve which we would not have anticipated, it gains plausibility. The alcoholic who recovers by means of Christian faith gains a new respect for Christianity, while one who sees the attempt to obey religious strictures as bringing only hypocrisy to her community may lose all faith in the religion. On a larger scale, the central stories of Judaism and Christianity have been reinterpreted to fit in with Platonic and Aristotelian systems, when those seemed the most plausible views of what there is. By dint of a lot of reinterpretation, they may yet be made to fit the results of modern science, but their emphases on revelation rather than empirical observation, and on devout commitment rather than critical theory building, do not sit comfortably with the methodology of modern science. And some of their traditional claims—to the central importance of the earth in the history of the universe, of human beings in the history of the earth, and of their own adherents' experience in the history of human beings—seem, to say the least, wildly overblown.

So Judaism and Christianity, like every other anciently rooted tradition, can at best be marginal cultures in a world dominated by modern science, and insofar as a Westerner (or anyone else for that matter) embraces the methods of science enthusiastically, his or her culture cannot be adequately described as "Jewish" or "Christian." The myth we have traced to Leibniz and Herder, on the other hand, fits modern science perfectly. The good it envisions is mysterious without being transcendent. It is not a supernatural governor of the universe but a structuring principle revealed in natural workings, and its rationality and naturalism encourage us to explore the world as a scientist does. At the same time, its infinite variety keeps it always somewhat obscured from us, keeps it something that necessarily lies beyond our self-centered experience and imaginings, something that continually holds out the possibility of learning a new and better way to live when our desires as given seem selfish and empty. The infinite variety of the world, if it is a good in itself, is thus simultaneously one in which the most hard-nosed scientist may believe and one by which the cynic who has despaired of finding any telos beyond immediate sources of pleasure can be inspired. Science, and all empirical exploration with the curiosity and openness of science, becomes not only pragmatically useful but intrinsically worthwhile. And if the world's infinite variety is especially reflected, as Leibniz argues, in intelligent forces ("souls"), and if, as Herder adds, cultures are as full an expression of intelligence as we can hope to find, then the exploration of cultures is particularly worthwhile.

In addition to its naturalism, however, the vision of Leibniz and Herder is a peculiarly sensible response to Western history. After Europe had been torn apart by religious wars in the sixteenth and seventeenth centuries, it is immensely reasonable that the children of those violent generations would seek a story allowing people of different faiths to live together harmoniously; after it became clear that the European merchants and missionaries in foreign lands were "trying to convert to their faith peoples whose property they stole, whom they robbed, enslaved, murdered, and deprived of their land and state," it is only to be expected that the most decent among their children and grandchildren would reject the universalistic pretensions in whose name such atrocities were committed. These events are the Egyptian slavery from which the Herderian story offers an exodus; nationalism is the first church or kingdom of that story. And while the failings of that church have done perhaps as much to discredit the story as Ahab and the Borgia pope did for their respective traditions, a series of psalmists and prophets, from Whitman and Max Müller, through Forster and Joyce, to Alvin Ailey, John Lennon, and Peter Brook, has kept the notion of going perpetually beyond one's own cultural borders, and of subduing the feeling that one has finally grasped the true and the good, an invigorating and ennobling ideal for which Westerners could strive.

To be sure, a lot of nonsense has been talked in the course of pursuing this ideal, but the absurdities of a tradition are not necessarily a point against it. By a culture's absurdities, you shall know its faith. If tradition and authority address those aspects of our decisions that depend on the limitations to the reasons we have at our disposal, then it is when reason alone cannot explain a pattern of activity that a society's authoritative traditions ought to appear. We cannot expect to find a distinctive culture in the fact that a society seeks food and shelter, makes marriages, or has an economic system. Only when the needs of the society are not sufficient to explain why it has some practice or festival, or conducts its marriages or business in some particular way, may we begin to make out the contours of its story about how to live and the way in which that story is integrated into the fabric of how, specifically, its members do live. In application to Western society, it is the success of chiropractic, acupuncture, "health food" stores, and Eastern meditative techniques in the face of all the scientific evidence that tells against what they claim to offer, and of nationalist and multiculturalist educational agendas in the face of all the historical evidence and humanistic arguments with which they conflict, that identifies starkly where reason fails to reach. The absurdities of multiculturalism are no more than the rituals of a new Western tradition.

I admit there is some ironic intent in these last remarks. Claims that all positive human achievements come from Africa or that Croats and Serbs need to be represented in separate political entities speak more of an ominous return to racist arrogance than of what faith in a tradition might add to our ethical practice. But these most extreme cases bring out clearly the fact that a faith lies at the heart of the belief in cultural diversity, and multiculturalism at its best—in Forster, say, or Clifford Geertz—is enough aware of that fact, of the fact that the West is also a culture deserving respect, and of the fact that what is worth respecting in Western culture depends in part on the West's other story, the freedom story, to combine its appeal to the intrinsic value of diversity with a deep rationality and humanism. Especially for those who have witnessed a great deal of bigotry and small-mindedness, those whose stomachs have turned, again and again, at the injustices their neighbors or parents have committed in the name of supposedly universal ethical standards, the Herderian story suggests a healthy and decent way of life as well as an intrinsically worthwhile one. It is this humanistic multiculturalism that I think has more to offer as an ethical tradition than the freedom story alone.

That is not to say it works flawlessly as a tradition. The Enlightenment may have given rise to an authoritative tradition of its own rather than the mere abandonment of authoritative traditions, but there could not but be limitations to how well it could perform this role given that it took itself to be an attack on both authority and tradition. The West may constitute a distinctive culture, but its unwillingness to *admit* that it is a distinctive culture has deprived it of much of the ethical power that other cultures have in their societies. This is apparent in ways that reflect both the ingredients making up the notion of culture.

In the first place, we in the West fail to study and revere our multiculturalist ideals and practices as a tradition. We do not make our children read Leibniz and Herder in school, let alone read and reread these figures ourselves, try to work out why they have such a hold over us, or see how they might be reinterpreted and reapplied as our circumstances change. Those who preach multiculturalism today tend to ignore altogether that it is itself a product of Western thought and history, and indeed ignore altogether the need for those who live in Western societies to study Western thought and history. This need should be obvious on an empirical level—just as one learns another language best when one has a good grip on one's own, so one learns most from other cultures when one has a deep familiarity with one's own—but it is also a consequence of the motivation for the whole multiculturalist project. We who live in the West must study Western culture not because it is the "best" of all cultures in the world, but because it is ours: a line of reasoning that those interested in culture recognize and respect when it comes from the mouths of adherents to non-Western traditions. There is nothing odd about the fact that Herder's greatest followers have sought to understand the "cultural Other" from a position firmly rooted in their own tradition. The irony, sometimes self-conscious, that T. E. Lawrence and E. M. Forster, like Paul Bowles and Bruce Chatwin after them, should combine such a thoroughgoing *English* manner with their empathy for Arabs and Indians is not accidental to their success in expressing that empathy. Multiculturalism is an ideal that requires going beyond one's own position, but that means one must have a position to go beyond.

In the second place, the West has lost all but a remnant of authority. Unwilling to place our trust in anyone, suspicious of disinterestedness, and disinclined to believe there is such a thing as moral wisdom, we tend not to see any middle ground between people who are trying to manipulate us and people we can reason with. We feel we simply "like what we like" and "are who we are," and do not readily allow our interests to be redirected. Where institutions of authority existed in the past, we have charlatans and tyrants today. We get advice from newspaper columnists, acquire values from the inanities of the quietly noble characters who are a staple of every soap opera and television comedy, and when all else fails, submit in blind obedience to spiritual and political gurus. It follows that we cannot hope to perceive clearly, let alone either accept or criticize in a healthy manner, the authoritative spokespeople who might make our tradition come alive. As a society, we lack trustworthy and thoughtful interpreters of our multiculturalism, and as individuals, we have trouble seeing it as a moral ideal at all, continually making the mistake of representing it instead as an empirical result or necessary tool of science, or a purely political goal. Rather than treating multiculturalism as an article of faith, something by which individuals may guide the decisions of their daily lives, we insist, contrary to fact, that all cultures are equally successful at finding empirical knowledge or making their members happy and free, or we try, contrary to the spirit of multiculturalism, to give cultures political power in the form of nationalist states.

If we learn to avoid these errors and build institutions to overcome the weaknesses that breed them, we may find we do have a culture. Those who bet on the methodology of modern science have reason to bring their children up on the stories, practices, and ideals that have accompanied that methodology. We in the West, like other peoples, need such stories: we cannot rely on universalizable reasons alone to provide our moral practice. That does not mean that we can look to science itself to supply us with stories. Like other peoples, we need at some point to rely on faith rather than reason in order to have a tradition: we need, not a science or a politics, but an ethics of culture.

Notes

1. LIMITS OF UNIVERSALISM

1. For discussions of this issue, see Gowans 1987.

2. MacIntyre 1981, Hauerwas 1981, Taylor 1989. See also Walzer 1980 and 1989, Sandel 1982, Nardin 1983, and Stout 1988. Bernard Williams (1985) shares the diagnosis but not the remedy, as, I think, does Stanley Cavell (1979: Part III).

3. In addition to the works cited in note 2, Gilligan 1982 is the main source for feminist objections to these theories; Nussbaum 1985 offers an Aristotelian alternative to Kantian and utilitarian theories; and Pennock 1981 superbly sums up the problems in natural law theory and intuitionism.

4. Elegant and clear presentations of the moral point of view, according to this understanding of it, can be found in Hare 1963 and Baier 1965.

5. Kant's work is the locus classicus for this position, although his belief that the universality of ethical judgments is a synthetic rather than an analytic truth may indicate that he did not hold it himself. The position is widely taken for granted, however, even by writers not at all concerned to argue for Kantianism. R. J. Vincent, a theorist of international law, writes that "the expression 'universal morality' is a tautology" (Vincent 1974: 74); Ruth Marcus, in the course of an argument on other topics, assumes that moral claims must involve "generalizing [one's] own choice to all" (Marcus, "Moral Dilemmas and Consistency," in Gowans 1987: 201). Even such a critic of the Kantian approach to ethics as Philippa Foot, who argues that moral statements are not unique in making their demands universally applicable, and that the fact they do so is in any case no reason for us to accept those demands, never denies that universal applicability is an essential feature of ethical speech (see Foot 1978). The most explicit and influential formulation of this claim, however, is to be found in the writings of R. M. Hare, who holds that it is definitive of moral language to be prescriptive and universal (see Hare 1963: 10–16).

6. Nardin 1983: 245. When "morality" is tied to "mores," of course, it becomes quite close in meaning to "ethics," with its root in "ethos." The Hegelian distinction between "morality" and "ethics" will not make much sense in the terms of this book.

7. Nardin 1983: 224–225.

8. Barrow 1986: 52–53.

9. Karsten Harries, of Yale University, has stressed the intrinsic connection between "morality" and "personhood" in conversation with me. See further discussion below.

10. Aquinas gives "aim at the Good" as the essence of the natural law, but he goes on, ingeniously, to derive more specific prescriptions from it (and the prescriptions he gives are not terribly far from the general conditions for counting something as a morality that I suggest in the next section of this chapter). See *Summa Theologica* I–II, Question 94, Article 2, translated in Aquinas 1953: 44–46.

11. I discuss the importance of these criteria later in this chapter.

12. See, for instance, Finnis 1980: 33–35.

13. See again Finnis 1980: 83, 96–97; and Nardin 1983: 320. Both refer especially to the work of Edel and Edel (1963).

14. Finnis 1980: 83.

15. Ibid.

16. For an account of the Ik, see Turnbull 1972.

17. Finnis, for instance, at least implicitly uses the claim that all societies have a form of religion to indicate that we in the secular West are missing something (1980), and he explicitly uses the universal "concern for the value of human life" as a basis for a case against abortion (1974).

18. "In 1961, the last Shaker brother, Delmer Wilson, died. In August 1965, the ruling ministry, which then consisted of Eldresses Emma King and Marguerite Frost of Canterbury and Eldress Gertrude Soule of Sabbathday Lake, ordained that the society be closed to new members and that further recruiting cease. The eldresses were quoted as agreeing with Elder Arthur Bruce, one of the last Shaker brethren, that as much bravery is required to walk through the end of an age as to found it" (see Horgan 1982: 181).

19. That is, we cannot use Donald Davidson's principle of charity to read universally acceptable principles into the society a priori, because Davidson asks us to interpret words and beliefs by taking as fixed what we, around here, hold true, and the truth we, around here, hold about universal standards of ethics is just what we are trying to find out.

20. Davidson has hinted, but not shown in detail, that he thinks his views on belief can extend to ethics (see Davidson 1980: 222n). David Cooper (1978) has written an admirable account of how this might be done.

21. See above, note 7, and text.

22. Kant 1964: 68–69, 78, 93, 95–98, 102–103, 107, 117 (Academy edition: 400–401, 411, 425, 427–430, 434–436, 439–440, 449–450).

23. Ibid.: 122 (454–455).

24. On Kamehameha II and taboo, see MacIntyre 1981: 105–107.

25. On Nazism, compare Barrow 1986: 52. On the Ik, see Turnbull 1972.

26. I shall argue in later chapters that the telos of an ethic is always in part obscure, even to insiders.

27. For suggestions that we abandon the notion of morality (at least as philosophically understood), see Williams 1985, Foot 1978, and Frankfurt 1982.

2. BEYOND UNIVERSALISM

1. Alexandre Koyré (1968) points out that Galileo was especially taken by Plato's notion that the "human intellect . . . participates in divinity solely because it is able to understand

the nature of numbers" (quoted on pp. 40–41). Galileo believed that science ought to be based on mathematics and that insofar as it is based on mathematics it can achieve divine comprehensiveness and certainty—"the human mind understands some propositions as perfectly and has of them as absolute certainty as Nature herself can have; and of that kind are the pure mathematical sciences" (Galileo, quoted in ibid., p. 41). These are of course also crucial convictions of Descartes and Newton.

2. Descartes's assertion of transrational possibilities (see Frankfurt 1977) and Hume's and Kant's insistence on the limitations of the human mind amount to such an admission.

3. Williams 1985: 135–140, Williams 1983, Williams 1978: 65–67, 211–212, 239, 245–249, 301–303, and Nagel 1986.

4. Descartes 1974: 112.

5. "And, finally, as it is [necessary], *before commencing to rebuild the house in which we live,* . . . that we be furnished with some other house in which we may live commodiously during the operations, so that I might not remain irresolute in my actions, while my reason compelled me to suspend my judgment, and that I might not be prevented from living thenceforward in the greatest possible felicity, I formed a provisory code of morals" (ibid.: Part III, first paragraph, my italics).

6. Williams 1981: 152.

7. Davidson 1984: 198.

8. Ayer 1952: 110–111.

9. "Overbelief in the truth," according to Kierkegaard, is a superstition of the most dangerous kind. "A superstitious belief which embraces an error keeps the possibility open that the truth may come to arouse it; but when the truth is there, and the superstitious mode of apprehending it transforms it into a lie, no saving awakening is possible" (Kierkegaard 1968: 385).

10. "I, Johannes Climacus, am a human being, neither more nor less; and I assume that anyone I may have the honor to engage in conversation with, is also a human being. If he presumes to be speculative philosophy in the abstract, pure, speculative thought, I must renounce the effort to speak with him; for in that case he instantly vanishes from my sight, and from the feeble sight of every mortal" (ibid.: 99).

11. "Every speculative philosopher confuses himself with humanity at large; whereby he becomes something infinitely great, and at the same time nothing at all. He confounds himself with humanity in sheer distraction of mind, just as the opposition press uses the royal 'we'" (ibid.: 126).

12. Ibid.: 108. See also p. 126: "It has indeed been said, that *die Weltgeschichte ist das Weltgericht* ['the history of the world is the judgment of the world' (Hegel)], and the word 'judgment' here seems to present a claim that the saying expresses an ethical view of life. For God it may perhaps be so"; and p. 192: "Suppose that the speculative philosopher is . . . the naughty child who refuses to remain where existing individuals belong, namely, in the existential training school where one becomes mature only through inwardness in existing, but instead demands a place in the divine council chamber."

13. "Ethics closes immediately about the individual . . . ; it does not make a parade of millions, or of generations of men; it does not take humanity in the lump, any more than the police arrest humanity at large. The ethical is concerned with particular human beings, and with each and every one of them by himself" (ibid.: 284). Compare also: "Each age has its own characteristic depravity. Ours is perhaps not pleasure or indulgence or sensuality, but rather a dissolute pantheistic contempt for the individual man. . . . Everything must

attach itself so as to be a part of some movement; men are determined to lose themselves in the totality of things, in world-history, fascinated and deceived by a magic witchery; no one wants to be an individual human being. Hence perhaps the many attempts to continue clinging to Hegel" (p. 317).

14. With the great exception, of course, of Kant, whose writings spawned a long history of skepticism about how much so-called social or human sciences can really tell us about ourselves (Wilhelm Dilthey and Ernst Cassirer are the two main conduits of this line of criticism).

15. Robespierre, quoted in Becker 1932: 142–143.

16. I take the failings of nationalism and Marxism to be fairly obvious. For good critiques of utilitarianism, see Taurek 1977 and Williams 1973.

17. Compare the well-known thought experiment showing the need for a unified consciousness to understand any single piece of information: "Take a sentence of a dozen words, and take twelve men and tell to each one word. Then stand the men in a row or jam them in a bunch, and let each think of his word as intently as he will; nowhere will there be a consciousness of the whole sentence" (William James, as quoted in Wolff 1963: 106; the discussion from which this quotation is taken, of the unity of consciousness in Kant, is an excellent account of the issue). Compare also Jonathan Bennett, endorsing Kant's emphasis on the first person singular: "A problem exists for me only if I have it. Someone else may have evidence which bears upon my problem, but I cannot take such evidence into account until I have it too. And when someone tells me what he knows about something, he provides me with new evidence only by confronting me with new sensory data: I hear him speak, and I have evidence as to his truthfulness, i.e. as to the likelihood that the sounds he makes will tally with my experience in appropriate ways; and I therefore treat the occurrence of my auditory experience in hearing him as evidence, *my* evidence, that such and such is the case" (Bennett 1966: 129–130).

18. Kierkegaard 1968: 275.

19. Reichenbach 1938: 348–357.

20. Compare the conditions Maimonides gives for regarding someone as a prophet: "Not every one showing a sign or token is on that account to be accepted as a prophet. Only if a man, by reason of his wisdom and conduct wherein he stands preeminent among his contemporaries, is already recognized as worthy of the prophetic gift, and his life, in its sanctity and renunciation, is favorable to the prophetic calling,—then, when he shows a sign or token and asserts that God had sent him, is it one's duty to listen to his message, as it is said, 'Unto him ye shall hearken' [Deut. 18:15]" (Maimonides 1981: 43b).

21. Reichenbach 1938: 357.

22. Lovejoy 1948: 80. Cf. also 82–85 and 172, and Lovejoy 1964: 6–10, 288–293.

23. Compare Ronald de Sousa: "[We learn] the vocabulary of emotion by association with *paradigm scenarios*, drawn first from our daily life as small children, later reinforced by the stories and fairy tales to which we are exposed, and, later still, supplemented and refined by literature and art. . . . An essential part of education consists in identifying [certain paradigm situations and their characteristic] responses, giving the child a name for [these responses] in the context of the scenario, and thus teaching it that it is experiencing a particular emotion" ("The Rationality of Emotions," in Rorty 1980: 142).

24. Hume 1969: 463.

25. Cf. Davidson 1980: 229–244 and Davidson 1984: 141–148, 158–160.

26. The desire is, after all, interwoven with other desires, such as that I and my fellow

human beings have happiness and freedom of thought, and other beliefs, such as that egalitarian societies provide their members with greater happiness and freedom of thought than other societies. Should scientific evidence show me that these other beliefs are wrong, or something outside science lead me to feel that these other desires are misguided, I will presumably revise my interest in egalitarianism.

27. The opening line of the *Critique of Pure Reason* (Kant 1965: A vii).

28. Cf. Kant 1965: A416 = B444 and A422 = B450.

29. "The substance of the absolute conception . . . lies in the idea that it could nonvacuously explain how it itself, and the various perspectival views of the world, are possible" (Williams 1985: 139). And again: "It is an important feature of modern science that it contributes to explaining how creatures with our origins and characteristics can understand a world with properties that this same science ascribes to the world" (ibid.: 139–140).

30. More precisely:

Thesis	*Antithesis*
There must be a nonrelative standard for truth, against which all other truth-claims can ultimately be measured.	Any judgment can be called "true" only relative to some prior contingent framework establishing what is to count as truth.

Proof	*Proof*
Let us assume that there is no such standard. Now it is part of the use of our very word "truth" that we evaluate every statement for truth or falsehood by means of other, logically prior statements setting truth-conditions for it. If there is no absolute ground for this process, all statements setting truth-conditions must themselves be empirical. But this leads to the following situation: P will be true if and only if it satisfies test y. We can state this in a new sentence (P_1): "P is true if and only if it satisfies test y." P_1 will itself be true if and only if it satisfies test y_1. This state of affairs can be formulated in yet another sentence P_2, which we must in turn subject to another empirical check . . . We thus reach an infinite regress. But truth-conditions, to be truth-conditions of a statement at all, must *sufficiently* determine the truth of that statement, which means that they cannot regress infinitely.	Assume that there is some nonrelative truth-claim or set of claims P, by which all modes of explanation and justification can be evaluated. Now we normally come to understand sentences as true by learning what it would be for them not to be true, by recognizing what condition of the world they rule out. And we come to accept modes of explanation and justification according to how well they fit in with this ordinary use of "truth," how well, that is, they direct us toward true sentences and away from false ones. We thus use the word "true" for sentences we might have considered false. But clearly there is no condition P rules out, because if there were any such condition, P's truth would be contingent on the failure of that condition to obtain, and we would accept P only relative to whatever lets us know that the condition in fact does not hold. By hypothesis P holds, and we accept P, absolutely, not relative to any contingent condition.
Nor is there any help to be found in the declaration that truth-conditions regress to a finite network of judgments	But if P holds, and we accept P, independent of the obtaining and failure to

serving as a framework for determining truth. For how would we evaluate this claim? Against what background judgments, what framework, could we declare the existence of finite, and possibly multiple, frameworks? Either such a declaration would have to be accepted by fiat, violating the condition that a true statement must have truth-conditions, or it will lead to an infinite regress of frameworks. The very supposition that there could be a multiplicity of finite frameworks for truth thus implies that there is a position beyond all of them from which we can see them *as* different—and we can see why we stick with the one we have.

obtain of every condition of the world, then it cannot serve as a ground for explanation. For the empirical claims and modes of evidence it is supposed to ground must show that certain conditions rather than others obtain, and a principle that holds regardless of all conditions can hardly guide us in making such distinctions. Hence P turns out to be empty, irrelevant to knowledge, meaningless when proposed as a foundation for knowledge.

These proofs are elaborated and brought close to Kant's arguments for his third antinomy in Fleischacker 1989 and Fleischacker 1992: chap. 4.

31. Kant 1965: A484 = B512.

32. Lewis White Beck gives an excellent account of this distinction in Kant (Beck 1960: 29–32); Alasdair MacIntyre, not citing Kant, expands on it wonderfully in MacIntyre 1981: 91–92; and Kant's own use of it (like MacIntyre's) is probably based, at least in part, on Adam Smith's exhaustive comparison of "spectator" and "person principally concerned" in Books I–III of *The Theory of Moral Sentiments* (Smith 1982).

33. See Mackie 1978 or Murphy 1982.

34. Kant 1956: 130–131 (Academy edition: 126).

35. Kierkegaard 1962: 55.

36. Ibid.: 59.

3. TRADITIONS AND THEIR STORIES

1. The intimate relationship between these two terms is the subject of Chapter 5.

2. The Hindu prohibition on eating beef is said to have been a way of making more economical use of the products of the cow.

3. Compare Eliseo Vivas, a fervent antirelativist who yet sees this kernel of justice in the relativist position: "[Cultural relativism has served] to defend nonliterates from the well-meaning, but often catastrophic, meddling of missionaries and the ruthless exploitation of imperialists. . . . Here are peoples who . . . have learned the hard way how to master nature for their own ends and are at least living a life of relative happiness and dignity in terms of their mores. A few years of meddling or of exploitation, and they become a pathetic lot. They lose their skills. Disorganization sets in. Their nakedness is covered—with ugly garments. They lose the urge to toil and they become beggars. In some cases they are destroyed not by somatic illnesses imported from the white world, but by something more insidious, moral illness, for somehow they lose their morale and their will to live . . . . True, in some

cases cannibalism is abolished by their exploiting masters, and in many cases modern medicine helps them. But what their 'benefactors' do not, cannot, see is that [in the process the] . . . people lose their identity and their dignity" (Vivas 1961: 65–66).

4. We might expect this, given the dual structure of human interests (see previous chapter). Perhaps these dualities are precisely what keep the good in part obscure—perhaps we cannot properly know what the good is until all our desires are satisfied, or find a satisfiable set of desires until we have achieved all knowledge.

5. That this, and not some optimistic estimation of human happiness, is what Leibniz meant by calling our world the "best of all possible worlds" has been shown superbly by Arthur Lovejoy (1964: 173–180). See also below, Chapters 5 and 8.

6. MacIntyre 1981: 203–204.

7. Ibid.: 1981: 207.

8. These three positions are established, respectively, on pp. 191–204, 204–205, and 205–206 of MacIntyre 1981.

9. We shall see in Chapter 5, however, that "religion" can be used as a name for the founding principles of ethics.

10. Consider the way mysticism, among Christians, Muslims, and Jews at least, pervades the readings of some communities and is almost entirely absent in others.

11. Chatwin 1987: 10–15.

12. Geertz 1968.

13. As, for instance, Fideists in anthropology and the philosophy of culture tend to do. See the excellent article on problems in this position by Robin Horton: "Tradition and Modernity Revisited," in Hollis and Lukes 1982: especially 203–210.

14. I am simplifying here. Judaism contains several other general themes, including the one it more commonly presents as primary: an attack on idolatry. This it understands to mean that true worship must always be directed beyond what we can conceive, that worshiping "the work of human hands" is ultimately empty self-worship, issuing in callousness, dishonesty, and violence. I choose a single theme to dramatize the point that there is such a thing as a distinctively Jewish way of looking at things (the point remains, but in a more complicated way, once we recognize several different themes: we just need to add that all the themes work together, establishing a "way of looking at things" as an interwoven band), and I choose a less obvious theme because it demonstrates well how the overall interpretation of a tradition may arise only from a detailed reading of its texts and practices.

15. Rousseau 1964: 160.

16. "[There] finally form[ed] in each country a particular nation, unified by customs and character, not by regulations and laws but by the same kind of life and foods and by the common influence of climate" (ibid.: 148). And earlier: "In proportion as the human race spread, difficulties multiplied along with men. Differences of soil, climate, and season could force them to admit differences in their ways of life" (ibid.: 143).

17. See Roger Masters, note 85 to his edition of Rousseau (Rousseau 1964: 245), and Geertz 1973: 356–358.

18. See Khadduri 1955: 141–145, 202–222. It has also reinterpreted its original, unworkable insistence that only oral testimony, and from a virtuous witness at that, is legitimate evidence in a courtroom (see Geertz 1983: 187–195).

19. The difference that tradition makes to a story was recognized, I believe, in the Roman distinction between "ancient religions" (e.g., Judaism), which were to be respected, and new cults (e.g., infant Christianity), which were not. (Wayne Meeks, of Yale University, tells me

that it is more or less a commonplace of Christianity's early history in Rome that anti-Christian polemics accuse the religion of being a "novel superstition" while Christian apologetics try very hard to show its antiquity (see, for instance, Celsus 1987: 87). The role I propose for tradition is also recognized, I think, in the Quranic limitation of tolerance to "People of a Book," especially since that was understood widely enough to include Zoroastrians, who have no Book (see Khadduri 1955: 176). The point seems clearly to be that some sort of text or story has been preserved over several generations, not that that text or story has been written down.

20. Arendt 1977: 93–94, 122–224, 140.

4. AUTHORITY

1. Arendt 1977: 91–92.

2. As far as I have seen, attempts in the contemporary literature to defend the legitimacy of relying on authority do not make this distinction and always wind up arguing for expertise rather than authority proper. This is certainly true of the essays collected in Harris 1976, in which, for instance, Richard DeGeorge argues that epistemic authority depends on the differential distribution of information across the population (p. 79), and W. H. Werkmeister sees moral authority as but an aid to the perception or implementation of universally acceptable moral principles (pp. 97ff).

3. Williams 1985: 148, 167–168. See also the whole of chapter 9. I take much of what I say in the paragraphs that follow to be an expansion and defense of this claim, albeit in terms of which Williams might disapprove.

4. Cf. Wittgenstein 1958: §217. There is an implied argument for authority, as essential to not just the learning but the constitution of rules, running throughout Wittgenstein's discussion of rule-following. See below, Chapter 6, notes 1, 5, and 6.

5. Perhaps better: interests are directed toward values (among other things), while values must speak to interests—if any final account of the good is (as Davidson, for one, would argue it must be) largely similar to what we pretheoretically take to be good.

6. See Smith 1982: III.4.4.

7. One wrinkle in using a rabbi as a model for authority is that the way of life for which rabbis speak privileges a text containing highly specific guidelines for how to live. It may seem that this is not the case for most other ways of life, and indeed even other scriptural religions, including Christianity, do not find in their scriptures more than a rough outline of how to conduct daily behavior. Yet Christian churches all over the world have found ways to translate their privileged text into a program for living. The modern secular world revolves around an array of texts, privileging, perhaps, Marx, Freud, and Nietzsche, but emphasizing the plurality of its grounds and prescriptions for living. Even the most proudly tolerant liberal, however, might well find more wisdom in the advice of one who, along with other moral features, has a good acquaintance with, say, Gibbon and Hume, Madison and Tocqueville, Austen, Eliot, Forster and James, than in one lacking such knowledge. As for how these texts can be translated into a way of living, that depends on how willing the listener is to recognize the institutions and social interactions they describe as his or her own milieu, and to welcome the virtues they recommend for that milieu—grace and subtly

compassionate decorum, in the case of Austen and James, tolerance and a new kind of courage, in the case of Forster—into his or her daily life.

8. I use the masculine pronoun throughout this paragraph because only orthodox rabbis offer *p'sak* to individuals, and they have always been male—up until this point at least.

9. This progress is misunderstood in both cases if it is seen as seamless, a mere accumulation of technical abilities: instead, it transpires by leaps, by shifts in ontological level. From crying to speaking is no less and no more a miracle than from behaving to acting freely. Cf. Wittgenstein 1958: §244 (together with §§6, 9, 32, 143, 157, 185) and Kierkegaard 1962: chaps. 1 and 3, especially pp. 15–18 and 53–54.

10. See Kant 1951: §40, and Gadamer's discussion of the *sensus communis* in Gadamer 1975.

11. Three notes: First, Kant, whom I generally follow in this account, distinguishes sharply between applying the general terms ("determinant judgment") and interpreting the cases ("reflective judgment"). "Determinant judgment" applies concepts or rules to particular cases, determining whether a particular thing is a house or flower or tree. "Reflective judgment" enables us to unify our particular intuitions into concepts in the first place. I see the two as inseparable (see also Chapter 6, note 4 and text, below).

Second, I here reject contemporary arguments to the effect that judgment is something *pre*-conceptual, something that operates *without* rules or generalities. John Kekes writes (in the beginning of a chapter that gets the phenomenology of judgment wonderfully right): "Unless it is possible to judge without principles, we could not, in the end, judge on the basis of principles either. The reason for this is that principles . . . are expressions of patterns of concurring judgments. So principles presuppose judgments, and, consequently, good judgment cannot merely be the application of principles to situations. Good judgment consists primarily in finding the right interpretation of complex moral situations in the absence of principles" (Kekes 1989: 128). I find the notion of a world without concepts ("principles," here) inconceivable, the notion of thought without concepts unintelligible. As soon as we think, we are always already in the midst of generalizations of some kind, such that we cannot interpret *any* situation, moral or otherwise, without trying to fit it under the rubric of various general patterns we have used for interpretation in the past. Now these patterns may very well be themselves comprised of "concurring judgments" of other situations, and in a particular situation we may very well wind up modifying the patterns we try out, in favor of a new constellation of judgments. So we are not *bound* by the concepts or principles we already have, and in the reinterpretation of old concepts and construction of new ones lies the significant role for judgment. It is in this sense quite true, as Kekes says, that "principles presuppose judgments." But the hierarchy he sets up is too neat—judgments also presuppose principles. To appreciate the importance of judgment, we do not need to make it prior to generalization, and to keep it intelligible, we must avoid any such claim. (See also the interpretation of Kant's account of judgment, below, and note 19.)

Finally, for similar reasons, I do not accept Lawrence Blum's claim that moral perception is a distinct capacity from moral judgment (see Blum 1991). Blum points out that in order to judge what features of a situation are morally relevant, we need first to perceive those features. We need to perceive *that* one person is humiliated, or another is displaying racism, before we can judge that a given act is motivated by prejudice, or cruelty, or insensitivity. Blum's account is elegant and thorough, but insofar as moral perception is informed by and directed toward moral categories (as Blum himself admits [p. 707]), I see no reason to separate it from reflective judgment. At any rate, the importance of moral perception extends exactly as far as the importance of moral judgment, and judgment offers more puzzling features and features more directly relevant to an account of authority. I shall therefore ignore perception, on the whole, in what follows.

12. Larmore 1987: 19.

13. I have noted above and shall consider again below, however, that *authoritative* judgment, at least, requires a certain distance from practice as well as a connection with it.

14. In Anglo-American common law, the need for judgments to submit to precedent is treated as simply a given. On the account of moral thought we have so far developed, we can offer it some grounding (both for legal and for other moral practice): We rely on histories of judgment as authoritative in order to join a particular case to one set of similar cases rather than another, for several reasons. First, the possibilities for linking up particulars with one another (which ones to link up and with regard to which properties) are endless, while we need to bring the process of judgment to an end in order to act. Second, we need, as social beings, to bring our judgments into some coherence with those of our neighbors, and a shared history of judgment provides a means by which that can be achieved. Third, by submitting to a preexisting pattern of judgment rather than positing a new one, we can express a faith that the good ultimately measuring our judgment is objective rather than invented by us. And finally, by insisting on a historical justification for our judgments, rather than trying to draw them from a universal theory or faculty of perception alone, we can express faith in a good that incorporates *temporal events* into its nature or mode of revelation, and thereby grants them intrinsic value. This is not to say, as I will emphasize shortly, that reliance on authority is enough for good judgments. Theory and experience, and the development of a capacity for moral perception, are also necessary and may in turn be used to judge our authorities. Indeed, since we must each use judgment to pick our individual authorities from among competing candidates for that role, our judgment *must* in part transcend the reliance on authority that also helps to comprise it.

In Chapter 6, I discuss the role of precedent in more detail and tie it to Wittgenstein's account of judgment in *On Certainty*.

15. Larmore 1987: 19–20.

16. Kant 1951, second introduction §§ IV and V.

17. Ibid.: §2.

18. Ibid.: §5.

19. When Kant writes that the "cognitive powers . . . are . . . in free play, [if] no definite concept limits them to a definite rule of cognition" (§9/p. 52), this must not be read to elide the word "definite." The free play of the faculties involves concepts, if not definite ones; it is a play not of the imagination alone, but *between* the imagination and the understanding. (The word "definite" or "determinate" qualifies "concept" over and over again in similar passages of the *Critique*: Compare Kant 1951: §4/p. 41, §12/p. 58, §22/p. 78.) I therefore speak of reflection as moving back and forth from sensations to concepts, rather than as unifying sensations in the imagination without a concept.

The latter is the more common interpretation of Kant. Donald Crawford writes, "In the case of the experience of the beautiful . . . no concept is forthcoming," and strongly implies that "free play" is an activity of the imagination alone (Crawford 1974: 89). Paul Guyer, wrestling explicitly with this issue, concludes that the word "definite" or "determinate" does no work in Kant's theory. Commenting on a passage that speaks of the imagination's work having to agree with the understanding's "presentation of a concept . . . (regardless of which concept)", he writes: "This somewhat inept wording might suggest the idea of a concept which is no concept in particular, much like the idea of a triangle that is 'neither oblique, nor rectangle, equilateral, equicrural, nor scalenon' to which Berkeley so vigorously objected. But it is surely more charitably interpreted as describing a state in which the ordinary condition for the application of a concept . . . obtains without the application of any concept at all. . . . Reflective judgment, it turns out, leads to aesthetic response not by finding a *possible concept* for a given particular, but by discovering that a given object fulfills the *general condition for the possibility of the application of concepts* without having any concept at all applied to it." In a footnote to this discussion, Guyer rebuts Mary Warnock's attempt to interpret Kant as supposing that the understanding provides an "indeterminate concept" to the imagination; he claims that Kant never uses any such phrase (Guyer 1979: 88–89 and 408–409 n. 60). See also p. 251: "It is clear that any actual occurrence of the harmony of the faculties requires the presentation of a manifold which is unifiable without concepts."

Guyer is right to refuse Warnock's interpretation, but not to ignore Kant's repeated emphasis on the word "definite" or "determinate." To think without a determinate concept is not, indeed, to think *with* an *in*determinate concept, but to use concepts without allowing any single concept to determine one's thought. "Without a determinate concept" might perhaps best be understood as "without a determin*ing* concept"; to think without a determining concept is then to allow a range or array of concepts (each quite "definite" in and of itself) to play with the contents of one's imagination instead of using one of them to fix the interpretation of that content. I note briefly here that Guyer raises a series of problems for his own reading of the *Critique of Judgment*—that it conflicts with the first *Critique's* insistence that there is no thought without concepts (pp. 96–99), that it makes no sense of the fact that aesthetic pleasure and reflection extend indefinitely over time (pp. 94–95), that it allows no active role to the understanding in the harmony of the faculties (p. 86)—none of which arises for the reading I am offering.

20. Cf. Kant 1951: §12/p. 58, §22/p. 80.

21. For a powerful evocation of the inadequacy of language, see Hugo von Hofmannsthal's "Letter of Lord Chandos," in Hofmannsthal 1952: 129–141.

22. Here, perhaps, I share Blum's emphasis on "moral perception" (see note 11, above).

23. The example is I. B. Singer's (see "A Piece of Advice," in Singer 1961).

24. Alasdair MacIntyre has an excellent discussion of the way Aquinas synthesized Augustinian and Aristotelian traditions (see MacIntyre 1988: 167–208).

25. Bloom 1973.

5. From Traditions to "Cultures"

1. Leibniz 1974: *Discourse on Metaphysics* §XXX.

2. Leibniz 1974: *Monadology* §60.

3. Since truths of reason cannot be derived from truths of fact, falsehood in the latter can have no bearing on the truth or falsehood of the former (see Lessing 1956).

4. Leibniz 1974: *Monadology* §60.

5. Allison 1966: 49, 165–166.

6. Ibid.: 44.

7. Act III, scene 7 (Lessing 1955: 78).

8. *Thoughts on the Moravians,* discussed in Allison 1966: 52–54.

9. Lessing 1956: 57–58.

10. Ibid.: 63 (§10).

11. Act V, scene 6 (Lessing 1955: 137). Sittah, the Sultan's sister, responds to these remarks by saying that such learning is "better then retained and . . . / Engrosses all the soul." Here especially, there is an obvious resemblance between Lessing's views and the argument of Plato's *Phaedrus.* I do not know whether Lessing, by this time, had sufficiently overcome his earlier misgivings about Plato for this to be more than a coincidence; in any case, the connection he draws between oral and parental teaching constitutes an original addition to the Platonic account.

12. Consider in this light, also, how Lessing condemns the nurse Daya's evangelical Christian beliefs while respecting the attachment to her homeland which he supposes underlies those beliefs (III, 1, especially lines 20–25). Throughout *Nathan the Wise,* historical religion is understood as worthy of respect when, but only when, it is a matter of family feeling.

13. If anyone did, it was Kierkegaard, but he transformed the loving teacher in question from one's literal parents to something else altogether.

14. Consider how, throughout the Hebrew Bible, religion is the hallmark of nation- or peoplehood: "Hath a nation changed its gods, which yet are no gods?" (Jeremiah 2:11). There was an acknowledgment throughout the ancient Near East that peoples define themselves by their relationship to their gods (evidenced, among other things, in the desire of successive empires to secure their political victories by having subject peoples worship their god), and the Bible shares this acknowledgment even when condemning the gods of other peoples as false and evil. See also Hannah Arendt's discussion of the Roman understanding of religion as that which binds one to the past of one's community, such that "religious and political activity could be considered as almost identical" (Arendt 1977: 121).

15. This is not to denigrate Lessing: his relative lack of influence is due in large part to his distaste for pure theory, and to the irony and adoption of masks in his style, but those very qualities make him better suited to moral thought than is Herder. Eventually, I shall recast Herder in terms for which Lessing is as much responsible as anyone.

16. For a study of Herder's influence, see Berlin 1976.

17. Bluestein 1963: 119. On Klemm's significance, see Kroeber and Kluckhohn 1952.

18. See Koepping 1983: 38–39 and Ergang 1966: 86. Koepping says that Herder took over the notion of "life-force" from Leibniz and posited it as the "energizing principle of living organisms, including cultures and societies, which all evolve and change through interaction, and are thus different, in their constant flux, from any mechanical assemblage" (pp. 38–39).

19. Herder 1961: 187. Compare Berlin 1976: 192: "[Herder] speaks as if history were indeed a drama, but one without a dénouement: as if it were like a cosmic symphony of which each movement is significant in itself, and of which, in any case, we cannot hear the whole, for God alone does so."

20. Herder 1968: 41.

21. Quoted in Bluestein 1963: 118.

22. Quoted in Shafer 1955: 19.

23. Quoted in ibid.: 24–25.

24. Quoted in ibid.: 26, 20.

25. Arciniegas 1951: 33.

26. On the connection of Bastian to Herder, see Koepping 1983: 83–86. On Bastian's seminal importance to the development of cultural anthropology, see (in addition to Koepping 1983: passim) Haddon 1934: 64; Penniman 1965: 111, 219, 238; and Lowie 1937: 29–38, 71–73, 105. Lowie points out the connection to Boas.

27. Benedict 1934: 42 (cf. Leibniz 1974: *Monadology* §17, on the way that monads differ as a whole from all their parts).

28. More directly, Ernst Cassirer, whose notion of cultures as symbolic wholes has had a major impact on the development of cultural relativism in the past three or four decades, was an astute and apparently sympathetic reader of Herder; it was he who first noted the influence of Leibniz (see Cassirer 1951: 230–233).

29. "Nationalism," as I use it here, refers strictly to the doctrine that every nation in the world deserves a state (exactly one state) and every state has legitimacy insofar as it reflects the wishes of a nation (exactly one nation). People do not join nationalist movements solely because they believe this doctrine. In addition to the opportunists, the confused, and the generally rebellious who join every political movement, people support nationalism because they feel socially or economically oppressed by another group or because they have suffered violence or humiliation at the hands of members of that other group. In his *Report to Greco,* Nikos Kazantzakis describes vividly how Turkish pogroms in his childhood made him a Greek nationalist; similar stories can be told by countless Jews, Armenians, Palestinians, Kurds, and others. But at bottom there is a question as to whether human beings ought to live in distinct social and moral groups. For when they do live in such groups, but within a state including other groups, the way is open for members of each to prefer their fellow group members for friendship, for business, and for marriage; therefore to exclude the others from their everyday discussions and interactions; therefore to weave more or less institutionalized patterns of socioeconomic discrimination and to build a general atmosphere of suspicion and mutual ignorance; therefore, finally, to lay the ground for a cycle of hostile incidents that can never be properly understood or compensated for, hence never forgiven, for a history that can only issue in a violent separation. Liberals, socialists, and even political conservatives (who, after all, support societal stability, not cultural preservation as an end in itself) generally become nationalists only when events have already come to a bloody pass, and then, at least if they are sincere in their liberalism, socialism, or conservatism, only reluctantly and provisionally, as a way station on the road to the overcoming of human differences. Nationalism is marked out as a doctrine of its own by a reluctant or joyful acceptance of the divisions between human groups as permanent and/or morally essential. It is this doctrinal core of the various movements it has inspired, and not the more than usually complex political configurations that have actually run those movements, with which I am here concerned.

30. A. C. Haddon (1934) describes how the word "folklore" and the establishment of societies for its collection came about in the service of nationalist interests (p. 110). See also Bluestein 1963.

31. Mead 1943: chaps. 13–14; Herskovits 1950: 653; and "Found in Translation: On the Social History of the Moral Imagination," in Geertz 1983.

32. Quoted and discussed in Kroeber and Kluckhohn 1952: 9, 43.

33. Every reference work I have consulted, from Singer 1968 through Voget 1975, cited Kroeber and Kluckhohn as the definitive text on the word "culture," and most discussions of the word seemed to be based directly on this work.

34. See, for instance, Kroeber and Kluckhohn 1952: 46–47, 50, 55, 56, 65, 70, 86.
35. Ibid.: 46 and Geertz 1973: 89.
36. Clark Wissler 1933, quoted in Kroeber and Kluckhohn 1952: 47.
37. Ibid.: 56.
38. Ibid.: 129.
39. On Herder, see Kedourie 1985: 59, 62. On his like-minded contemporaries, Albert Gallatin and Wilhelm von Humboldt, see Haddon 1934: 96.
40. Kroeber and Kluckhohn 1952: 43.
41. Cassirer 1944: 22–23.
42. Kroeber and Kluckhohn, 1952: 122, 123.
43. Ibid.: 120.
44. Ibid.: 115.
45. Kedourie 1985: 59.
46. See the discussion of post-Kantian philosophy in Taylor 1979: 1–14.
47. Kedourie 1985: 58, Kohn 1965: 36, and Schmidt 1956.
48. Kedourie 1985: 62.
49. Ibid.: 64.
50. Ibid.: 67–68, Leaf 1979: 83, and Koepping 1983: 43.
51. Kedourie 1985: 72.
52. For Fichte, see Kedourie 1985: 64–70; for Kant, see Kant 1951: 105, 201–202, and especially 281 (Kroeber and Kluckhohn inexplicably overlook this richest source of what "culture" might mean to Kant). Fichte, it should be noted, took an interest in both *Nation* and *Kultur:* while the work Kedourie discusses is called *Reden an die Deutsche Nation,* Kroeber and Kluckhohn (p. 24) quote a passage from another work holding that *"Cultur"* [*sic*] is "die Übung aller Kräfte auf den Zweck der völligen Freiheit" [the exercise of all powers toward the goal of complete freedom] (although, like Kant, Fichte means by *"Cultur"* something more like "the cultivation of the mind" than what anthropologists would mean). As we have seen, Herder uses the term *Volk,* as well as *Volksgeist,* for something that can probably mean either "culture" or "nation" (in the latter he was followed by Hegel [see Avineri 1972: 16 and Taylor 1979: 86–87, 96–100]).
53. Koepping 1983: 43, 83, and passim.
54. Haddon (in 1934) writes happily of the close relationship between anthropologists and "Colonial Governments," and of the latters' recognition that one needs to understand "the native point of view" and "as far as possible, . . . build upon what is best and most stable in the native polity" (p. 141). He says that the possibility that anthropologists can provide advisory roles in colonial administrations indicates that there is a "great future of immediate practical utility for anthropologists" (p. 142). T. K. Penniman (1965) notes that James Hunt, the founder of the Anthropological Society (a breakaway from the Ethnological Society) in mid-nineteenth-century America, was a champion of the cause of the American South and a "firm believer in taking anthropology into politics" (pp. 90–91), that Otto Ammon and H. S. Chamberlain used anthropological arguments derived from August Weisman and C. L. Morgan to show the superiority of the Teutonic race and the advisability of avoiding interclass (and presumably interracial) marriages (p. 96), and that James Frazer, more than any other single person, made the European world "aware of the interest and value of studying the peoples of their empires," to the extent that a background in anthropology became desirable or even necessary for those who had any part in the administration of colonies (p. 142). Penniman also remarks that "every teacher of anthropology has but to

think of his own pupils who are district officers, missionaries, or special investigators all over the world" (p. 252). Lowie gives us an idea of the motivations of Gustav Klemm when he says that Klemm hoped and expected "priestly dominion" to be supplanted by "nations" (Lowie 1937: 11–12), and notes that Henry Maine, the extremely influential author of *Ancient Law* (1861), served in the Indian colonial government (p. 49).

In reaction to this discomfiting history, Dell Hymes edited a collection in 1972, entitled *Reinventing Anthropology*, devoted to the proposition that "if anthropology did not exist, [it would not] have to be invented[, and] if it were reinvented, [it] would [not] be the anthropology we have now" (Hymes 1972: 3). The anthropology we have now, he says, citing Claude Lévi-Strauss, "cannot perhaps escape its history as an expression of a certain period in the discovery, then domination, of the rest of the world by European and North American societies" (p. 5).

55. "After the Revolution: The Fate of Nationalism in the New States," in Geertz 1973: 237.

56. Ibid.: 239.

57. Hodgen 1964: 211–212.

58. Geertz 1973: 240.

59. Ibid.

60. Williams 1973: 116–117.

61. "The Politics of Meaning," in Geertz 1973: 317.

62. See Kedourie 1985: 36n; Taylor 1979: 117; Avineri 1972: 35, 45–46, 69, 115, 240–241; Hegel 1971: 272–273 ("it is the one sole aim of the state that a nation should *not* come to existence, to power and action, . . . [insofar as it is] a shapeless, wild, blind force"—which, of course, is precisely the respect in which a romantic nationalist would *want* nations to come to power); and Hegel 1967: §§35, 349.

63. Hegel 1967: §35.

64. Ibid.: §349.

65. Ibid.

66. An alternative account of made nationhood appeals to education, instead of positive law, as the primary function of the state. Ernest Gellner argues that our technological age has made it necessary for any "viable political unit" to have an educational pyramid supporting universities at which people can be trained to handle the complexities of contemporary management and engineering. The possibility of such a pyramid, together with the difficulties of our technology itself, in turn requires the existence of an accepted mode of "explicit and reasonably precise communication" (Gellner 1983: 33) among the population that the political unit is to serve. Not a peculiarity of nationalist ideologies, therefore, but the nature of our times demands that our states establish a certain homogeneity over a population of some minimal size (large enough to support the pyramid). Nationalist ideology merely reflects this need and inspires groups with the passion to try to turn their own language and culture into the dominant one within a given political unit (ibid.: 39, 46) Gellner defines the state by a monopoly of legitimate education rather than the traditional monopoly of legitimate violence and thereby provides a way out of some of the problems that come of turning positive law into an ethical decision procedure. Schools use a wider range of means of persuasion than law does and can therefore deal with a wider range of issues. Teachers can represent more aspects of a community than can legislators and judges, because they are free to speak as a plurality while law must have a single voice. But with this return to plurality we lose the decisiveness of positive law, and to Gellner's credit, he does not view the nation-

state as a cultural arbiter. The state performs a pragmatic role, and its unitary education is geared to that role. Some attitudes and norms are bound to come with the scientific instruction it provides, but these may continue to vary from and conflict with one another, and they need not obliterate the norms a child learns from her parents, her religious institutions, her friends, and the books she reads. If a nation is made in Gellner's way, it will carry out programs in pursuit of the limited ends all people tend to agree on (health and physical comfort, for example), not define and refine an entire conception of how to live.

67. "Now this interconnection, relationship, or this adaptation of all things to each particular one, and of each one to all the rest, brings it about that every simple substance has relations which express all the others and that it is consequently a perpetual living mirror of the universe" (Leibniz 1974: *Monadology* §56). See also §§1, 14.

68. Ibid.: §§20–23.

69. Ibid.: §62.

70. Of course, for Leibniz, neither stones and missiles nor groups could possibly be minds (perceivers): they can merely serve as the bodily counterpart of a mind. But that the having of relations is equivalent to perception is quite clear in Leibniz's doctrine of small perceptions (see the discussion in Allison 1966: 128–129).

71. Leibniz himself indicates that every religion functions like a monad, as "a confused expression of the ultimate truth, . . . consequently contain[ing] a relative truth, . . . [and as] merely one among a number of possible perspectives, . . . wrong [only] in denying the validity of opposing standpoints" (Allison 1966: 130). He also moves tentatively toward taking philosophical standpoints as monads, insofar as he tries to find a kernel of truth in every position with which he disagrees. "This tendency to find a measure of truth in diverse standpoints," says Henry Allison, "serves, more than anything else, to distinguish his philosophy from that of such rationalists as Descartes, Spinoza, and Wolff, and . . . is grounded in his deepest philosophical insight—the universal harmony [of all perspectives]" (ibid.: 128).

72. Leibniz 1974: *Monadology* §§11, 7, 51.

73. "Do you see this river, flowing on, how it springs from a tiny source, swells, divides, joins up again, winds in and out, and cuts farther and deeper but, whatever the intricacies of its course, still remains water. . . . Might it not be the same with humankind? . . . No one lives in his own period only; he builds on what has gone before and lays a foundation for what comes after. . . . The Egyptian could not have existed without the Oriental, nor the Greek without the Egyptian" (Herder 1961: 187–188). Compare Koepping, citation in note 18, above.

74. Herder 1961: 181.

75. Cf. Leibniz 1974: *Monadology* §§4–5, 7.

76. For a general discussion of biological and cultural myths on which nationalism has been based, see Shafer 1955: chaps. 3 and 4.

77. Cf. note 18, above.

78. The debate between Leibniz and the Newtonians turns on whether the structuring principles of empirical science are mathematical or metaphysical, with mathematical principles being understood as not, strictly speaking, an *alternative* to empirical investigation (rather, perhaps, a way of organizing empirical results). Says Leibniz, "It appears . . . that although all the particular phenomena of nature can be explained mathematically or mechanically by those who understand them, yet nevertheless, the general principles of corporeal nature and even of mechanics are metaphysical rather than geometric" (Leibniz 1974:

Discourse §XVIII). Compare also Leibniz/Clarke 1956: 20 (§1) and 25 (§1). Neither Leibniz nor Clarke (nor Wolff, Hume, Voltaire, or anyone else involved in this debate) so much as raises the possibility that moral thought might constitute a third alternative.

79. Herder himself, claiming that "history may not manifestly be revealed as the theatre of a divine purpose on earth . . . for we may not be able to espy its final end" (see text to note 19, above), seems to share the skepticism of common human goals, and the corresponding notion that the human telos might be in some way obscure, that I earlier suggested was a prerequisite for traditions to be essential to the revelation of that telos.

80. Herder 1968: 98.

81. Ibid.

82. Cf. Geertz 1973: especially the opening essay.

83. There are, after all, severe constraints on what one can allow to constitute a culture at all. When looking for their culture, agents turn to traditions of literature and proverbs, religious practices, and political institutions, from which most of them can reasonably pick out not more than three or four significantly different groups that might have a strong influence on them. From this much pluralism, they are unlikely to be overwhelmed by dilemmas.

84. Compare Ruth Marcus's position on moral dilemmas. Marcus argues that we can define a set of rules as consistent as long as "there is some possible world in which they are all obeyable in all circumstances in *that* world" (Marcus, "Moral Dilemmas and Consistency," in Gowans 1987: 194). As an example she gives the rules for "a silly two-person card game," in which higher cards trump lower ones and black trumps red (p. 195). Such a game is consistent in that there need not be any situation in which high reds are faced off with low blacks; sometimes, if not always, the game can be played to a conclusion. Inconsistency will apply only to a set of rules inconsistent in *all* possible circumstances, in which case the rules provide "*no* guide to action under any circumstance." (p. 195). According to Marcus, our ethical rules are not inconsistent in this sense, only, like the card game, incomplete: they do not provide a guide to action in every circumstance. Moreover, they are much more complete than the card game, and their conflicts inspire us to reflect on them, change them, and reflect on and change those of our institutions helping to create circumstances conducive to moral dilemma.

85. Compare Marcus, who notes that the choices agents do make among their various norms and options are sometimes taken to be "a way in which, given good will, an agent can make explicit the rules under which he acts[, . . . can discover] a priority principle under which he orders his actions." Although she is not willing to agree that in this way they really uncover *rules,* she concedes that they may determine, and reveal to others, "the kind of persons they [wish] to be and the kind of lives they [wish] to lead" (ibid.: 201).

6. BEYOND CULTURES (I): JUDGING OTHERS

1. Wittgenstein, in *On Certainty* especially, beautifully describes the fact that we are able to judge without being able to say in general what constitutes judgment. "My judgments themselves characterize the way I judge," he says, or, more unsatisfyingly yet, "*This is* judging" (Wittgenstein 1977: §§149, 128). Since "judgments . . . characterize the nature of judgment" (§149), since "we use judgments as principles of judgment" (§124), we cannot learn the game independent of playing it; we cannot develop a capacity to judge if we have none

to start with. We must grow up with it, as human beings always do (and most do, and some perhaps do not, get the hang of it—those who fail may be "stupid," as Kant claims (see Kant 1965: 178) or impractical, as Aristotle says about Anaxagoras, or utterly monstrous in some sense, like those we call "psychotic," "sociopaths," or simply "inhumanly" abstract and cold): "From a child up I learnt to judge like this. *This* is judging. / This is how I learned to judge; *this* I got to know as judgment" (Wittgenstein 1977: §§128–129).

2. *Nicomachean Ethics*, Book VI, 1141^{b}14–21, 1142^{a}13–19, 1142^{a}24–31, in Aristotle 1941.

3. Ibid.: 1141^{b}4–8.

4. Kant distinguishes sharply between determinant judgment, the application of a rule to a particular, which is supposed to be quite definitive or "complete," and reflective judgment, an indefinite process without any clear end, which seeks the specific rules we might want to apply (see Kant 1951: second introduction §§IV and V). I agree with the later Wittgenstein, however, whose argument that rules can be defined only by the way they apply can be taken as showing that every determinant judgment entails a new reflective one and vice versa.

5. "Must I not begin to trust somewhere? . . . somewhere I must begin with not-doubting; and that is not, so to speak, hasty but excusable: it is part of judging" (Wittgenstein 1977: §150; also §§310, 493). See also Chapter 4, note 14 and text, above.

6. Wittgenstein returns again and again in *On Certainty* to common law as a model for how we ought to conceive of knowledge. "In a law-court," he says, to correct some misconceptions about the word "know," " 'I am certain' could replace 'I know' in every piece of testimony" (§8). Wild counterfactuals "wouldn't ever be taken into consideration there," he remarks pointedly (§335), implying that in philosophy we ought not to regard them as challenges to our knowledge either. He quotes, in English, the British legal phrase "certain beyond all reasonable doubt" (§§416, 607), with obvious admiration for its pragmatic vagueness; uses "der vernünftige Mensch" in much the way British courts use "the reasonable man" as a standard for what assumptions to accept and what questions to take seriously (§§220, 254, 325, 334, 453; for a discussion of the "reasonable man" standard, see Devlin 1965: chap. 1); and at one point asks whether "learned judges" would consider reasonable some of the things philosophers so consider (§453; see also §§325, 500).

7. The way is always indefinite, because precedents, being particular, can take various and conflicting interpretations, but when a judge deviates radically from them, even if he gives a clever reading to justify his decision, others in the community will judge that he is wrong (if a higher court does not overturn his decision, at least the individuals making up his community will exercise their powers of judgment to condemn it). Here, as elsewhere, the correct use of judgment, the appropriate extrapolation of a way of judging, can be determined only by further judgment.

8. See Katz 1989: chap. 4, especially pp. 58–59.

9. See Geertz 1983: 187–195.

10. I mention these particular institutions because Sir Geoffrey Howe, James Baker, Cardinal O'Connor, and Rabbi Immanuel Jakobovits all made mealymouthed statements that attempted to effect a compromise by condemning both Khomeini and Rushdie. Jakobovits made the following remarkable comparison: "Both Mr. Rushdie and the Ayatollah have abused freedom of speech, the one by provocatively offending the genuine faith of many millions of devout believers, and the other by a public call to murder" (Letter to the London *Times*, March 4, 1989: p. 11). O'Connor said he would not read the book but announced "his sympathy for the aggrieved position the Muslim community has taken on this

publication" (*New York Times*, Feb. 20, 1989: A6). Howe told the BBC that his government understood "that the book itself has been found deeply offensive by people of the Moslem faith," remarked that the book was also offensive to his administration, but added that "we cannot allow the overturning of the principle of the freedom of speech" (*Washington Post*, March 3, 1989: A29). Baker could not bring himself to call Khomeini's death threat anything more than "regrettable," and went out of his way to add that his administration had not read the book and was not "endorsing some of the statements that might be contained" in it. He added, "We, of course, endorse the right of any to make those statements and to write such. We endorse the freedom of speech rights" (*New York Times*, Feb. 22, 1989: A7).

11. I might appeal, for instance, to Rabbi Avraham Yitzchak Kook's claim that *ahavat chinam* ("groundless love") ought to be the basis of the modern Jewish community. (*Sinat chinam* ["groundless hatred"] is said to be the sin for which the second Temple was destroyed. See Babylonian Talmud: *Gittin* 55b–56a.) Consider also the suggestion in Babylonian Talmud Gittin 59a and b, that the whole Torah was given "for the sake of the ways of peace," Rashi's opinion that at times one can "abrogate words of the Torah" in order to seek peace (which he understands as a higher form of acting for God, in such cases), or the famous remark of Rabbi Hanina that rabbinic scholars are supposed to be "builders of peace." See the discussion of these texts and an analysis of modern heresy that would preserve peace among rival Jewish groups, in Berkovits 1983: 26, 76–78, and 106–108.

12. For a wonderful comparison of metaphors and legal fictions, see Barfield 1962. For an argument that dead metaphors turn into literal speech, see Davidson, "What Metaphors Mean," in Davidson 1984.

13. Berger 1979: 9–10.

14. Ibid.

15. *Summa Theologica* I–II, Q93A4, Q93A2, in Aquinas 1953.

16. Vitoria 1917: 144, §13.

17. *Summa Theologica* I–II, Q93A2, Reply, Obj. 3, in Aquinas 1953.

18. Vitoria 1917: 146.

19. Ibid.

20. Ibid.: 147.

21. Grotius 1901: 248.

22. *Summa Theologica* I–II, Q94A2, in Aquinas 1953.

23. Ibid.

24. Vitoria argues specifically against coercing the Indians because of pederasty, bestiality, or lesbianism (see 1917: II, §16, p. 146). Cf. *Summa Theologica* I–II, Q96A2, where Aquinas suggests that human law can enforce only the more grievous violations of the natural law "from which it is possible for the majority [of a particular country] to abstain." (See also Q94A4, which hints that responsibility for knowing and obeying the secondary principles of the law of nature may vary from country to country.) Grotius (1901: 247–248) limits the right of sovereigns to make war as a means of punishment to cases of "gross violations of the law of nature and of nations"—in particular, cases that threaten "the peace and welfare of society"—and even to establish this he feels he must argue against the more anti-interventionist attitude of "Vitoria, Vasquez, Azorius, Molina, and others."

25. See the excellent discussion of this history in Benson 1976.

26. Babylonian Talmud: *Sanhedrin* 56a. This is the most famous but not the only list of Noachide commandments given in the Talmud. Some opinions offer expanded or altered versions of the list, including such things as interbreeding; some narrow the list such that,

in application at least, only idolatry, murder, and adultery (or idolatry alone) are universally prohibited. Cf. ibid.: 56a–60a.

27. Khadduri 1955: 165–166.

28. Ghoshal 1959: 778.

29. Gluckman 1967: 204, 207.

30. It is arguable that Christian, Jewish, and Muslim principles resemble one another only because they have interacted a great deal and have all been influenced in important ways by Plato and Aristotle. I have offered Buddhist and especially Lozi practices precisely in order to show that some general notion of humanity and standard of how to treat human beings who don't belong to one's own culture exist even where the universalist philosophies of Western civilization have had little or no impact. Each time we rediscover this fact in a new people we can have more confidence that there is indeed a road to humanitarianism via culture. At the same time, attempting to follow that road has the advantage of helping us avoid the temptation to crush cultures in the name of a humanitarianism that we imagine we alone possess.

31. Gluckman 1967: 220, 207, 203.

32. Vitoria 1917: 156; Grotius 1901: 202, 205–209; Khadduri 1955: 165; and Gluckman 1967: 208.

33. Gluckman 1967: 207–208.

34. Vitoria 1917: 127, §23.

35. This may be an appropriate point at which to record my skepticism of the well-known anthropologists' claim that some human groups apply their word for "human being" only to members of their own tribe. It may well be true that the local word for "human" is often the same as the name of the tribe, but what does that prove? Perhaps the tribe regards its members as special, superior human beings or as the norm for what a human being should be like. These alternatives are not only more plausible than the supposition that the tribe fails to recognize nonmembers as human at all—it is methodologically almost impossible to get to the latter position. For how can the anthropologist know that the tribe does not consider outsiders human? If it does not treat them as human, how did he or she ever get to talking with its members, let alone to setting up a complete translation manual? If it does treat them as human—if its members talk to outsiders, barter with them, make war on or peace with them, have sex (licitly or illicitly) with them—then he or she is surely translating the wrong linguistic element into our word "human": *whatever* they call beings they treat in such a manner deserves to be translated into that term. This is so according to the way we use our *own* terms. If the anthropologist chooses to translate the tribal name into our word "human" regardless of these facts about usage, he simply fails to grasp the logic of his own native language. (Of course, this does not prevent us from condemning certain cultural practices, and attitudes toward nonmembers, as "dehumanizing." On the contrary, it strengthens such condemnation: a group that calls outsiders "pigs" [*Marranos*], or breeds, buys and sells, and works other people like pack animals, violates the terms of its *own* recognition that all humans are kin. We can *call* other humans "animals," but we cannot believe it.)

36. As I, here, am proposing the distinctions in Jewish, Muslim, Buddhist, and Lozi groups as a model for how post-Enlightenment Europe and America might reinterpret its own *ius gentium* and *ius naturale*.

37. Cf. Michael Walzer in Beitz et al. 1985: 181: "The ban on boundary crossings is subject to unilateral suspension . . . when the violation of human rights within a set of

boundaries is so terrible that it makes talk of community or self-determination or 'arduous struggle' seem cynical and irrelevant."

38. Vitoria 1917: 156, 159.

39. See text to note 19, above.

40. Vitoria 1917: 116–117.

41. Quoted by E. C. Stowell, in Laqueur and Rubin 1979: 173.

42. Vitoria 1917: 158.

43. See Hehir 1974: 128.

44. Nardin 1983: 67.

45. The first such case concerns the 1827 Greek struggle for independence against the Turks, which Henry Wheaton, a standard source for international law, justifies as the "interference of the Christian powers of Europe in favour of the Greeks, who, after enduring ages of cruel oppression, had shaken off the Ottoman yoke" (quoted in Moore 1974: 234). Then, in 1860, the European powers won the reluctant consent of the Ottomans to defend the Lebanese Maronites against an attack by the Druze. Ian Brownlie ("Humanitarian Intervention," in Moore 1974), on the whole a staunch opponent of humanitarian intervention, considers this one of the few cases in which it might have been legitimate, while Thomas Franck and Nigel Rodley point out that even here the situation was hardly clearcut: the Maronites had been planning a similar onslaught on the Druze for months, encouraging their followers with the claim that "their endeavor to attain undisputed possession of the Lebanon would be warmly countenanced by the Powers of Christendom" (Franck and Rodley 1973: 282). Finally, Russia intervened against Turkey in 1877–88 on the purported grounds of the "outrageous persecution" of the Christians in the Balkans and was joined by others against the same foe in Macedonia in 1903. The only major exception to this pattern in the nineteenth century is the U.S. invasion of Cuba in 1898, which Brownlie, at least, does not consider a real case of humanitarianism (see Moore 1974: 220–221). Quite as striking is the absence of even the mention of humanitarian intervention, by European and American leaders, during the pogroms against Jews in nineteenth-century Russia (see Franck and Rodley 1973: 290–291).

7. BEYOND CULTURES (II): JUDGING OURSELVES

1. Blackburn 1981: 171, 174.

2. In his discussion of natural law, J. R. Pennock (1981: especially 10–12) treats the problems with such putative grounds for a transcultural standard.

3. Lovibond 1983: 128.

4. Blackburn 1981: 171.

5. See d'Entreves 1970: chaps. 2–4.

6. See d'Entreves 1970: chap. 4, and Lauterpacht 1945: chap. 3.

7. Montaigne 1958: 110 and Rousseau 1964: 141.

8. "What! must we destroy societies, annihilate thine and mine, and go back to live in forests with bears? . . . Oh you, to whom the heavenly voice has not made itself heard and who recognize no other destination for your species than to end this brief life in peace; you who can leave your fatal acquisitions, your worried minds, your corrupt hearts, and your unbridled desires in the midst of cities; reclaim . . . your ancient and first innocence, go into the woods . . . and have no fear of debasing your species in renouncing its enlightenment in

order to renounce its vices. As for men like me, [our] passions have forever destroyed [our] original simplicity, [we] can no longer nourish [our]selves on grass and nuts, nor do without laws and chiefs" (Rousseau 1964: 201–202).

9. Midgley 1975: 80–81.

10. Strauss 1953: 184.

11. Hobbes 1968: 187.

12. Quoted in Lovejoy 1948: 14–15.

13. See references in Chapter 3, note 17, above.

14. Rousseau 1964: 103.

15. Ibid.: 105.

16. This seems to have been the position of both Baius and Jansen (as well as such contemporary—and more acceptable—theologians as Karl Rahner) (see Burke 1967: 1033).

17. Rawls 1971: 137, 162, 192.

18. Ibid.: 92.

19. Benjamin Barber raises a very similar objection: "Certain Christian ascetics may even complain that the Rawlsian standard deprives them of the austerity and struggle for survival they regard as necessary to their otherworldly beliefs" (Barber 1975: 299; see also 313–314). Rawls might well respond to Barber that such an ascetic could simply give up any primary goods he doesn't need, after the distribution agreed on behind the veil of ignorance is completed. The point in my example (perhaps also, implicitly, in Barber's) is that having too many primary goods might constitute an irresistible temptation, for *some* people, to fail in their spiritual mission. Thus a traditional Hindu—or Christian ascetic—might, quite without envy, will that *others* be deprived for their own spiritual good. Whether this hierarchical view of liability to temptation is true or not (or a fair representation of any Hindu or Christian beliefs) is of course beside the point: if it is so much as rational, it brings out a problem in Rawls's separation of the right from the good. The latter position is a common target for criticism: in addition to Barber, see for instance Sandel 1982.

20. Eckhart 1941: 96.

21. See Meeks 1986: 52–55.

22. At the same time, Heidegger believed that truth must be established and communicated in the discourse of the "they": precisely because discourse is capable of so exalted a role, it is capable of falling into the corruption of falsehood and triviality. I am therefore simplifying Heidegger, but a subtler exposition would be unnecessarily complicated for present purposes.

23. Heidegger 1962: 315–316.

24. Kierkegaard 1974: 106.

25. "Praying, reading, singing, watching, fasting, and doing penance—all these virtuous practices were contrived to catch us and keep us away from strange, ungodly things. Thus, if one feels that the spirit of God is not at work in him, that he has departed inwardly from God, he will all the more feel the need to do virtuous deeds. . . . But when a person has a true spiritual experience, he may boldly drop external disciplines, even those to which he is bound by vows, from which even a bishop may not release him" (Eckhart 1941: 115–116). M. O'C. Walshe reports some doubt as to the authenticity of this sermon, although he himself appears not to share this doubt (see Walshe 1979: 36 n. 1).

26. Eckhart 1941: 110.

27. Heidegger 1971: 71.

28. The more the work of art is able to "open" a new truth for us, Heidegger says, "the

more essentially is the extraordinary thrust to the surface and the long-familiar thrust down." And "to submit to this displacement means: to transform our accustomed ties to world and earth and henceforth to restrain all usual doing and prizing, knowing and looking, in order to stay within the truth that is happening in the work" (ibid.: 66). Compare also p. 76: "A beginning . . . always contains the undisclosed abundance of the unfamiliar and extraordinary, which means that it also contains strife with the familiar and ordinary."

29. Heidegger 1977: 390.

30. Truth happens "always in some particular way" and "becomes historical"; that is, occurs in a different way for each "historical people" (see Heidegger 1971: 60, 78, 75).

31. Cf. note 28, above.

32. I here disagree with Bernard Williams, who considers conversion part, if at the extreme end, of a continuum: "Even conversion," he says, "had better be something which can be lived sanely, . . . [which means] 'retaining [one's] hold on reality' . . . [not] engaging in extensive self-deception, falling into paranoia, and such things" (Williams 1981: 139). I prefer Kierkegaard's use of the term: "In consequence of receiving [the truth and] the condition [for truth], the course of [the disciple's] life has been given an opposite direction, so that he is now turned about. Let us call this change *Conversion*" (Kierkegaard 1962: 23). And similarly, Stanley Cavell writes, "Conversion is a turning of our natural reactions; so it is symbolized as rebirth" (Cavell 1979: 125). Here conversion is clearly the antithesis to a normal pattern, not its limit, and that is how I see its relationship to normal ethical reflection and argument. We may well, taking up the naturalistic perspective, attribute someone's conversion to her losing grip on reality, engaging in self-deception, etc., while the convert herself feels she has moved closer to reality and self-knowledge without being able to explain to us, trapped in the "old ways," how she has come to this new light. (Faith and dementia, says Kierkegaard [1974: 116], are as close as the divine and the demoniac.) Or we may consider the conversion sane, sincere, and even healthy, while the convert, although she probably agrees, feels we are missing the main point. And if we are concerned with what is truly *right* rather than the well-being of this particular individual, we *are* missing the main point, for the strange or nutty shift may be the true conversion while the healthy reorientation of manner and practice may not be a conversion at all.

33. And not merely in the sense of appealing to one part of an "imperfectly coherent" community against another, cf. pp. 181–182 above.

34. There are limits to this comparison, however: here we insist on the possibility, there we might refuse to recognize it. At the same time, this possibility cannot be adequately realized in experience, whereas the other we just do not expect to see.

8. Western Culture

1. Note that insofar as Gandhi and Sukarno were revolutionaries, they were very much part of the West's story about itself. In the latter case, this is not terribly surprising: Sukarno's various ideologies were highly influenced by Western political traditions. Gandhi's thought was also influenced by Western traditions (he acknowledges the powerful impact Thoreau and the Gospels had had on him), but he understood himself—correctly—as trying to use those traditions to bring out long-standing aspects of Hinduism. His heroic stature in the West, however, is not due to this side of his personality and thought.

2. Marx and Engels 1947: 53.

3. Sforno 1987: 19. Bracketed interpolations added by the translator, Raphael Pelcovitz.

4. Even Marx believed that when we reach the communist ideal, our desires, themselves a product of our labor conditions, will change, such that then, but only then, can we lead rich and satisfying lives by doing "just what we have a mind" to do.

5. *War and Peace*, vol. 1, part 2, especially chaps. 2 and 3.

6. Having wagered his soul that he would never utter the words, "Stay, fleeting moment, you are so beautiful"—at the time quite certain that nothing in life, no moment of it, could possibly be worthwhile—Faust dies while saying that he *might* utter those words if he could witness a world in which lush fields were maintained at the cost of a constant battle to keep the sea away: as happened in Holland, a century or so after the time of the historical Faust. The conditional tense and the constant struggle that here sets the terms for full happiness express ironically Faust's rejection of the very terms of his original bet, the very notion that happiness could consist in a moment of fulfilled desire. More explicitly, Faust says, "He only earns both freedom and existence who must reconquer them each day" (Goethe 1976: Part II, Act V, lines 11575–11576). Goethe underlines this point, in the final scene and especially the final chorus, by envisioning even heaven as a place of eternal striving. His notion of the human telos as something that can be a telos only by continually eluding us, and his metaphor of a community at the edge of the sea—a hard-working and democratic community, if the model is indeed Holland—is one of the most important sources for my own account of the good in Chapter 3.

7. Mill 1973: 414.

8. This has been widely reported about Francis Ford Coppola's film *Peggy Sue Got Married* and the recent *Pretty Woman*. It seems also to be true of *Something Wild* and *Sea of Love*, both of which have clear, appropriately tragic endings shortly before an extremely strained happy scene with which they formally close.

9. It finds the notions *scientifically* unsound because they violate the principle of sufficient reason, which is methodologically fundamental to all believers in science.

10. Berlin 1976: 161.

11. Ibid.: 184–185.

12. Gene Bluestein (1963) shows how deeply Herder influenced Whitman, on the importance of slang, folk culture, folk music, nationalism, and internationalism. For the influence of Whitman on Forster, see Beer 1962: 147 and Levine 1971: 157. John Colmer (1975: 267) discusses the importance of travel and the *genius loci* to Forster's writing.

13. Berlin 1976: 175–176.

References

Allison, Henry. 1966. *Lessing and the Enlightenment*. Ann Arbor: University of Michigan Press.

Aquinas, Thomas. 1953. *The Political Ideas of St. Thomas Aquinas*. Ed. Dino Bigongiari. New York: Hafner Press.

Arciniegas, German. 1951. "Culture—A Human Right." In *Freedom and Culture*. Ed. UNESCO. Intro. Julian Huxley. New York: Columbia University Press.

Arendt, Hannah. 1977. *Between Past and Future*. New York: Penguin.

Aristotle 1941. *Nicomachean Ethics*. In *The Basic Works of Aristotle*. Ed. Richard McKeon. New York: Random House.

Avineri, Shlomo. 1972. *Hegel's Theory of the Modern State*. London: Cambridge University Press.

Ayer, Alfred. 1952. *Language, Truth, and Logic*. 2d edition. New York: Dover.

Baier, Kurt. 1965. *The Moral Point of View*. Abridged edition. New York: Random House.

Barber, Benjamin. 1975. "Justifying Justice." In *Reading Rawls: Critical Studies on Rawls' A Theory of Justice*. Ed. and intro. Norman Daniels. New York: Basic Books.

Barfield, Owen. 1962. "Poetic Diction and Legal Fiction." In *The Importance of Language*. Ed. Max Black. Englewood Cliffs, N.J.: Prentice-Hall.

Barrow, Robin. 1986. "Socrates Was a Human Being: A Plea for Transcultural Moral Education." *Journal of Moral Education* 15: 50–57.

Beck, Lewis White. 1960. *A Commentary on Kant's "Critique of Practical Reason."* Chicago: University of Chicago Press.

Becker, Carl. 1932. *The Heavenly City of the Eighteenth-Century Philosophers*. New Haven: Yale University Press.

Beer, J. B. 1962. *The Achievement of E. M. Forster*. London: Chatto & Windus.

Beitz, Charles, Marshall Cohen, Thomas Scanlon, and A. J. Simmons, eds. 1985. *International Ethics*. Princeton: Princeton University Press.

Benedict, Ruth. 1934. *Patterns of Culture*. New York: Mentor.

Bennett, Jonathan. 1966. *Kant's Analytic.* Cambridge: Cambridge University Press.

Benson, Robert L. 1976. "Medieval Canonistic Origins of the Debate on the Lawfulness of the Spanish Conquest." In *First Images of America*, vol. 1. Ed. Fredi Chiappelli. Berkeley: University of California Press.

Berger, Peter. 1979. "Are Human Rights Universal?" In *Human Rights and U.S. Foreign Policy.* Ed. Barry Rubin and Elizabeth Spiro. Boulder, Colo.: Westview Press.

Berkovits, Eliezer. 1983. *Not in Heaven: The Nature and Function of Halakha.* New York: Ktav.

Berlin, Isaiah. 1976. *Vico and Herder.* New York: Viking.

Blackburn, Simon. 1981. "Rule-Following and Moral Realism." In *Wittgenstein: To Follow a Rule.* Ed. Steven Holtzman and Christopher Leich. London: Routledge & Kegan Paul.

Bloom, Harold. 1973. *The Anxiety of Influence.* New York: Oxford University Press.

Bluestein, Gene. 1963. "The Advantages of Barbarism: Herder and Whitman's Nationalism." *Journal of the History of Ideas* 24: 115–126.

Blum, Lawrence. 1991. "Moral Perception and Particularity." *Ethics* 101: 701–725.

Burke, E. M. 1967. "State of Pure Nature" (s.v. "Pure Nature, State of"). In *New Catholic Encyclopedia*, vol. 11. New York: McGraw Hill.

Cassirer, Ernst. 1944. *Essay on Man.* New Haven: Yale University Press.

——. 1951. *The Philosophy of the Enlightenment.* Trans. F. C. A. Koelln and James Pettegrove. Princeton: Princeton University Press.

Cavell, Stanley. 1979. *The Claim of Reason.* New York: Oxford University Press.

Celsus. 1987. *On the True Doctrine.* New York: Oxford University Press.

Chatwin, Bruce. 1987. *The Songlines.* New York: Viking.

Colmer, John. 1975. *E. M. Forster: The Personal Voice.* Boston: Routledge & Kegan Paul.

Cooper, David. 1978. "Moral Relativism." *Midwest Studies in Philosophy* 3: 97–108.

Crawford, Donald. 1974. *Kant's Aesthetic Theory.* Madison: University of Wisconsin Press.

Davidson, Donald. 1980. *Essays on Actions and Events.* Oxford: Clarendon Press.

——. 1984. *Inquiries into Truth and Interpretation.* Oxford: Clarendon Press.

d'Entreves, A. P. 1970. *Natural Law.* London: Hutchinson.

Descartes, René. 1974. *Meditations.* In *The Rationalists.* Trans. John Veitch. Garden City, N.Y.: Anchor.

Devlin, Patrick. 1965. *The Enforcement of Morals.* New York: Oxford University Press.

Eckhart, Meister. 1941. *Meister Eckhart: A Modern Translation.* Trans. and ed. R. E. Blakney. New York: Harper & Brothers.

Edel, Abraham, and May Edel. 1963. "The Confrontation of Anthropology and Ethics." *Monist* 47: 489–505.

Ergang, Robert. 1966. *Herder and the Foundations of German Nationalism.* New York: Octagon.

Finnis, John. 1974. "The Rights and Wrongs of Abortion." In *The Rights and Wrongs of Abortion*. Ed. Marshall Cohen, Thomas Nagel, and Thomas Scanlon. Princeton: Princeton University Press.

———. 1980. *Natural Law and Natural Rights*. New York: Oxford University Press.

Fleischacker, Samuel. 1988. "Kant's Theory of Punishment." *Kant-Studien* 79: 434–449.

———. 1989. "A Fifth Antinomy." *Philosophia* 19: 23–27.

———. 1992. *Integrity and Moral Relativism*. Leiden: E. J. Brill.

Foot, Philippa. 1978. "Are Moral Considerations Overriding?" and "Morality as a System of Hypothetical Imperatives." In Foot, *Virtues and Vices*. Berkeley: University of California Press.

Franck, Thomas, and Nigel Rodley. 1973. "After Bangladesh: The Law of Humanitarian Intervention by Military Force." *American Journal of International Law* 67: 275–305.

Frankfurt, Harry. 1977. "Descartes on the Creation of Eternal Truths." *Philosophical Review* 86: 36–57.

———. 1982. "The Importance of What We Care About." *Synthese* 53: 257–272.

Gadamer, Hans-Georg. 1975. *Truth and Method*. Trans. Sheed & Ward Ltd. Ed. Garrett Barden and John Cumming. New York: Seabury Press.

Gandhi, Mohandas. 1951. *Non-Violent Resistance*. Ahmedabad: Navajivan.

Geertz, Clifford. 1968. *Islam Observed*. Chicago: University of Chicago Press.

———. 1973. *The Interpretation of Cultures*. New York: Basic Books.

———. 1983. *Local Knowledge: Further Essays in Interpretive Anthropology*. New York: Basic Books.

Gellner, Ernest. 1983. *Nations and Nationalism*. Ithaca: Cornell University Press.

Ghoshal, U. N. 1959. *A History of Indian Political Ideas*. Oxford: Oxford University Press.

Gilligan, Carol. 1982. *In a Different Voice: Psychological Theory and Women's Development*. Cambridge: Harvard University Press.

Gluckman, Max. 1967. *The Judicial Process among the Barotse of Northern Rhodesia*. Manchester: Manchester University Press.

Goethe, J. W. 1976. *Faust*. Trans. Walter Arndt. Ed. Cyrus Hamlin. New York: Norton.

Gowans, Chris, ed. 1987. *Moral Dilemmas*. New York: Oxford University Press.

Grotius, Hugo. 1901. *The Rights of War and Peace*. Trans. A. C. Campbell. New York: Walter Dunne.

Guyer, Paul. 1979. *Kant and the Claims of Taste*. Cambridge: Harvard University Press.

Haddon, A. C. 1934. *History of Anthropology*. London: Watts.

Hamilton, Bernice. 1963. *Political Thought in Sixteenth-Century Spain*. Oxford: Clarendon Press.

Hare, R. M. 1963. *Freedom and Reason.* London: Oxford University Press.

Harris, R. Baine, ed. 1976. *Authority: A Philosophical Analysis.* Tuscaloosa: University of Alabama Press.

Hauerwas, Stanley. 1981. *A Community of Character.* Notre Dame: University of Notre Dame Press.

Hegel, G. W. F. 1967. *Philosophy of Right.* Trans. T. M. Knox. New York: Oxford University Press.

———. 1971. *Hegel's Philosophy of Mind.* Trans. William Wallace and A. V. Miller. Oxford: Clarendon Press.

Hehir, J. Bryan. 1974. "The Ethics of Intervention." In *Human Rights and U.S. Foreign Policy.* Ed. P. G. Brown and Douglas MacLean. Lexington: D. C. Heath.

Heidegger, Martin. 1962. *Being and Time.* Trans. John Macquarrie and Edward Robinson. New York: Harper & Row.

———. 1971. "Origin of the Work of Art." In *Poetry, Language, Thought.* Trans. and intro. Albert Hofstadter. New York: Harper & Row.

———. 1977. "The End of Philosophy and the Task of Thinking." In *Basic Writings.* Ed. D. F. Krell. New York: Harper & Row.

Herder, J. G. 1961. *J. G. Herder on Social and Political Culture.* Trans. and ed. F. M. Barnard. Cambridge: Cambridge University Press.

———. 1968. *Reflections on the Philosophy of the History of Mankind.* Trans. and ed. Frank E. Manuel. Chicago: University of Chicago Press.

Herskovits, Melville. 1950. *Man and His Works.* New York: Alfred A. Knopf.

Hobbes, Thomas. 1968. *Leviathan.* Ed. C. B. Macpherson. Harmondsworth: Penguin.

Hodgen, Margaret T. 1964. *Early Anthropology in the Sixteenth and Seventeenth Centuries.* Philadelphia: University of Pennsylvania Press.

Hofmannsthal, Hugo von. 1952. *Selected Prose.* Trans. Mary Hottinger and Tania and James Stern. New York: Pantheon.

Hollis, Martin, and Steven Lukes, eds. 1982. *Rationality and Relativism.* Cambridge: MIT Press.

Horgan, Edward R. 1982. *The Shaker Holy Land.* Harvard, Mass.: Harvard Common Press.

Hume, David. 1969. *A Treatise of Human Nature.* Harmondsworth: Penguin.

———. 1975. *Enquiries.* Ed. L. A. Selby-Bigge. 3d edition revised by P. H. Nidditch. Oxford: Oxford University Press.

Hymes, Dell. 1972. *Reinventing Anthropology.* New York: Random House.

Kant, Immanuel. 1951. *Critique of Judgment.* Trans. J. H. Bernard. New York: Hafner Press.

———. 1956. *Critique of Practical Reason.* Trans. L. W. Beck. Indianapolis: Bobbs-Merrill.

———. 1964. *Groundwork of the Metaphysic of Morals.* Trans. H. J. Paton. New York: Harper & Row.

———. 1965. *Critique of Pure Reason*. Trans. N. K. Smith. New York: St. Martin's Press.

Katz, Jacob. 1989. *The "Shabbes Goy": A Study in Halakhic Flexibility*. Philadelphia: Jewish Publication Society.

Kedourie, Elie. 1985. *Nationalism*. 3d edition. London: Hutchinson.

Kekes, John. 1989. *Moral Tradition and Individuality*. Princeton: Princeton University Press.

Khadduri, Majid. 1955. *War and Peace in the Law of Islam*. Baltimore: Johns Hopkins University Press.

Kierkegaard, Søren. 1962. *Philosophical Fragments*. Trans. David Swenson and Howard Hong. Princeton: Princeton University Press.

———. 1968. *Concluding Unscientific Postscript*. Trans. David Swenson and Walter Lowrie. Princeton: Princeton University Press.

———. 1974. *Fear and Trembling*. Trans. Walter Lowrie. Princeton: Princeton University Press.

Koepping, Klaus-Peter. 1983. *Adolf Bastian and the Psychic Unity of Mankind*. St. Lucia: University of Queensland Press.

Kohn, Hans. 1965. *Nationalism: Its Meaning and History*. Princeton, N.J.: D. Van Nostrand.

Koyré, Alexandre. 1968. "Galileo and Plato." In Koyré, *Metaphysics and Measurement: Essays in the Scientific Revolution*. Cambridge: Harvard University Press.

Kroeber, Alfred L., and Clyde Kluckhohn. 1952. *Culture: A Critical Review of Concepts and Definitions*. Cambridge, Mass.: Peabody Museum of American Archaeology and Ethnology.

Laqueur, Walter, and Barry Rubin, eds. 1979. *The Human Rights Reader*. Philadelphia: Temple University Press.

Larmore, Charles. 1987. *Patterns of Moral Complexity*. New York: Cambridge University Press.

Lauterpacht, Hersch 1945. *An International Bill of the Rights of Man*. New York: Columbia University Press.

Leaf, Murray. 1979. *Man, Mind, and Science*. New York: Columbia University Press.

Leibniz, Gottfried. 1974. *Monadology* and *Discourses*. In *The Rationalists*. Trans. George Montgomery with revisions by A. R. Chandler. Garden City, N.Y.: Anchor.

Leibniz, Gottfried/Clarke, Samuel. 1956. *The Leibniz/Clarke Correspondence*. Ed. H. G. Alexander. Manchester: Manchester University Press.

Lessing, Gotthold. 1955. *Nathan the Wise*. Trans. B. Q. Morgan. New York: Frederick Ungar.

———. 1956. *Lessing's Theological Writings*. Ed. and trans. Henry Chadwick. Stanford: Stanford University Press.

Levine, June Perry. 1971. *Creation and Criticism: A Passage to India*. Lincoln: University of Nebraska Press.

Lovejoy, Arthur. 1948. *Essays in the History of Ideas.* Baltimore: Johns Hopkins University Press.

———. 1964. *The Great Chain of Being.* Cambridge: Harvard University Press.

Lovibond, Sabina. 1983. *Realism and Imagination in Ethics.* Oxford: Basil Blackwell.

Lowie, Robert A. 1937. *The History of Ethnological Theory.* New York: Farrar & Rinehart.

MacIntyre, Alasdair. 1981. *After Virtue.* Notre Dame: University of Notre Dame Press.

———. 1988. *Whose Justice? Which Rationality?* Notre Dame: University of Notre Dame Press.

Mackie, John. 1978. "The Law of the Jungle—Moral Alternatives and Principles of Evolution." *Philosophy* 53: 455–464.

Maimonides, Moses. 1981. *The Book of Knowledge* (vol. 1 of the *Mishneh Torah*). Ed. and trans. Moses Hyamson. Jerusalem: Feldheim.

Marx, Karl, and Friedrich Engels. 1947. *The German Ideology.* Ed. C. J. Arthur. New York: International.

Mead, Margaret. 1943. *Coming of Age in Samoa.* Harmondsworth: Penguin.

Meeks, Wayne. 1986. *The Moral World of the First Christians.* Philadelphia: Westminster Press.

Midgley, E. B. F. 1975. *The Natural Law Tradition and the Theory of International Relations.* New York: Harper & Row.

Mill, J. S. 1973. *Utilitarianism.* In *The Utilitarians.* Garden City, N.Y.: Anchor.

Montaigne, Michel de. 1958. *Essays.* Trans. J. M. Cohen. Harmondsworth: Penguin.

Moore, John N., ed. 1974. *Law and Civil War in the Modern World.* Baltimore: Johns Hopkins University Press.

Murphy, Jeffrie. 1982. *Evolution, Morality, and the Meaning of Life.* Totowa, N.J.: Rowman & Littlefield.

Nagel, Thomas. 1986. *The View from Nowhere.* New York: Oxford University Press.

Nardin, Terry. 1983. *Law, Morality, and the Relations of States.* Princeton: Princeton University Press.

Nussbaum, Martha. 1985. *The Fragility of Goodness.* New York: Cambridge University Press.

Penniman, T. K. 1965. *A Hundred Years of Anthropology.* 3d edition. London: Gerald Duckworth.

Pennock, J. R. 1981. "Rights, Natural Rights, and Human Rights—A General View." In *Human Rights.* Ed. Pennock and J. W. Chapman. New York: New York University Press.

Rawls, John. 1971. *A Theory of Justice.* Cambridge: Belknap Press of Harvard University Press.

Reichenbach, Hans. 1938. *Experience and Prediction.* Chicago: University of Chicago Press.

Rorty, Amelie, ed. 1980. *Explaining Emotions*. Berkeley: University of California Press.

Rousseau, Jean-Jacques. 1964. *First and Second Discourses*. Ed. Roger Masters. Trans. Roger and Judith Masters. New York: St. Martin's Press.

Sandel, Michael. 1982. *Liberalism and the Limits of Justice*. New York: Cambridge University Press.

Schmidt, Royal J. 1956. "Cultural Nationalism in Herder." *Journal of the History of Ideas* 17: 407–417.

Sforno, Ovadiah. 1987. *Commentary on the Torah*. Trans. Raphael Pelcovitz. New York: Mesorah Publications.

Shafer, Boyd. 1955. *Nationalism: Myth and Reality*. New York: Harcourt, Brace.

Singer, Isaac Bashevis. 1961. *The Spinoza of Market Street*. New York: Fawcett Crest.

Singer, Milton. 1968. "Culture." In *International Encyclopedia of the Social Sciences*. Ed. David Sills. New York: Macmillan.

Smith, Adam. 1982. *The Theory of Moral Sentiments*. Indianapolis: Liberty Classics.

Stout, Jeffrey. 1988. *Ethics after Babel*. Boston: Beacon Press.

Strauss, Leo. 1953. *Natural Right and History*. Chicago: University of Chicago Press.

Taurek, John. 1977. "Should the Numbers Count?" *Philosophy and Public Affairs* 6: 293–316.

Taylor, Charles. 1979. *Hegel and Modern Society*. New York: Cambridge University Press.

——. 1989. *Sources of the Self*. Cambridge: Harvard University Press.

Turnbull, Colin. 1972. *The Mountain People*. New York: Simon & Schuster.

Vincent, R. J. 1974. *Non-intervention and International Order*. Princeton: Princeton University Press.

Vitoria, Francisco de. 1917. *De indis et De iure belli relectiones*. Ed. Ernest Nys. Trans. John Bate. Washington, D.C.: Carnegie Institution of Washington.

Vivas, Eliseo. 1961. "Reiteration and Second Thoughts on Cultural Relativism." In *Relativism and the Study of Man*. Ed. Helmut Schoeck and James Wiggins. Princeton, N.J.: Van Nostrand.

Voget, Fred. 1975. *A History of Ethnology*. New York: Holt, Rinehart & Winston.

Walshe, M. O'C. 1979. *Meister Eckhart: Sermons and Treatises*. Vol. 1. London: Watkins.

Walzer, Michael. 1980. *Just and Unjust Wars*. Harmondsworth: Penguin.

——. 1989. *Spheres of Justice*. Oxford: Basil Blackwell.

Williams, Bernard. 1973. "A Critique of Utilitarianism." In J. J. Smart and Williams, *Utilitarianism: For and Against*. Cambridge: Cambridge University Press.

——. 1978. *Descartes: The Project of Pure Enquiry*. Harmondsworth: Penguin.

——. 1981. *Moral Luck*. Cambridge: Cambridge University Press.

——. 1983. "Auto-da-Fé." Review of Richard Rorty's *Consequences of Pragmatism*. *New York Review of Books*: April 28.

References

———. 1985. *Ethics and the Limits of Philosophy*. Cambridge: Harvard University Press.

Wittgenstein, Ludwig. 1958. *Philosophical Investigations*. Trans. G. E. M. Anscombe. New York: Macmillan.

———. 1977. *On Certainty*. Ed. G. E. M. Anscombe and G. H. von Wright. Trans. Denis Paul and G. E. M. Anscombe. Oxford: Basil Blackwell.

Wolff, Robert Paul. 1963. *Kant's Theory of Mental Activity*. Gloucester, Mass.: Peter Smith.

Index